# REGIONAL PLANNING AND SOCIAL CHANGE

*To B*

# Regional Planning and Social Change

A responsive approach

DAVID GILLINGWATER
*University of Technology,*
*Loughborough*

SAXON HOUSE | LEXINGTON BOOKS

*Published by*

SAXON HOUSE, D. C. Heath Ltd.
Westmead, Farnborough, Hants., England.


*Jointly with*

LEXINGTON BOOKS, D. C. Heath & Co.
Lexington, Mass. USA.


ISBN 0 347 01086 5

Library of Congress Catalog Card Number 75-28615

Printed and bound in Great Britain
by Butler and Tanner Ltd, Frome and London

# Contents

# List of figures

# Preface

*'Well then', said the king in a bit of excitement, 'could you please open it up for us'? Frank, whom all this time had been reclining with his eyes closed, suddenly opened them both up as wide as a tiger. 'And just how far would you like to go in'? he asked and the three kings all looked at each other. 'Not too far but just far enough so's we can say that we've been there', said the first chief. 'All right', said Frank, 'I'll see what I can do', and he commenced to doing it.* (Bob Dylan, 1968.)

This book is about planning, one kind of planning — *public* planning — of which *regional* is one strand. It is also a book about change — the need to comprehend and understand change in all its forms — and not to simply plan for it. The book is therefore indirectly concerned with the politics of change — the relations between politics and planning, the political administration of planning, and political administrations' attempts to plan. It is not about the techniques of planning or their administration, neither is it a manual of form and content. If it is about anything it is a concern for *processes* — those relationships and connections which influence planning and which planning in turn influences. It is a book which emphasises the importance of viewing planning in conceptual and conceptualisable terms, rather than with observations about actual planning practice. To use Faludi's distinction, it is concerned more with contributions of theories for planning toward a theory of planning, not with the use of theory in planning practice.

The book is divided roughly into two parts, the first concerning the idea of planning and public planning, the second the idea of regional planning and its relations with public planning. The assumption underpinning this approach, and one which permeates the whole of what follows, is that we need to understand and assimilate what is and what is not regional planning *qua* public planning at the same time as we attempt to accommodate it into the 'present order of things'. It is contended here that what currently passes for public planning, especially in western capitalist societies, is that based on one particular model of planning which in turn rests on one particular model of social change. At the risk of considerable oversimplification these 'good currency' approaches, reflected in 'current best practices', are respectively the rational model of action and the integration model of social change. But these two approaches neither constitute the final irreducible bed of reality on the subject of planning and change, nor do they imply that the alternative is 'muddling through' or 'non-planning'. Like so many other ideas which pervade current planning practice, the situation is neither a causal nor an either-or one. It would seem to be much more appropriate to treat them as continuums of shades of grey rather than black-or-white alternatives. It will be argued throughout this book, more implicitly than explicitly, that it is this openness of thought and flexibility of action which needs to be made a central feature of planning practice.

The objectives of the book are threefold: (a) to outline some of the key facets associated with the 'good currency' approaches to planning and planning practice, whilst at the same time trying (b) to assess their relevance and applicability to a view of planning which sees it as primarily a highly politicised process attempting to achieve politically emotive things in the arena of politics, whilst at the same time trying (c) to outline the requirements of a sketch for a responsive theory of planning. Implicit in this triad of aims is the assumption that both theory and practice are necessary conditions for planning practice, but taken individually they are not sufficient conditions. It is only through the fusion of theory with practice, and its mobilisation, that planning can set about the task of achieving those things to which it can only aspire — political respectability and legitimacy. It is contended here that these are the only ways in which planning can ever be 'successful'.

Chapter One is concerned with interrelationships between the problem of planning and the need for conceptualising about planning. Chapter Two is an attempt to grasp the nettle of public planning by considering the 'good currency' approaches to it and its relationships with public policy-making. The final part concerns relations between public planning, the legitimacy associated with public intervention, and some of the grounds on which intervention may be deemed appropriate. Chapter Three is concerned with the relevance of 'good currency' approaches to the kind of demands with which they are faced. In this respect they are found to be seriously wanting, and so some other potential avenues are explored — notably deductive alternatives. The chapter culminates in an attempt to outline a sketch for a theory of the processes of planning along indeterminist-deductive lines, and to set it within the context of the processes associated with the environment within which it is located, and the nature of social change itself. Chapter Four is an attempt to map-out the institutional context within which public planning fits and which to some extent planning determines. The emphasis here is on planner—state—societal relations, and in particular with the kind of images of reality which planning constructs and which are reflected in certain styles of planning. The chapter concludes with an assessment of a deductive alternative − the skeleton of a responsive approach − by making comparisons of it with these styles in terms of their respective ideological, institutional, operational, and administrative requirements and differences. Chapter Five is in many respects a continuation of this institutional context, but at the next level down, so to speak. The emphasis here is on the administrative setting of public planning, the political administration of the United Kingdom being taken as an illustration of 'current best practice' in a relatively formal, heavily centralised political and administrative system. Chapter Six represents a shift in emphasis away from public planning *per se* to regional planning. A case is presented as to why regional planning should be treated as one strand of public planning by comparing it with 'good currency' approaches to regional planning. These are again found to be wanting. The chapter ends with an attempt to consider the interrelationships between problem regions and regional problems within the context of public planning and the emergence of political problems. The penultimate chapter, Chapter Seven, is devoted almost entirely to a sketch for a theory of a responsive approach to regional planning. This is set within the context of a problematic approach to a paradigm for public planning itself. The chapter concludes with a brief assessment of the core of a responsive approach − the idea of the continuous recasting of problems with respect to the consequences of action and inaction. The concern of the final chapter, Chapter Eight, is with three of the particular problem areas which have arisen out of the previous seven chapters. These are, firstly, the idea that the political process has been the subject of serious neglect − the missing dimension − in most 'good currency' if not all 'current best practice' approaches. A responsive approach is seen to be one way of not simply accounting for or including the political process − which some of the more recent books on public policy and planning have mistakenly intimated − but with a style of planning which is based on those very processes and on which that process itself is based. The second problem area is a brief look at the implications of and kind of problems which could be expected to emerge if regional planning *qua* public planning is to be recast − but within the context of a responsive approach. The final problem area stems out of this latter point. If regional planning is to be recast then where are the principal entry points for change to be found? A brief review is then made of the minimum requirements associated with the introduction of some level of responsiveness into the political administration of planning.

It would be an impossible task to acknowledge all those individuals who have had some influence on the eight chapters which follow. However, I especially wish to thank Derek Diamond (LSE), Andreas Faludi (now of University of Delft), and particularly Douglas Hart (University of Birmingham). All three have contributed in any number of diverse ways to the development of the ideas to be found in these pages. In this respect I must also include my undergraduate students, who have suffered in more ways than one as a result. I must also acknowledge the help and generous assistance which the Editor, John Irwin, has consistently offered me; Vivia Johnson for deciphering and preparing the bulk of the manuscript; and Derek Glenister for preparing most of the diagrams and illustrations.

Since there is an exception to every rule, there is one person who defies classification — to her this book is dedicated.

Because it was begun in earnest in September 1974 it has been possible to have the manuscript commented upon only in bits and pieces. The usual proviso must therefore apply, but more forcefully in this case — I alone am responsible for what it contains, and perhaps also for what it does not contain. The inclusion—exclusion idea of selective perception seems to operate in the writing of books too.

David Gillingwater
June 1975

# 1 Introduction

## The problem of planning

That planning means all things to all men, particularly governments, is self-evident. As is the observation that all men and most governments indulge in broadly similar kinds of activity and label it planning. But when taken together these two truisms make for a paradox which illustrates one of planning's principal weaknesses and yet probably reflects its only real source of strength. For unlike the other social sciences planning has no developed philosophical or theoretical roots, or body of knowledge, which it can legitimately call its own. Instead it tends to be associated with two kinds of institutional activity: firstly, as a simple and politically expedient extension of the concept of the 'inevitability' of intervention by the state, where planning is tacked-on to those branches of the social sciences which are deemed to lend themselves to such normative extension. So, for example, economics becomes translated *ex ante* fashion into the need for intervention via economic planning, and then justified in *ex post* terms on the basis of that original need. Secondly, this kind of circular argument is taken one step further by an ingenious and often subtle process of political manipulation which manages to somehow conceptually separate, for example, the economic content from economic planning. Theory − in this case economic theory − is translated into a set of practices via institutional, administrative and political arrangements, and then divorced from it. It is as if a surgeon's knife magically separates the theoretical content from the practical content once it has become institutionalised and labelled planning. So when planning − be it economic, social, physical, etc. − has been deemed to have failed politically, the brunt of the attack is generally directed at either the folly of attempting to plan in the first place (the 'external' attack) or the general lack or watering down of the political and resource commitment originally promised (the 'internal' attack). Whereas planning takes the brickbats, economics for example somehow escapes direct criticism. In other words it is generally accepted in political terms that planning is principally concerned with 'doing' rather than 'thinking', with action rather than words, with practice rather than theory. Economics retains its reputation and legitimacy whereas the reputation of planning is more than simply tarnished. If not

1

quite regarded as irresponsible it retains certain qualities which are regarded as the (inevitable) perjorative characteristics associated with public intervention.

Whether this amounts to a 'grand conspiracy theory' against public planning is not at issue here, and not a cul-de-sac which will be pursued either. But it does illustrate a point of crucial and significant proportions: that somewhere along the line the process of translation from a substantive theoretical base, for example economics, into an institutionalised form of interventionist activity, for example economic planning, results in some measure of failure and fragmentation. Theory becomes largely divorced from the experience of practice, not irrevocably but certainly in a way which gives this author the impression that a gap exists – and is possibly widening – between theory and practice, between original intentions and eventual form of impact, and a concomitant extention of the division of labour between those who primarily 'think' and those who primarily 'do'.

## The concern of the book

The primary concern of this book then is with the kind of issues raised above. If it has a purpose then it is not so much an attempt but more of a plea (a) to improve our understanding of the nature and practice of planning and regional planning; (b) to prepare the groundwork necessary for the development of a theory for public planning, whilst at the same time (c) assessing its general utility for and applicability to regional planning.

It is therefore a tentative exercise in trying to explore what constitutes the nature and practice of planning by an examination of the roles of the social, economic, political, historical and administrative components of societal relations *vis-à-vis* planning. Societal relations which on the one hand give the impression of stability and yet appear to be in a state of continuous change; of apparent integration but creating the impression of being in continuous conflict; of presenting a picture of consensus, but a consensus which appears to be based on a degree of coercion which seems to be at the very least paradoxical, if not highly questionable. These and other paradoxes, it is argued, are of crucial importance for any study of the nature and practice of public planning – especially with regard to its general social acceptability or total political rejection, to its complex social legitimation or simple political destruction.[1] But what is not of concern in what follows is an attempt to produce solutions or rational explanations for these kinds of paradox, or to construct a 'new' theory of social change. Both are beyond the capability of this particular author. But this is not to devalue in any way the power and influence which they clearly exert, and which all planners in the public arena must consider if they are to reconcile their individual actions with those of society's. For in the final analysis it is society which not only creates and maintains their positions but which succeeds in broadly tolerating their very existence and intrusion — and accords them authority and status for doing it.

In the light of this apparently muddled and paradoxical state of affairs it is possible to make a plea for, together with an attempt to construct, an outline of the critical assumptions, assertions and actions — covert and overt, implicit and explicit — which when taken together constitute the foundations on which public planning is based, and of which regional planning is but one part. This constitutes the groundwork necessary for a study of the nature and practice of planning.


**The need for theory**

One particular avenue which can be explored in this respect — one of a potentially infinite range of possibilities — is to make two critical and arbitrary assumptions concerning the need for, first, a working outline of planning, and second, a theory for planning. To counter the criticisms which can be levelled against this approach, and to substantiate some of the reasons for its adoption, two assertions can be made in its defence. First, we need to outline what is meant by the term planning in order to map-out the boundaries as to what might legitimately constitute public planning; also to help to identify what may not constitute legitimate areas of intervention. This is not necessarily a particularly determinist position to adopt. For by attempting to identify what might constitute the core of planning does not infer that we are trying to define its totality — core and periphery — with absolute precision, only that it might help to clarify the substantive issues which underpin the second key assertion — the need of a theory for planning. An attempt to construct a working outline of planning in this manner is not seen as a static once and for all exercise. Rather as a formulation of some of its key components, emphasising the strands which tie them together in the form of an internally consistent set of assumptions and propositions. These can then be opened up to criticism, assessment, probable refutation and hence to some general reformulation. This approach therefore places the onus on two crucially important concepts, concepts which permeate almost every page of what

3

is to follow in this book: first, the fundamental importance of the temporal dimension — in terms of the manner in which it has an impact on what we think, how we think, and how we translate that thought into action; and second, the importance of regarding a state of continuous conflict and positive criticism as a potentially useful device from which to improve our understanding of what planners can do, how they can set about doing it, and so in the longer term improve on the very foundations of planning itself.

These perhaps utopian views of the need for a theory for planning may be brought down to earth with a simpler pragmatic argument: we need a theory for public planning in order to provide a base from which to map-out the boundaries as to what might constitute legitimate and non-legitimate tasks for planning activity. This also need not be as deterministic a position for similar reasons as those outlined above.

Quite clearly to adopt an approach like this begs answers to an almost infinite range of questions, questions which query the very basis of what planning is, and what it is trying to achieve, how it is setting about it, etc. To narrow this range to more manageable proportions, and to construct a bridge-head for the rest of the book, it is possible to identify four areas of concern which require some examination in the light of the comments and assertions outlined above. A discussion of these four areas, taken together, constitutes the concern of the first part of the book:

1   Is there such a unique societal activity as planning?
2   If so, can it be usefully defined?
3   Can public planning be justified as a legitimate activity?
4   If so, is it possible to map-out potential areas for planned intervention?


**Notes**

[1]   See for example R. Dahrendorf, 1959, Chapter V.

# 2 The Idea of Public Planning

## The concept of planning

To begin with the term 'planning' covers a multiplicity of possible interpretations. It is no overstatement to say that the concept of planning is confusing because of its inherent ambiguity. Indeed it probably has as many interpretations as practitioners.[1] A useful starting point is to consider some of these contemporary interpretations.

For example, the Oxford Dictionary defines only the verb 'to plan', meaning *'to make a plan of, to make a design for, to arrange beforehand'*. Roget's Thesaurus provides a more comprehensive and formidable list of synonyms: *'approach a problem, attack; make a plan, design, draft, blueprint; project, plan out, map out, lay out; organize, systematize, rationalize, schematize, methodize; schedule, programme, phase; contrive, devise, engineer; hatch, concoct, mature'*. These descriptions begin to yield some interesting insights. As Peter Hall has stated: 'In the general sense of planning we mean, take thought to determine an action or a series of actions beforehand'.[2]

This contemporary interpretation may be usefully taken as the minimum requirements necessary to identify that activity called planning. As such it can be taken to represent what Schon calls a 'good currency' view of planning.[3] According to this interpretation any purposeful action of an anticipatory nature can be considered planning.[4] For example, the preparation of this book has by this definition been the subject of planning: an overall framework has been prepared within which this particular chapter fits; a framework has been prepared for this particular chapter; it has been planned in advance to use certain key words and phrases. To quote Peter Hall again:

> Each of these acts has a *main aim* and a series of subsidiary operations which further describe the achievement of that main aim; . . . if this is . . . planning, almost any sphere of life can be planned and *is* planned to some degree.[5]

As a minimum definition, any action which can be thought of as being premeditated or anticipatory in nature can be labelled planning. This is not really very helpful. Unless we are prepared to accept the truism that planning is what people do all the time anyway, we must dig deeper into the notion of purposeful action. In fact a distinction has to be made between basically two forms of purposeful action:

1   purposeful action of a formal nature,
2   purposeful action which is informal.

The distinction is crucial. It recognises that western capitalist society is structured in some basic way. In other words it is organised. By adopting these two categories we can say that informal or unstructured purposeful action is what everybody does most of the time, and that formal or structured purposeful action is what the organised component of society does most of the time.[6]

It is this split which marks the parting of the ways between, on the one hand, theories which attempt to explain the way individuals act in society (psychology and sociology) and, on the other, theories which attempt to explain the actions of groups of individuals (sociology and politics). Quite clearly this split opens up some agonising problems which any theory for planning has to face up to. In fact there are essentially three paths which can be taken:

1   to develop a theory for planning which centres around the rôle of individuals in society,
2   to develop a theory centering around the rôle of groups in society,
3   to develop a theory which combines the rôles of both individuals and groups.

It is at this point where we have to take a stand on the issue of which approach to follow: theories which stress individualism or theories which stress societal relations. The issue presented here is clearly an over-simplification. It is not as simple or black-and-white as might at first appear, but it does illustrate the idea that all theories are based on sets of assumptions, and it is these very assumptions which need explicit formulation, be open to criticism and therefore to general reformulation. What follows here is certainly no exception. And so we have to make a fairly arbitrary decision as to which path to follow, in other words which set of assumptions regarding theories of society are deemed to be somehow more relevant or less ambiguous. In fact the path which will be followed is the societal relations approach, in other words to concentrate primarily on the organised component of society. By doing so we are by definition stating a position, for *theory of this kind is essentially social and political theory,* incorporating the philosophical foundations of those theories.[7]

6

Instead of debating the pros and cons of the concept of formal purposeful action — an ambiguous, clumsy and all-meaning phrase — it is more useful to refer to the making and implementation of decisions: primarily that kind of decision-making which takes place in institution-alised environments, that is within organisations.[8] In other words with the manner in which decisions are made by groups of individuals acting in some kind of coalition or corporate manner. But this is still too shallow a response. How are decisions made? What group of individuals? What is the framework within which decisions are reached?

To answer these kinds of question we need to consider organisational decision-making in more detail.[9] The first move which can be made is to attempt to give greater meaning to the concept of decision-making. A decision in itself does not give very much away. For example, the British Government's many pronouncements and apparent changes in policy regarding the Channel Tunnel is one such instance. But what were the pros and cons, the pressures, which Cabinet's considered and discussed which led up to the making of those particular decisions? In other words, the essence of the sequence of decisions from the perspective of the social and political sciences is therefore with the way in which those decisions were reached. In other words, what can be called the decision-making process. Abstracting from this example we can now say that what is of particular interest from a planning point of view is the process by which decisions are made and the organisational framework within which that process takes place.[10]

But what about the types of decision with which planning is interested? Although it might be revealing to know the process by which some of the more trivial organisational decisions are made, it can be reasonably assumed that their substantive impact on the principles, procedures and objectives of a particular organisation would be fairly minimal. The kinds of decision-making of greater interest are those decisions where issues of substance are involved, issues involving those very principles, procedures and objectives which organisations are attempting to pursue. In other words, the process of the making, implementation and coordination of policies, and in particular public policy-making. [11] It is at this stage that the case for a more robust and purposeful meaning of planning can begin to be made. But first it is necessary to consider this concept of public policy-making in more detail.


## Planning and policy-making

According to the Oxford Dictionary policy means *'statecraft; course of action adopted by government, party, etc; sagacious procedure'*. The last of these meanings is perhaps of most relevance because it implies that policy requires the maker(s) to have or show 'insight and practical wisdom', or as some writers have noted, reticulist skills. [12] In this context the interpretation can be refined to an assertion that policy is an implicit or explicit statement or declaration of intent, intended action or commitment on the part of policy-makers to pursue and implement a particular course or courses of action. [13] In terms of policy-*making*, and in particular a contemporary and widely accepted and respected interpretation of public policy-making, we can do no better than to follow the outline proposed by Dror. This view, which corresponds to another what Schon has called an 'idea in good currency', [14] argues that:

> Public policy-making is a very complex, dynamic process whose various components make different contributions to it. It decides major guidelines for action directed at the future, mainly by governmental organs. These guidelines (policies) formally aim at achieving what is in the public interest by the best possible means. [15]

With regard to the implications of his definition, Dror outlines twelve significant features. Policy-making, he argues, is very complex because it involves a configuration of highly interrelated and interconnected components which interact in a multiplicity of ways. Some parts of the process are explicit and open to observation, but many others are implicit, hidden and therefore difficult to detect. It is also a dynamic process, a continuous activity which changes over time, and with sequences which vary internally and with respect to each other. Furthermore, it requires a continuing input of resources and motivation. This complexity and dynamism is, he argues, directly related to the variety and number of the components or substructures involved at any one point in time. (The substructures most involved being the political institutions or the political system of a society.) Every substructure therefore makes different contributions to public policy, depending in part on the formal and informal characteristics of each. But most importantly, Dror argues, policy-making is a type of decision-making which takes an aggregative form rather than with the making of discrete or individualistic decisions. Public policy therefore tries to lay down general directives or major guidelines rather than to set-down a detailed list of decisions to cover all possible situations. Furthermore, a kind of decision-making which results in external action, in changes in the decision-maker(s), in both, or in neither, but which is intended to result in action. For Dror one of the most significant characteristics of policy-making is that it is directed at the future: in other words, it recognises explicitly the 'ever-present' elements of uncertainty and doubtful prediction and therefore introduces them into the policy equation.

A principal difference between private and public policy-making is that the latter mainly concerns actions which are taken and implemented mainly by governmental organs. Here Dror incorporates semi-government and quasi-government institutions into the equation as well as government itself. A significant claim made by public policy-makers and most contemporary political institutions is that they formally aim at achieving things. They all try to establish their legitimacy, and hence gain continued support, by presenting policies usually couched in terms of the public interest. Or rather the political image of what constitutes the public interest by the best possible means — that is, public interest achieved less cost of achievement.[16]

These working definitions of policy and policy-making have stemmed from the idea of decision-making and the process by which supra (rather than trivial) decisions are made.[17] But what of planning, and in particular public planning? Is planning a 'special case' of public policy-making or is it subsumed by it? Dror argues that decision-making is a broader concept which incorporates policy-making, but that planning — like policy-making — is a species of decision-making which often overlaps with policy-making: 'Sometimes planning is a major means of policy-making, characterised by being relatively more structured, explicit and systematic, and by presuming to be more rational.'[18]

It is doubtful whether many contemporary planners or policy-makers would violently disagree with these observations. Indeed if these observations are accepted it is possible to argue that neither decision-making, public nor private policy-making, nor planning can be regarded as a mutually exclusive activity. Rather they can be viewed as a set of similar activities, layered and overlapping, one upon the other (Figure 2.1).

Having established that relationships exist between decision-making, policy-making and planning, the position has been reached where it is possible to set up a working definition of planning, and in particular for public planning. Having followed Dror as the principal protagonist it is useful to observe what he has to say about planning: 'Planning is the process of preparing a set of decisions for action in the future, directed at achieving goals by preferable means.'[19]

It is also doubtful whether many contemporary planners or policy-makers would violently disagree with this interpretation, so it too may be taken as being broadly representative of an 'idea in good currency' *vis-à-vis* public planning.[20] This definition then incorporates a number of significant elements, elements which when taken together make planning a

Fig. 2.1   Planning and policy-making

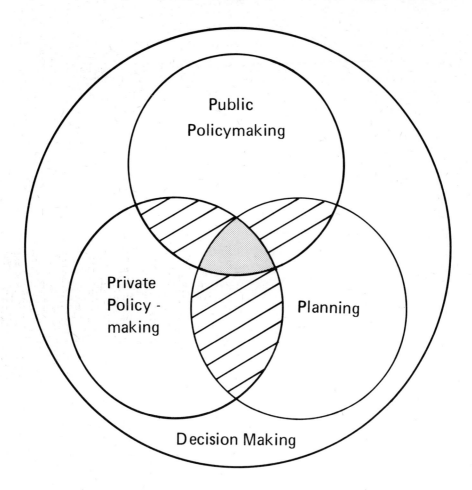

distinct and definable social activity. The first of these elements is that, like policy-making, planning too is a process: a continuous activity requiring resources and commitment in order for it to be sustained. It is also a process of preparing — formally and often legally — a set of decisions to be approved and implemented by some other institution or organisation. Whereas planning is a kind of decision-making and policy-making, according to Dror its principal identifying characteristic is that it attempts to deal with a set of decisions, a matrix of interdependent and sequential decisions which are systematically related. It is therefore primarily concerned with action and action directed at the future. Like policy-making planning is also concerned with problems of prediction and uncertainty which impact on and pervade all aspects, problems and features of planning.

Dror also argues that planning is concerned with the achievement of goals; in fact he goes so far as to say that the planning process cannot operate unless it has clearly defined goals with which it can focus its attention and hence direct its recommendations and commitment to action. The manner in which it sets about this task is therefore to match goals and intent via action by identifying the most preferable means in combination with a feasible input of resources.

So Dror's interpretation of planning is a fairly tight and unambiguous working definition. But there is one further point that should be stressed here, and that concerns the often confused relationships between what is meant by the 'process of planning' with what is meant by a 'plan'. In many instances the two concepts are used interchangeably, and often with unfortunate consequences. [21] In specific instances it is possible to consider a 'plan' as an outcome of the process of planning, but not necessarily as the only or natural outcome. [22] As Dror points out: 'A plan can be defined as "a set of decisions for action in the future" and can be arrived at either through planning, or through some other — rational or irrational — method of decision-making.' [23]

According to this notion of the separation of the concept of the process of planning from the concept of a plan, it is possible to arrive at a more refined interpretation of the concept of planning in 'good currency'. According to Faludi: 'Planning is the application of rational methods to the setting of objectives and their translation into public policies and concrete action programmes. It is future-oriented and geared towards social values.' [24]


**Planning and change**

The parallels between Faludi's and Dror's definitions are obvious enough, but there are two differences of some significance between them. The first concerns the different emphasis each places on the need for planning to be aiming at some desirable future state of affairs: Dror stresses the idea of the need for 'goals' to be explicitly stated as a formal part of the procedure of planning, whereas Faludi stresses the 'setting of objectives'. The difference is more than one of semantics. It is not the intention here to pursue what constitutes a 'goal' or 'objective', or how different they may or may not be. Rather the distinction between Dror and Faludi can be discussed in a more positive and potentially useful way in terms of 'ends' and 'means'.

Dror implicitly argues that goals, according to his terminology, are desirable 'ends' to be achieved through planning ('means'). Faludi's point is that objectives are simply a series of 'means' by which policies are formulated and articulated into action programmes ('ends'), and that this overall procedure constitutes planning. But Faludi takes his argument one step further: these action programmes are in turn concerned with having an impact on society — in other words his actions are not 'ends' in themselves but merely 'means' to achieving other 'ends'. So quite clearly not only can we criticise Dror for implicitly arguing that goals are desirable 'ends' to be achieved in and of themselves, but more importantly that the very 'ends-means' distinction is tautological — an 'end' is simply another 'means' by which some other activity is or might be pursued.

The second significant difference between Faludi and Dror stems to a certain degree from this initial distinction. This concerns the emphasis each author gives to three of the critical components of planning and policy-making: what policy hopes to achieve in a given situation (policy *intent*), how that policy is to be articulated and pursued (policy *implementation*), and to what extent policy has achieved what it sets out to do (policy *impact*).[25]

Whereas Dror tends to concentrate on planning as primarily intended action (policy intent), playing down the rôles for and relationships between policy implementation and impact, Faludi clearly takes a different tack. He also stresses policy intent but gives more emphasis to policy implementation. It is perhaps interesting to note that both authors appear to neglect the actual impact side of planning and policy-making — the concern for assessing whether or not what was intended has been matched by reality — what has in another context been called policy evaluation and policy review.[26] But it serves to illustrate the view that any comprehensive working definition of planning must be capable of incorporating all three of these components into its structure, if it is to have any viable utility. In other words, that planning must be as equally concerned with the impact of perceived outcomes of policies as much as if not more than with their original creation and mobilisation.[27]

This in turn has some rather interesting implications for a study of the nature and practice of planning. In the first place it indicates that planning is broadly concerned with the idea of 'change' — however defined. Second, that one of its underlying principles concerns a more normative relationship between the idea of planning and change: planning for change. Third, that this dualism — between descriptive/positive and normative/deductive — is a continuous process of mutual interaction which relates what is substantively legitimate in theory to what is regarded as reasonably legitimate in practice.

So this concern of planning with and for change is a crucially important characteristic. But it also serves to illustrate the fact that the very idea of change itself is neither a neatly defined nor definable concept. The concept of change is messy and confusing precisely because it is ubiquitous and continuous rather than orderly and discrete. The powerful implication which this has for planning is therefore crystal-clear: if the notion of planning is to be justified on the grounds that it is concerned primarily if not principally with change — and change is messy, confusing, ubiquitous and continuous by definition — then presumably it must follow that this disorderly state of affairs has to be, if not one of its distinguishing features, at least reflected in the mechanisms, ideas, techniques and principles which planning marshals in its general defence of and search for the boundaries of its legitimacy. In other words that planning as an institutional activity reflects the requisite variety which characterises the environment — broadly defined — with which it is principally concerned.[28,29]

If 'change' is a heterogeneous rather than homogeneous commodity, is it not possible to discern broad types of change which, when taken together, would allow for a reasonably generalised level of examination at the expense of detail? In fact Cattell proposes just such a typology of interdependence, a model of change. He distinguishes between five 'ideal' types of change:

1   change in a 'fixed' trait or channel,
2   change in the levels of temporary states,
3   change in environmental relations,
4   change as a tendency to change,
5   change as a characteristic configurational sequence or process.[30]

This typology, or more meaningfully range of types of change, could be of some importance to planning, if it is accepted that a concern of planning is with change. In other words, any formal attempt at planning would have to be able to illustrate that it recognises the nature and importance of change as well as its basic distinguishing characteristics. To argue that it would be concerned with change *per se* is a truism and not a sufficient condition for its legitimation. Likewise if it is accepted that another of its conditions is that of planning for change. If this too is a reasonable position to adopt, any formal attempt to institute planning would have to be able to illustrate that it recognised the importance of different kinds of change and the way in which that change could be identified, accommodated and indeed subjected to some measure of control or influence across the full interlocking spectrum of types of change.

This assessment of the relationship between the nature of planning and the concept of change has been concerned primarily with the legitimation of planning as an institutional activity in and of its own right. It has been pursued 'internal' to the idea of public policy-making and planning, not with the broader 'external' relationships between planning as an institutional activity and the social system or environment within which it clearly operates. A fine and often tenuous relationship of crucial dimensions.

## The need for public planning

If it can be agreed that Faludi's interpretation is in principle representative of the current state of the art, we must consider, given the present structuring of western capitalist society and its concomitant system of social values, whether or not such an activity can really be justified and justifiable. After all, what are the implications of what we have been saying? In brief it is this: if it is accepted that such an interpretation is legitimate, we are passively condoning an activity which involves a minority of individuals (planners, policy-makers, etc.) who are mostly elected by nondemocratic, if not undemocratic, means, and whose resultant actions impinge in some form or other on the actions and aspirations of the majority of individuals in that society. [31] The parallels with the dilemmas of political philosophy in the sense of involvement by the state are therefore obvious: how can such interference be justified and reconciled with the freedom and liberty of the individual? Such arguments usually involve what have been referred to as the antagonisms of planning. [32]

Arguments about the need for planning and public intervention usually involve a debate with a particular political and economic doctrine of liberalism: the philosophy of 'Laissez-faire'. In its indiluted form this doctrine — 'laissez-faire et laissez-passer' ('let things continue without interference') [33] — which is generally totally opposed to planning, especially public planning and state intervention, usually objects on four fundamental and interrelated grounds:

1  Planning interferes with the accepted axioms of economics, and hence with the smooth and natural functioning of the market mechanism (the 'invisible hand'), leading to inefficiency in the use of scarce resources by a general and inevitable distortion of the market.
2  Planning seriously restricts, to an intolerable degree, the freedom of the individual to determine his own actions, and hence destiny, within the

framework which society provides him and which he as an equal member contributes to.

3   Planning is wholly undemocratic and stands condemned on its own admission: it allows a minority of individuals to impose their collective authoritarian will on the majority who neither want nor need such intervention.

4   Planning, especially public planning, is totally inflexible and hence unable to accommodate the needs and aspirations of the individual, imposing order on individuals and groups of individuals where previously no such order existed or was merited.

The first point to note about these dissensions is that those who do not generally believe in the need for public planning or policy-making of the kinds which have been outlined usually have some naive individualistic or atomistic view of society that sees all men as being somehow 'free' and 'equal' at any point in time and at any stage of social or economic development. Any differentials which may be apparent or which might appear, for example, in the distribution of income or entrance to higher education, merely reflect 'natural forces' and the 'abilities' of individuals to realise or not realise their potential or position in society.[34]

The second point is equally basic: if any form of planning is to be opposed on the grounds outlined above, then surely *any form of government or any form of government activity is to be opposed by definition:* Adam Smith, in a much quoted passage from *The Wealth of Nations,* illustrates the position adopted by the eighteenth and nineteenth century physiocrats — in the United Kingdom typified by the 'Manchester School' — with real precision. Writing in 1776, Smith asserted that:

> The Statesman, who should attempt to direct private people in what manner they ought to employ their capitals, would not only load himself with a most unnecessary attention, but assume an authority which could safely be trusted, not only to no single person, but to no council or senate whatever, and which would nowhere be so dangerous as in the hands of a man who had folly and presumption enough to fancy himself to exercise it.[35]

To some extent the extreme position which this reflects indicates many of the broader criticisms, internal conflicts and paradoxical arguments which abound within the very philosophy of 'laissez-faire' itself. [36] For example, as Edmund Dell points out (in the context of public intervention in industry):

> *Laissez-faire* means government abstention from action on principle, and hence the rejection on principle of responsibility in the social

and economic fields . . . (but) it is far more a *feeling* about the way government should behave than a *principle* as to how it should behave. . . . This is the dilemma about *laissez-faire*. It cannot realistically imply repudiation of government responsibility for the economy or for industry. Government can disengage from industry. It cannot disengage from responsibility.[37]

From this brief discussion it is possible to arrive at a very simplistic justification for public planning. But it is an unsatisfactory justification because it does nothing substantive to satisfy or negate the kind of opposition outlined above. Simply stated the argument runs like this: the rôle of government, in the broader sense of representing, indeed constituting, politics and the political process, can be described and indeed justified in terms of the need to balance and reconcile conflicting interests. As Crick puts it, this rôle is therefore both evaluative and predictive, not only because it involves an act of selection from a potentially infinite range of relevant factors, but also because it has to be justified as in some way significant.[38] Therefore so long as we have a society which is basically tolerant of this kind of activity in the form and name of government, then we have a sufficient justification for government intervention and planning.[39]

## Public planning and public intervention

Having established a simple justification for planning we are now in a stronger position to tackle an issue of arguably greater significance: given that some degree of public intervention is legitimate is it not possible to identify and map-out the broad boundaries of this legitimacy, between what is deemed permissible intervention and what is not? One approach to this problem is to consider the kind of parameters which would be of some use in assessing the degree or level of such intervention by considering the implications of two simple concepts:

1   planibility,
2   welfare economics.

Derived by Bićanić, the concept of 'planibility' is a crucial one, and means roughly what it implies: the fundamental ability to plan.[40] It is possible to identify at least three components of planibility:

1   technical planibility,
2   economic planibility,
3   social and political planibility.

The concept of technical planibility means pretty much what it implies. It is the basic technical expertise and ability, the technical feasibility required to plan a particular activity or set of activities. Economic planibility concerns a 'trade-off' between the potential 'benefits' of public action (intent) measured against the probable 'costs' associated with various forms and degrees of planned intervention (impact). For intervention to be legitimate on these grounds the 'benefits' (however measured) must be equal to or greater than the possible effects or 'costs' attributable to other forms of intervention or non-intervention. In other words the balance between whether it would pay to intervene and the form such intervention might take. [41] Social and political planibility concerns the social and political feasibility of intervention, given the possible constraints imposed on action by particular sections of the social system and the political machine. Obviously if an activity is to be planned it must be regarded as being both socially and politically legitimate.

These three components are by no means mutually exclusive characteristics. They are all concerned with the ability to plan. But when taken together they recognise that there are different facets, imposing a multiplicity of constraints, each with a different potential, which need to be identified and which require radically different treatment, and which generate implications which are − potentially anyway − at some variance. [42] They indicate that what might be a legitimate area of concern in one respect, for example to intervene technically, might not be regarded as legitimate in another, for example in the political context. So whereas the concept of planibility does not map-out the precise boundaries of legitimate intervention it does indicate some of the constraints which would have to be considered before any attempt to intervene were made. In this context all three components of planibility appear to have at least one thing in common: each requires a basic prior knowledge and understanding of the process of planning *vis-à-vis* the degree of intervention in terms of the other two components. For example, to implement a policy set which is technically legitimate demands that similar requirements are fulfilled for the economic, social and political components. In other words, that the policy set itself is capable of legitimation.

Welfare economics, or rather concepts made use of in that branch of applied economic theory which is concerned with 'welfare', is potentially of some value in mapping-out the legitimate area of concern for planning and public intervention. [43] As Winch notes, welfare economics concerns the study of the well-being of society, *in so far as it is affected by the decisions and actions of its members and agencies concerning economic variables.*[44] Welfare economics is therefore concerned with 'mainstream' microeconomic principles and concepts — factors of production, determinants of production, costs, etc. — but from a subtlely different perspective. Whereas it is as equally concerned with notions of economic efficiency as much as with any other branch of microeconomics, its principle difference is that it stresses the equity or distributional aspects of economic development. It is, as Winch notes, concerned not so much with factors, production and costs *per se* but more with the extent and nature of the use of factors of production, with the types and quantities of goods and services produced both individually and collectively, and with the differential impact or distribution of the benefits as well as the costs resulting from economic activity. An interest of welfare economics is therefore concerned with the satisfaction of social wants as well as private or individual wants. Or as Winch puts it:

> The private interest and the public interest can and do conflict. If a particular course of action would result in some persons being privately better off and some worse off, the economics of individual behaviour alone stops short of telling us whether it is *on balance* a desirable policy.[45] (Italics added.)

It is contended here that the notions of welfare economics and planning coalesce on this issue of 'on balance'. Neither provides cut-and-dried solutions, but when taken together they reflect and map-out the broad boundaries and dimensions of this balance between public and private involvement, and in turn yield some interesting insights into the nature of the processes of the legitimation of economic planibility.

On this basis the use of applied welfare economics helps to identify at least four broad themes where public intervention and planning might be considered justifiable and hence legitimate. These correspond to notions of:

1  public or collective goods,
2  externalities,
3  indivisibilities,
4  public welfare.[46]

Where a market for the provision of certain (non-free) goods and services does not exist, or where one cannot be effectively made use of, then welfare economics illustrates that a legitimate alternative may be to supply them as a public service.[47] Indeed, the notion of 'collective' goods — catering for a group want, where consumption cannot be confined to those who are prepared to pay for them — is the *raison d'être* for the

18

provision of public goods. Examples of pure and semi-pure public goods —
if supplied to one are supplied to many if not all — include national
defence, streetlighting, flood protection, police, etc. On this basis the
marginal or 'grey' areas for legitimate public intervention concern those
aspects of consumption for which a market cannot be effectively made
use of for providing primarily semi-pure public goods (for example, state
education, a national health service, roads, etc.)

Where private costs (and the benefits associated with them) differ from
social costs (and benefits), then welfare economics indicates that there
may be certain additional grounds for legitimate public intervention. In
particular in those cases where private costs (or benefits) incurred (or
received) as a result of a particular activity diverge from total, real or
social costs (or benefits), and where the difference is not borne (or
received) by the individual responsible for producing or consuming that
activity. In other words where external costs (or benefits) are involved. [48]
These 'externalities', according to Peters, [49] can be of broadly four types:

1  production-to-production externalities;
2  production-to-consumption externalities;
3  consumption-to-consumption externalities; and
4  consumption-to-production externalities.

By 'production-to-production' externalities Peters refers to the kind of
situation where the activity of one individual 'producer' impinges directly
or indirectly on the nature and scale of operations of another, other things
being equal. A classic example is provided by river basin development: for
example, a dam built upstream from existing electricity generating plant
may serve to increase total generating capacity by controlling river flow,
but at no additional cost to the electricity company concerned.

By a 'production-to-consumption' externality Peters refers to the
situation where the activity of one individual 'producer' impinges directly
or indirectly on the welfare and actions of 'consumers'. He cites as
examples smoke nuisance, noise intrusion and water pollution.

By 'consumption-to-consumption' externalities Peters refers to those
situations where the activity of one 'consumer' or group of consumers
impinges directly or indirectly on the welfare and activities of other
consumers. He cites the playing of transistor radios in parks as an
example. A more relevant one for planning might be delays and traffic
congestion attributable to, say, the conflict between private cars and
pedestrians in city centres.

By a 'consumption-to-production' externality Peters refers to the kind
of situation where the activity of one 'consumer' impinges directly or

indirectly on the nature and scale of operations of a 'producer' or producers. The example he cites is where a group of ramblers trample over growing crops, a situation where the farmer has no form or means of redress or compensation.[50]

The idea of indivisibilities as a legitimate area of concern for public involvement stems not so much from the principles of welfare economics as from some of the implications arising out of their application. Pure theory treats factor inputs — land, labour, capital, entrepreneurial talent — and methods and scales of production (output) as being 'perfectly divisible'. A situation where both factor inputs and productive processes can be thought of as being continuous rather than discrete entities. The problem of this ubiquitous assumption is that it is at some variance to and irreconcilable with the 'real world'. For example, it is patently absurd to treat labour as a continuous factor input. We can only usefully refer to either one man, two men, or three men, etc. Labour is therefore a discrete variable: we cannot sensibly refer to it or treat it in terms of a continuous progression from one man, to one-and-a-half men, to two men, etc. Likewise with productive capacity. For example, to increase the capacity of a fixed pipe-line operating at full capacity requires not some magical continuous mathematical adjustment but rather a discrete physical operation: the construction of a new, larger capacity pipe.

The argument is by no means restricted to these kind of more trivial examples. Consider a major capital investment decision: to build a new aluminium smelter.[51] The decision requires a simple answer to a very simple question. The scale of investment is such that if it is to operate at all it has to be built either in its entirety or it is not built. There is no room for marginal or continuous adjustment to existing capacity. It is an all-or-nothing situation requiring all-or-nothing commitment. This example serves to illustrate the twin ideas behind the concept of indivisibility: the problem posed by large-scale production and the need for integration of effort. That is, where capital investment is primarily 'lumpy'; where it is beyond the scope and capacity of private individuals to implement; where it has a significant impact in terms of altering price structures and cost levels, spatially and sectorally; and where a joint or state effort would achieve more for society than the sum of potential individual actions.[52] Classic examples of investment decisions where indivisibilities, or 'lumpiness', can be identified are in the fields of electricity generating capacity and rail transport.

In terms of comparative costs and 'technological progress' in electricity generation, contemporary debates in this country at least have hinged on whether capacity should be increased by re-equipping present power

20

stations together with the possible addition of one or two 'intermediate technology' stations — coal- or oil-fired — or opting for the 'total technology' approach, for example nuclear power. The need for additional capacity has not been in serious dispute, only the means by which it is to be realised. Both schemes are 'lumpy' in the sense with which the term is usually employed and both are indisputably beyond the scope and means of individuals to either finance or operate.

Similarly with the problem of developments in rail transport. 'Present technology' approaches emphasise diesel-powered modes, but in terms of improving and redeveloping rail transport an alternative and attractive 'intermediate technology' solution exists: electrification. But this kind of investment is inherently 'lumpy'. It is not really feasible to embark on a programme of electrification based on marginal additions or extensions in the form of some kind of continuous extrusion. Rather the problem is discrete. Broadly speaking, sections of track need to be electrified in full — at one and the same time — or not at all. There are no long-term half-way solutions which can be justified on either economic or operational grounds. Likewise with the power units. Moreover it too is beyond the scope of individuals to either finance or operate.

The notion of indivisibilities therefore provides a useful 'catch-all' category for potential legitimate activity by the state on at least five by no means mutually exclusive grounds: first, where the scale of production of an activity is of significant proportions (for example, as measured in terms of proportion of total GDP); second, where the scale of production requires a level of investment — not just finance — which is of significant proportions (for example, as measured in terms of the proportion of total investment); thirdly, where that level of investment is significantly 'lumpy', or where a threshold or step-function is identified such that unless investment takes place at that rate or scale it is impossible to effectively or efficiently operationalise the project in either economic or technical terms; fourthly, where that level of investment is a more or less 'once and for all' exercise (for example, a nuclear power station, city centre development, an aluminium smelter) with a long project life; and finally, where that investment requires a significantly high level of integrated effort on the part of private individuals and/or organisations, and which is beyond the scope of any one of them.

The fourth and arguably the most important and contentious area of potentially legitimate intervention concerns the idea of intervention by the state in the interests and (latterly) promotion of public welfare. [53] As Sleeman notes, in terms of the contemporary history of government involvement in public welfare (particularly in the United Kingdom), the state has legitimately and historically performed three, what can be called remedial, rôles: maintaining law and order; arbitrating in disputes and upholding the sanctity of contracts; and providing relief in acute cases of need or inequality. But more recently, and in the case of this country from 1945 onward, successive governments have tended to adopt a fourth more positive interventionist rôle. Sleeman describes it thus:

> ... there is no doubt that we have seen a change in the concept of the rôle of the Government in the community which is one of kind rather than merely of degree. The term 'welfare state' reflects an attitude towards the state, which sees it as *a positive agent for the promotion of social welfare* ... Not only should the Government provide social services, such as social security, medical treatment, education, welfare facilities and subsidized housing, but these should go beyond the provision of a bare minimum . . .[54] (Italics added.)

There are at least two important themes which need to be disentangled and examined here: first, what is generally referred to as the deferment of consumption criterion, and second, the criterion of the public interest.

To argue that welfare economics provides solutions to the problems of general public welfare is clearly too speculative, but — as has been argued earlier — this is to misinterpret the value of welfare economics *to* public planning. The idea of deferred consumption is a good example, and illustrated perfectly by Peters:

> Is there a distinction between the time preferences of *private individuals,* which in the last analysis must be related to the length of human life, and that of *society as a whole,* which must at least be regarded as somewhat longer?[55] (Italics added.)

There are at least three interrelated issues here. First, do the preferences of individuals sum to reflect the preferences of society? Second, is the notion and value of time to an individual the same as that of society in the context of social change? Third, on what basis do individuals prefer consumption now to consumption in the future? It has already been argued that private and social preferences may indeed differ — and differ significantly. A case for the rôle of welfare economics in this context has therefore already been made, but it also gives some interesting insights into the second and third issues: that of the relationship between perceptions of private and social time, and private and social preferences.

The pure theory of economics intimates that private and social do not, or rather need not, necessarily diverge — they can be considered as one and the same thing. In terms of equating present consumption to future

22

consumption, the 'invisible hand' is deemed to be the rate of interest: consumption now is 'traded-off' against consumption in the future via 'price'. But the point has already been made that private and social can and indeed often do diverge. [56] If this is the case, is it not more valid to argue that what might be an optimal 'trade-off' for the individual might not necessarily be an optimal 'trade-off' for society as a whole? Is it not also equally valid to argue therefore that what might constitute the private rate of discount as reflected by the market may not coincide or even remotely reflect the rate at which society discounts the foregoing of consumption now in favour of consumption for future generations? If this is the case then welfare economics indicates that where, as Peters puts it, capital is used to 'strengthen the framework of society for the future', and where the short-term returns to that investment are concomitantly low, then intervention by the state may be 'allowable'. He cites as good examples the reclamation and conservation of land, but perhaps better examples are provided by the National Health Service and state-controlled education. A case can also be made to include the interventionist policies of governments with respect to regional development. [57]

The link between welfare economics and the public interest can be considered as a simple extension of the idea of social discounting and deferment of present consumption. That a function of the private rate of return on capital is to allocate it between competing uses is as axiomatic as that it reflects private preferences as between present and future consumption. That in practice the private rate diverges from the social rate is something less than axiomatic. In fact it is very much open to debate. With respect to the public interest therein lies its inherent theoretical weakness — but also its source of political strength.

Cannot the same argument then be made for the function of the social rate of return as that for the private? That the social rate of return reflects the social allocation of social capital between competing social uses, representing social preferences as between present and future consumption. In other words, that the social rate of return reflects the interests of society at large — the public interest. This theme can be taken one step further. The fact that the social rate of return is generally assumed to be lower than the private rate of return may constitute a truism, since society's time margins are substantially longer than those of the individuals which make up its structure. So investment made on society's behalf is likely to be of a more longer-term nature and involving — potentially anyway — lower rates of return, especially rates of return in the short run.

The criterion or criteria to be used to evaluate whether or not this kind of project is deemed socially desirable is therefore not a specific cardinal rate reflecting the return to be made in the private market for capital, but rather a rate — cardinal or ordinal — which is deemed to be relevant to the long-term interests and development of society, if it only implies the deferment of consumption now. So a rôle for intervention by the state, or rather a justification based on the notion of the public interest, could be not to try and beat the market system at its own game (and therefore according to its own rules), but rather to draw-up a set of different rules which incorporates the rôle of the private sector, within which the private sector may or may not operate. The political ramifications are clearly immense.[58]

But there is one particular outcome of this approach which has a bearing on the relationship between public planning, welfare economics, and the public interest. Simply stated it is that the social rate of return need not or should not be tied to or indeed set in the perspective of private rates of return. Rather an argument can be made that it should be the other way around: private rates of return should be considered within the context of social rates when questions of general public welfare are deemed important — that is, within the context of the public interest. In this relational situation it is the state which is deemed to be the guardian or custodian of public welfare. It is therefore these state-societal relations which maps-out, indeed constitutes, the legitimacy-conferring idea of what is or is not in the public interest. In other words the political and public policy-making domain.

The point is simple and yet potentially emotive.

But what is the alternative? The contemporary view is that intervention by the state should reflect, if not follow, not only the spirit and purpose of economic efficiency as prescribed by contemporary liberal economic doctrine, but also by the views of respected industrialists. In the context of the private-versus-social rate of return argument, this means that enterprise conducted by the state should broadly follow market principles — in other words, public enterprise should attempt to keep in step with the cardinal rates of return currently reflected in the capital markets, or at least something approximating to them.[59] The problem associated with this view is that liberal economic theory — or rather the theory proposed by liberal economists — is in a state of considerable turmoil regarding what type of rate is even applicable let alone appropriate. There is no consensus view, apart from the notion that the public sector should roughly follow market trends set by the private sector. The chaos is admirably summed-up by Peters:

> Indeed it is now widely held that choice of an appropriate rate is purely a *value-judgement* and that it is impossible to lay down any

clear-cut rules of procedure. But if this is so does it not reduce the whole procedure from an exact science to an 'art' dependent on personal judgement, preferences and perhaps prejudice? [60] (Italics added.)

Without entering the controversy as to whether or not liberal economic theory treats the rate of interest and discount problem in a manner approximating to the demands of an exact science, the message is nevertheless clear: economic theory is not particularly helpful. But implicit in Peters viewpoint is the black-and-white notion that if economics as a 'science' cannot help (economics being 'good') then any alternative – presumably politics – is by definition not only as equally doomed to failure but is not 'science' and therefore 'bad'. This ideological shadow-boxing in the guise of rigorous analysis is displayed by the Editor of the Institute of Economic Affairs in the preface to Peters' *Eaton Paper:*

> If . . . theory is defective, it cannot be used as an argument for taking decisions out of the market and putting them into the corridors of political power . . . It cannot yet be said that the 'economic and social priorities' laid down by government reflect very much more than good intentions or political pressures. [61]

But what is inherently wrong, 'bad', or necessarily perjorative about value judgements, preferences, prejudices, good intentions or political pressures? Such is the stuff of politics and the political process. Indeed, according to Crick it is precisely these notions which constitute the very essence of political choice: to balance and reconcile conflicting interests. In fact Sir Geoffrey Vickers argues that by definition politics, the political process and the formulation and implementation of public policy itself is an 'art of judgement'. [62]

Quite clearly then, these four interdependent themes – public goods, externalities, indivisibilities, public welfare – when taken together indicate a potentially legitimate area for some state involvement if not total public intervention. Areas of involvement and intervention which are in turn the subject of the continuous checks and balances of political debate, public scrutiny and social accountability. Indeed it can be argued that this process itself helps to identify the boundaries of what is legitimate intervention by the state. But boundaries also act as constraints to action – the private interest can and often does conflict, as we noted earlier, with the public interest. In this context welfare economics clearly does not provide us with clear-cut analyses or cut-and-dried policy prescriptions. As Winch points out, a rôle for welfare economics in public planning is to pinpoint the issues about which value judgements regarding intervention by the state must be made, to reason from those value judgements, and to comment on their appropriateness as means of identifying areas for *ex ante* action and *ex post* assessment. [63] In these respects welfare economics can only provide a framework, but an important framework grounded in a set of assumptions and arguments which are capable of being critically and politically evaluated. In this respect welfare economics provides broad directions outlining the scope of state involvement. Nothing more, nothing less. It says very little indeed about the scale or the magnitudes of such involvement. For example, in considering the four potential areas of legitimate intervention, what is really meant or implied by 'considerable' externalities? By 'beyond the scope of private action'? By 'short-term interests'? By 'for the sake of public welfare'? It is contended here that answers to these kind of questions can only be provided by a responsive pragmatism based on informed discussion and essentially political debate.

This political debate in some respects determines, reflects and is the reflector of potentially legitimate intervention, as well as that of the concept of planibility itself. This process is clearly dynamic and so interpretations of these constantly change and undergo continual evaluation and recasting through time. [64] To some extent, therefore, the very concept of intervention itself undergoes a similar process of constant evaluation, reevaluation and recasting. [65] The degrees of intervention can therefore be seen to be heavily dependent on the perceived pragmatics of the need to intervene and the means of intervention, in other words, with the problem of how to plan. It is this concept which will occupy the next two chapters.

## Notes

[1]  See A. Faludi, 1970, p. 1.
[2]  P. Hall, 1970, p. 1.
[3]  D. Schon, 1971, pp. 123–4; as an example see W. Solesbury, 1974, p. 9: planning must be *seen* in an administrative context, the *role* of politics must be explicitly *recognised*.
[4]  On purposive behaviour see H. Simon, 1957, p. 84–96.
[5]  Hall, 1970, op. cit., p. 1.
[6]  Obviously the distinction is a blurred one, compare with A. Etzione, 1964, pp. 89–94; for a dissenting view see M. Hill, 1972, pp. 32–47.
[7]  See A. Gouldner, 1970, pp. 26–9 and pp. 46–9; S. Grabow and A.

Heskin, 1973; J. Friedmann, 1973b, Chapter 1; also A. Faludi, 1973a, Part I, Introduction.

[8] See D. Silverman, 1970, Chapter 1.

[9] For an alternative approach see A. Faludi, 1973b, Chapter 4.

[10] See Simon, 1957, op. cit., pp. 8–11; Sir G. Vickers, 1965, Chapter 9; on decision-making see P. Levin, 1972.

[11] See Y. Dror, 1968, pp. 86–8; Sir G. Vickers, 1965, op. cit.; also J. Friend and N. Jessop, 1969, Chapter 5.

[12] The concept of 'reticulist skills' appears to have been coined by J. Power, 1971; see also J. Friend, J. Power and C. Yewlett, 1974, pp. 364–72.

[13] It is perhaps interesting to note that many writers on public administration and policy-making do not outline what they mean by 'policy'. For example, see Simon, 1957, op. cit. and J. Stewart, 1971. Simon distinguishes between four types of policy – legislative policy, management policy, working policy and practices (p. 59).

[14] Schon, 1971, op. cit., p. 123.

[15] Dror, 1968, op. cit., p. 12; Dror also has another working definition: 'The blind leading the lame and the lame leading the blind.' Conference on policy-making in local government, London, 24–5 June, 1974.

[16] Dror, 1968, op. cit., pp. 12–17.

[17] For an alternative discussion see D. Hart, 1974. Compare with G. Page, ex-Cabinet Minister responsible for implementing the 1972 Local Government Act. He argues that there are two stages to policy-making: (1) before declaration of a policy, and (2) after declaration of a policy statement. Stage (1) consists of 'fitting policy to facts', whereas stage (2) consists of 'fitting the facts to the policy'. Conference of policy-making in local government, London 24–5 June, 1974.

[18] Dror, 1968, op. cit., p. 17.

[19] Y. Dror, 1963, p. 51.

[20] Compare with R. Ackoff, 1970, pp. 2–4: planning as anticipatory decision-making.

[21] See Hart, 1974, op. cit.

[22] See also Chapter 5: The Administrative Setting.

[23] Dror, 1963, op. cit., p. 51.

[24] A. Faludi, 1969; for a more recent and modified version of this approach see Faludi, 1973b, op. cit.

[25] See D. Hart, 1975, Chapter 1.

[26] On relationships between policy evaluation and policy review, see F. Wedgewood-Oppenheim et al., 1975.

[27] See Hart, 1974, op. cit., pp. 27–9.

[28] On the 'law of requisite variety' see W. Ashby, 1956, Chapter 11, pp. 202–18; on an application in a public planning context see J. McLoughlin, 1973, Chapters 8 and 9, especially pp. 218–24.

[29] Whether this is the case is not at issue here; this thread will be picked-up in Chapters 6 and 7.

[30] R. Cattell, 1966.

[31] See in general F. von Hayek, 1944 and J. Dewey, 1927.

[32] The concept of antagonisms of planning has been coined by Faludi, 1969, op. cit.

[33] P. Taylor, 1968, p. 63.

[34] For a critique of this position see R. Miliband, 1969, H. Marcuse, 1964, J. Rawls, 1972 and A. Giddens, 1971. In an urban context, see D. Harvey, 1973.

[35] A. Smith, 1776, Book IV, Chapter 2.

[36] For example, see J. Robinson, 1964, Chapter 3.

[37] E. Dell, 1973, p. 16.

[38] See B. Crick, 1964, Chapter 1, especially pp. 32–3.

[39] For alternative discussions see J. Coleman, 1972, P. Self, 1972a and J. Dewey, 1927, op. cit.

[40] On the concept of 'planibility' see R. Bićanić, 1967, pp. 74–5.

[41] See note 16.

[42] For an alternative derivation see Dror, 1963, op. cit.

[43] On the problems associated with this approach see H. Rittell and M. Webber, 1973, R. Zeckhauser and E. Schaeffer, 1968 and C. Foster, 1972.

[44] D. Winch, 1971, p. 13.

[45] Winch, 1971, op. cit., p. 13.

[46] Faludi, 1969, op. cit.; see Solesbury, 1974, op. cit., for an alternative treatment.

[47] On public goods see R. Musgrave, 1959, pp. 13–14.

[48] On external costs and benefits of economic actions see E. Mishan, 1971, Chapter 16.

[49] G. Peters, 1966, p. 15.

[50] The examples which Peters makes use of to illustrate these types of externality are of interest in themselves. They indicate the problems which welfare economists face in attempting to track-down and identify, let alone quantify, different impacts. As he notes: 'Problems associated with the existence of externalities and group wants are among the most intractable in economics.' (Peters, 1966, op. cit., p. 45.)

[51] On the political problems of locating aluminium smelters in the UK see Dell, 1973, op. cit.

[52] A major implication in this respect concerns strategic or defence

requirements, where for reasons of national security the state controls, for example, nuclear energy supplies and its production.

[53] On the problem of public welfare in general see J. Sleeman, 1973.

[54] Sleeman, 1973, op. cit., pp. 4–5.

[55] Peters, 1966, op. cit., p. 19.

[56] On the problem of present versus future consumption see M. Feldstein, 1964.

[57] On an assessment of British regional economic policy in general see A. Brown, 1972.

[58] See for example the attempt in the UK to initiate 'planning agreements' between industry and government, see Secretary of State for Industry, 1975; also G. Polyani and P. Polyani, 1974, pp. 37–41, on the record of the public-sector industries; also S. Brittan, 1975, pp. 113–119, on a market-solution proposal to de-politicise state-industry relations.

[59] For example, government 'advice' to public-sector industries in the UK has been that capital investment projects should create a return of about 10 per cent per annum on the capital employed.

[60] Peters, 1966, op. cit., p. 19.

[61] Peters, 1966, op. cit., pp. 6–7.

[62] Crick, 1964, op. cit., and Vickers, 1965, op. cit.

[63] Winch, 1971, op. cit., Introduction.

[64] For an incisive assessment of the dilemma's of planning for change along these lines see A. Hirschman, 1967.

[65] For example, the way in which total administrative planning is tacitly accepted by society in conditions of impending catastrophes and their aftermaths, e.g. large-scale conflicts, natural disasters, etc.

# 3 Sketch for a Theory of Public Planning

The argument presented in the first two chapters has focussed attention on a number of areas of interest. This argument was formulated largely within the framework provided by what were referred to as 'ideas in good currency' *vis-à-vis* contemporary views as to what constitutes planning and policy-making. This perspective presented a case for planning as a unique and ubiquitous social activity, that its prime area of concern was the process by which decisions are made and implemented, together with the organisational framework within which that process takes place. In other words, that contemporary planning was concerned with the process of making policies, and in particular public policy. But this argument does not present or indeed prepare a sufficient case for the manner in which that planning and public policy-making takes place: the concept of what to plan cannot be neatly separated from the means at the planners disposal to plan. In other words, questions concerning what to plan cannot be divorced from questions of how to plan.[1]

Immediately a problem of major proportions arises, for on what foundations can a case be made for outlining the way in which planners plan and make policy? There are essentially three paths which can be taken here:

1   to observe what individuals who label themselves, or who are labelled, 'planners' actually do, and then critically assess the underlying assumptions on which their actions appear to be based (empirical approach); or
2   to develop a conceptual schema of what planners do from a more theoretical and philosophical viewpoint (conceptual approach); or
3   to attempt to do both (conceptual and empirical).

The best approach would clearly be the third — to attempt both at the same time — but it is dubious whether this is possible given the current 'states of the arts'. However, by introducing a division-of-labour into the problem it is possible to treat both simultaneously, but only by according one or other some initial priority or emphasis. The approach adopted for the remainder of this book will be to give initial priority to the conceptual side, and only then consider the behavioural component in more depth.[2]

31

So what are the theoretical assumptions and constructs which underpin a schematic approach to the problem of the means of public planning? Any attempt to provide insights into this problem must begin with a measure of the concept of planibility — cardinal or ordinal. In other words, with some idea of the degree of public intervention which can be deemed legitimate.[3] The argument whether or not to plan has already been illustrated to be to some extent a tautology. But there is obviously a potentially infinite range of different degrees of planning activity, from trivial public involvement to total state control. Fortunately there are no simple solutions to the kind of problem which this continuum begins to pull-out. There is no such thing as a 'best' form of public planning because the 'best' form of government simply does not exist. In fact it is possible to argue that there are potentially as many varieties of public planning as there are varieties of government.

This state of affairs is not especially helpful in a search for a solution to the problem of how to plan. One way out of this impasse is to delve into political theory, and in particular, theories of government and democracy. But this would be too restrictive. In the first place most classical theories of government and democracy do not have much to say about specific contemporary issues, for example the process of policy-making — which, we have argued, are critical to ideas concerning the very nature and purpose of public planning in 'good currency'.[4] In the second place, most classical theories rely on grossly over-simplified, holistic or individualistic perceptions of the way society operates. For example, by making use of notions like 'obligation' and 'social contract'.[5] Such notions have little to offer in the way of explanatory power; they do not contribute much to solving the problems associated with levels and degrees of public intervention.[6] These formal theories may be of some relevance in specific instances but are generally unsatisfactory for particular examination at this stage. They are certainly of obvious use in planning, but they do not assist much in what is arguably the major task with which we are faced: a theory for public planning.

### The idea of a theory for planning

The problem here is that any proposal for a theory for planning, particularly of the public genre, is plagued by a succession of fundamental ambiguities. Indeed some opponents have argued that it is precisely because of these ambiguities — which they argue are unavoidable if not insurmountable — that the search is at least doomed to the inevitability of failure, or at best akin to a search for the philosophers stone of planning.[7] These kinds of criticism, whilst carrying a good deal of intuitive weight, carry little in the way of explanatory power. Because ambiguities, however inevitable they may appear to be, are present, there are precious little grounds on which it can be argued that they are unavoidable, or more importantly insurmountable. To equate ambiguity with the inevitability of failure stretches credulity to the limit. Indeed it is possible to present an argument which is in many respects diametrically opposed to the internal logic of this dubious equation. In fact it can be argued that ambiguities, whilst reflecting fundamental weaknesses, are also a source of considerable strength, if not a vital ingredient, for the nature and practice of planning itself.

Ambiguities reflect, aid in the creation of, and sometimes reinforce complex and often messy social and organisational situations. These facets, when taken together, make for a further addition to the process of mystification, distortion and disorientation which surrounds and permeates much of our understanding of the social construction of reality.[8] The inevitability-of-failure argument outlined above can be interpreted as a simple reflection of this process, albeit in the context of what constitutes planning. (In fact the more extreme positions appear to demonstrate the reinforcement element quite clearly.) So if a theory for planning is to be dismissed as irrelevant and/or utopian, it needs to be based on firmer foundations than those associated with the problem of ambiguity. But what of the qualities which a theory for planning might offer? According to Faludi[9] this is the equivalent of asking the question: what can planning theory usefully do? He argues from a behaviourist position, from the perspective of the planner at work, and from the viewpoint of the social and political scientist. Such a theory can do at least three positive things: first, by providing a framework which might enable planners to reach a better understanding of the phenomenon of planning — it might sharpen their consciousnesses. Second, by enabling both planners and interested social scientists to make systematic comparisons of the planning context in different social systems. And third, by — potentially at least — helping in the process of institutional innovation in planning.

In this context, the complexity-of-ambiguity argument serves at least two useful and significant purposes. By standing the argument on its head, as it were, this complexity indicates, first, that there may be not one single theory for planning, but rather a series of partial theories which when taken together might constitute the basis for such a theory; and second, that this loose and messy theory might itself be multilevelled as well as multifaceted. The implications are of some importance.

33

If this supposition is roughly correct – that planning may be thought of as a series of jointed partial theories reflecting different emphases and content at different levels – then it is clearly important that the components which might contribute to it are given some consideration. Whether the result is termed a theory for planning is thus a matter for individual choice and judgement – its substantive content is what is really at issue.

There appear to be three levels at which this kind of theory for public planning can be disentangled: first, a theory or set of theories which attempts to account for the actual processes of planning itself (wholly methodological and 'internal'); second, a theory or set of theories which attempts to map-out the relationships between the institutionalised planning component and the broader environment within which it operates ('internal-external'), and third, a theory or set of theories which accounts for the processes of change within society as a whole, of which institutionalised planning may be at least an integral part or at most a substantial contributor (wholly 'external').

The first kind of theory accords roughly with what can be called the methodological nature of planning, emphasising the *operational/administrative* components. The second accords with what can be referred to as the relational nature of planning, emphasising the *institutional/operational* components. The third kind of theory accords more clearly with the broader political and social nature of planning, emphasising the *ideological/institutional* components. The first can therefore be seen as being the concern of methodology, and in particular the philosophy of method; the second with political and organisation theories; and the third with theories of social change. That these are by no means mutually exclusive areas of concern is axiomatic.

The remainder of this chapter, and subsequent ones, will therefore be concerned with the problems which this relational approach gives rise to, and in the sequence with which they were raised: the processes of planning, the environment of planning, and social change.


### The processes of planning

The idea of a theory or theories which might account for the internal methodology of planning cannot be adequately considered without recourse to two fundamental questions: 'What do we mean by theory?' and 'Why do we need a theory to explain the processes of planning?'

The first of these questions can be tackled with few problems. We can argue that any 'good' theory provides an orientation to the subject under study and thereby makes a further contribution to the level and body of existing knowledge. [10] In other words it provides what Faludi refers to as: 'a constituent element on which to base facts and provide directions.'[11]

Furthermore, as Karl Deutsch has admirably stated:

> ... a theory is not a simple proposition but (a) configuration of interrelated propositions ... Progress in knowledge changes our knowledge of single facts or propositions, leaving the larger ... configurations of thought substantially unchanged.[12]

There are two components which need to be considered in dealing with the second question: 'Why do we need a theory of the processes of planning?' The first strand stems from the previous discussion concerning the use, or rather inapplicability, of existing formal theories, and in particular theories of government and democracy. In other words *the sum total of those theories which are of use in and which impinge upon the study and practice of planning do not add up to a satisfactory fully worked-out theory of public planning.* [13] In fact it could be said that the persistent doubts which have been cast on the need for public planning have arisen because as yet no formal theoretical base has been developed from which to argue. [14] The corollary to this 'grand conspiracy theory' is that such a theory has not been allowed to develop because these doubts and criticisms have had a very powerful formal historical, political and theoretical base: the philosophy and practice of 'laissez-faire'.[15]

The second strand stems from the argument presented in the previous section. In presenting the three relational components of a theory for planning – internal, internal-external, and external – it was argued that the internal component could be considered as a problem of methodology, and in particular a problem of the philosophy of method. In fact Faludi goes one step further by arguing that the problem is more than one of method but rather the application of scientific method – however crude that might be – to the making of public policy. [16] This position – especially since the approaches of Faludi and Dror can be interpreted as representing 'ideas in good currency' – is of no small significance. Implicit in each authors argument is the assumption that we need a theory for the processes of planning in order to understand how to set about the task of planning itself. The whole of this second strand is therefore important for two reasons: because it sets the tone for much of what is to follow in this outline of a theory for planning, and because it is a contentious approach to adopt – in the light of some of the views of a number of contemporary writers on the problem of public planning. [17] (This dichotomy will be returned to in the next chapter when different types of planning activity are considered.)

So the need to account for the internal nature of planning – that is the concept of a theory for the processes of public planning – is quite an important one for a study of the nature and practice of planning itself. Exactly what level of importance is attached to it clearly depends on the view one takes of the importance of public involvement and intervention in society's affairs. But the two are inextricably interwoven: the 'state of the art' of planning, especially public planning, cannot sensibly be divorced from the process of its legitimation. Its level of sophistication and relevance – the state of the theory – will impact on the response by society to it and the manner in which it is implemented and the concomitant status which it is or is not accorded. It is also clearly a two-way relationship.

From the point of view of the internal component of planning, the importance of this conclusion concerns the way in which the idea of theory can be moulded with the idea of methodology. In other words to be at all 'policy-relevant' the proposal here must be seen to be internally consistent and to represent an improvement over what has been the traditionally accepted point of view. It is here that we begin to depart from those 'ideas in good currency' which have been outlined, and so develop a sketch for a theory of planning substantively different from them.

The starting point for this departure is the manner in which the two strands outlined above – theory and methodology – relate to one another. Both Faludi and Dror argue from a theoretical standpoint which sees planning as a form of the making and implementing of decisions and policies, public planning being a more complex, multilevelled and formalised version of this generic decision-making. This is not in dispute here. What is in dispute is the method which each author proposes in order to explain the manner in which decisions and policies are made, but more importantly how they should be made. The theory of method which underpins the work of both Faludi and Dror, and represents 'good currency' in planning practice, is that of rationality, or rather the rational method of decision-making. The implication is that decisions and policies are and should be made according to the axioms of one particular methodology. This methodology assumes that a sequence of clearly identifiable stages are systematically worked through, stages which accord with the manner in which rational (and hence 'good') decisions are made. According to Hart these stages are:

> . . . (1) A clearly formulated problem exists; (2) the objectives of the policymakers are known and it is possible to at least approximately

36

determine whether they are being achieved; (3) an 'envelope' defining the action space available is both known and well-defined with regard to all possible alternatives; (4) there is also an outcome envelope containing all the possible consequences of (all) the available options; and (5) the policymakers have a preference function with regard to the outcome envelope which allows them to select and rank preferred alternatives.[18]

If this approximated to the only (available) approach to the problem of methodology then it would be legitimate to critique each part of this five stage sequence. But the rationality model, as it can be more properly referred to, is only one approach. Indeed by relating it to the philosophy of method, and in particular to the philosophy of scientific method, it is possible to see rationality — not as an end in and of itself — but rather as corresponding to one end of a methodological continuum. What is of interest here is what lies at the other end. In other words, is there a corollary to the rational model of scientific method, and if so, what is it?

Instead of mapping-out the possible form of this corollary in direct terms for public planning, it is perhaps of greater utility at this stage to concentrate on the idea of the philosophy of method, or rather the competing philosophies of method. Of the philosophies of inquiry available, the least highly developed are those concerning methods of social inquiry (methodology of the social sciences). The most highly developed, in terms of their respective explanatory powers, are without a shadow of doubt those competing philosophies which attempt to explain the nature of scientific discovery and the development of scientific knowledge. These are the respective philosophies of scientific method. If it is accepted that a concern of planning is with the theory of method, then it is possible to opt at this stage for one of two approaches: either to consider the less developed philosophies of social method or to consider the more highly developed philosophies of scientific method.

The problem is by no means simple or straightforward to resolve. We can either opt for an approach which is either arguably more relevant but with little explanatory power, or one of less direct relevance but with a higher potential level of explanation. Subject to the caveat that public planning is not necessarily solely concerned with the application of scientific method to social problems, for the purposes of the processes of planning it is proposed to opt for the more refined approach — the philosophy of scientific method. This is not to argue that planning is scientific method; rather that planning can learn much from the debate and discussion concerning the development of scientific discovery. At most scientific method has a rôle to play in public planning; but it does not constitute either the rôle or public planning *per se.* (In certain respects this differs substantially from the approaches of both Faludi and Dror.[19])

The first point which can be made is that there is no such thing as *the* philosophy of *the* scientific method, but rather a series of competing philosophies of what might constitute scientific methods. [20] A second point, at risk of considerable oversimplification, is that these correspond to two currents of thought which can be regarded as opposite ends of a conceptual continuum, together with an emergent third force. At one extreme are to be found the inductivists (those philosophies – chiefly positivism – which regard scientific method as corresponding to the process of verification by inducing 'facts' from observed 'phenomena').

At the other are the deductivists (those philosophies – chiefly indeterminism – which regard scientific method as corresponding to a process of theorising (conjecture) and theory testing (refutation)). Nestling somewhat uncomfortably in between these two gargantuans are the emergent philosophies which attempt a crude synthesis between induction and deduction. Following Medawar these are referred to as the hypothetico-deductive approaches to the logic of scientific method.[21]

Of these three philosophies the hypothetico-deductive approaches are the least well-formulated and therefore the most tentative. The two competing giants remain – induction versus deduction, determinism versus indeterminism, empiricism versus theorising. The distinction is therefore by no means academic or arbitrary. If method is important to an understanding of the processes of planning, then it is absolutely crucial to point up the implications for planning of making use of one or other approach. The process of induction views the process of scientific discovery as *the evolution of 'hypotheses', and thus 'theories', and then to the formulation of 'laws' which somehow emerge out of or can be inferred from that total body of information which the scientist has amassed via experimentation through the course of time.* The scientist in essence is therefore searching for empirically-determined proof, for consistency, for uniformity, for pattern which is seen to emerge 'naturally', though with some manipulation, from the empiric observations which have been made. The principle of induction is therefore based on the critical assertion that somewhere 'out there' are fundamental regularities and consistencies waiting to be found which, if found, can be interpreted as axioms or iron laws ... as objective facts. The problem for the philosopher and the scientist is simply to find them via the systematic process of making and sifting through observations of these phenomena. The onus is therefore on the principle of proof, of verification.[22]

The process of deduction is very much the antithesis of the process of inductive logic. The essence of the deductive method is the bringing together of theories and their evaluation by the mutual interaction between conjecture and refutation. According to the deductive school it is impossible and therefore undesirable to attempt to prove or verify anything. [23] All that can be honestly done is to set up working propositions (conjectures) and then attempt to refute them. In such cases scientific discovery proceeds not by inducing facts ('truth') but rather by (a) critically assessing the existing body of knowledge and defining a particular problem or issue which that critique raises; (b) proposing a particular solution (tentative theory) to that particular problem from a mass of competing possible solutions; (c) by deducing a number of testable propositions from that tentative theory (hypotheses); (d) by attempting to refute, by experimentation and debate, those propositions; and (e) by establishing a preference or otherwise for the tentative theory. The principle of deduction is therefore based on the critical assertion that both the philosopher and the scientist are concerned with problems, and in particular with the problem of the development of knowledge (in this case scientific knowledge). The problem is therefore to focus attention on the weaknesses, the ambiguities, the gaps in our knowledge ... with problems *per se*. As Popper succinctly puts it: 'We are not students of some subject matter but students *of problems*.' [24]

According to this view the crux of scientific discovery involves two dual notions about the rôle of scientific method:

1  *that the logic of scientific method involves the constant formulation and reformulation of ideas and theories (problems) via the process of continuous conjecture and refutation (between problems and tentative solutions);*
2  that the logic of scientific method is characterised by the *qualities of continuous mutual interaction and constant iteration* between the impact of existing problems and intentions to solve them − conjecture and refutation − resulting in the gradual *extrusion* of revised ideas, principles and theories. [25]

From the perspective of the processes of planning, which of these could be adopted as a basis for a tentative theory of the 'internal' component of a theory for planning: induction or deduction? In some respects the question is a misleading one, because the decision has already been taken implicitly in the brief outline of the structure of the rationality model. The key factors which need to be considered can best be evaluated in the context of Hart's schema − the five stages of rational decision-making.

The first point which can be made is that the rational model attempts to abstract from the 'general' to the 'specific' by means-reduction methods. In other words (a) the 'ends' are given (objectives), so the problem remains (b) to map-out all possible alternative 'means' open to the decision-maker, (c) to evaluate them against the objectives, and proceed to narrow the range by throwing out those whose performances do not meet the requirements, and (d) to set before the decision-maker a set of alternatives which do roughly match up to the performance demanded of them; (e) the decision-maker then has the apparently simple task of ranking and selecting a preferred alternative. The process is therefore one of beginning the sequence by identifying the total range of alternatives, and by a systematic elimination process, to narrow them down to a single viable solution.

The second point which can be made concerns the ends-means relationship of this schema. Although the dualism between ends and means was discussed earlier, it does illustrate the manner in which the objectives of the proposed process — the ends — are held to be reasonably inviolate, 'given', held constant. In other words the problem has been clearly spelt-out — achieve the objectives by the most relevant means available within the legitimate action space. The central concern with the pure rational model is therefore more or less solely with the mobilising, manipulation and reduction of means. In other words with mapping-out all possible alternative ways of meeting the objectives, the ends, of the action space. How is this to be tackled? By a systematic analysis of the decision area, the action space; by collecting and amassing information, facts, observations on the ends-means relationship; by surveying the 'real world' and abstracting from that survey broad generalisations about its nature, its construction, its substance. In other words by an empirical assessment of the state of the real world, matched with alternative possible means available to change it — simple cause and effect relationships.

How then does the 'good currency' rational model stand in the realm of the methodological debate? According to the inductive/deductive continuum it is reasonable to venture to suggest that it ties-in quite neatly with the inductive approach to the philosophy of scientific method. It is cause-effect related, albeit in a naive manner, and clearly empirically based; the stress on observations, facts and evidence are some of its critical, indeed distinguishing features. It therefore has significant and distinctive positivistic leanings and, according to Popper, is a wholly deterministic methodology.

So if the 'good currency' rational methodology represents one approach — indeed it was stated earlier that it could be regarded as one end of a continuum of methodologies — and that its approach is wedded to principles of positivism and induction, is it not conceivable that as a corollary a methodology wedded to the principles of indeterminism and deduction is a practicable and viable alternative? In other words with the development of an alternative approach to the theory of the process of planning based not on some notion of rational-positivism but rather on some form of deductive-indeterminism.

## Deductive-indeterminism and the processes of planning

The principal argument for deductive-indeterminism as a process of scientific method has been made by Sir Karl Popper.[26] His approach to the problem of deduction rests on the assertion that the growth and development of 'objective knowledge' is based on the continuous search for knowledge and the solving of problems. In fact he argues that *all societal action is a continuous engagement in problem-solving*. Popper has characterised the underlying pattern of this process in terms of a simple and elegant logical construct:

$$P_1 \longrightarrow TT \longrightarrow EE \longrightarrow P_2$$

To use Popper's terminology, a deductive approach to the problem of scientific method is concerned with the interrelationships between 'problems', 'tentative theories', and the 'elimination of error' between conceptions of theories matched with perceptions of problems:

> . . . all scientific discussions start with a problem ($P_1$), to which we offer some sort of tentative solution — a *tentative theory* (TT); this theory is then criticised, in an attempt at *error elimination* (EE); and as in the case of dialectic, this process renews itself: the theory and its critical revision give rise to new *problems* ($P_2$). (In other words,) . . . *science begins with problems and ends with problems.*[27]

There are a number of points of fundamental importance which can be made concerning this alternative approach to inductive determinism. The first is to note from Popper's interpretation that such a process is not cyclical, because $P_2$ is always different from the original starting point, $P_1$.[28] As Bryan Magee puts it:

> . . . even complete failure to solve a problem teaches us something new about where its difficulties lie, and what the minimum conditions are which any solution for it must meet — (this) therefore alters the (initial) problem situation.[29]

41

The second is to note Popper's concern with the importance attached to the idea of problem-solving. [30] In adopting this kind of approach he focusses attention first and foremost on the concept of problems defined in the broadest possible way. Attention, he argues, needs to be centred on the problem or set of problems which faces the inquirer, and in particular with the reasons for it being considered a problem in the first place. The key to Popper's schema is therefore with the fundamental importance which he gives to the idea of the initial formulation of the problem or problem set before giving any consideration whatsoever to its possible solution. In making use of the term 'problem' in this manner Popper does not necessarily give it the kind of interpretation or meaning which is usually and almost exclusively associated with it: a situation or set of circumstances which is deemed to be undesirable and requiring remedial action, by some individual or institution, of an immediate nature. Popper gives it a much broader and more positive interpretation: a situation or set of circumstances, which includes this narrower contemporary meaning, but which also encompasses the seeking, identification and grasping of opportunities and their development. He therefore incorporates both the negative and the positive attributes of the concept of what constitutes a problem, setting them up as central components of the nature and practise of scientific method. As Magee asserts, a methodology of this type:

> . . . puts the greatest premium of all on boldness of imagination; and it holds that we never actually *know* — that our approach to any and every situation or problem needs to be always such as to accommodate not merely unforeseeable contributions but the permanent possibility of a radical transformation of the whole conceptual scheme with which, and even within which, we are operating. It is fundamentally at variance with all views of science or rationality which see these as excluding passion or imagination or creative intuition. . . .[31]

By constantly and continuously defining and redefining problems in this way Popper explicitly recognises the qualities of interdependence and extrusion. He stresses the importance of these two ideas by arguing that attention should be explicitly centred on six basic organising concepts:

1 concern for continuity,
2 concern for process,
3 concern for dynamics,
4 concern for uncertainty,
5 concern for impact,
6 concern for intent.

The theme which permeates each of these is temporal; in other words an understanding of the nature and impact of time, and in particular change through time: changing ideas, changing concepts, changing values, changing theories, changing priorities, etc.

In fact Popper recognises the impact of change in his own organising schema by incorporating the temporal dimension into its structure. This revamped schema recognises that not only does the nature of the problem change following one iteration, but rather that the tentative theories and attempts to eliminate error also change. This is shown by Figure 3.1 below.

Fig. 3.1    Popper's schema of deductive-indeterminism

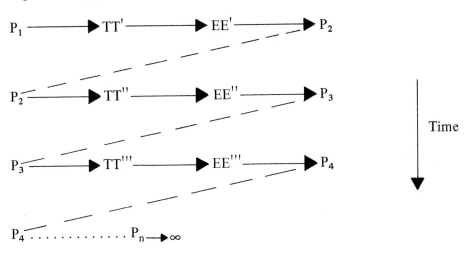

The schema illustrates quite clearly the dynamic and process orientation of a deductive, problem-oriented approach to the problem of scientific method. What it does not illustrate particularly well is the explicit relationship, the interaction, between problems and uncertainties surrounding potential outcomes to those problems. In other words, in the interaction between the problems thus identified, the actions proposed to overcome them, and assessments of how those actions are of relevance or otherwise. In other words, in the interaction between problem, intent and impact. Translating this into a policy- and planning-oriented context implies that the process of planning itself can be seen as a series of continuous interactions between policy problem, policy intent and policy impact. In terms of Popper's schema outlined in Figure 3.1 these additional critical points mean that policy-making can be viewed not as a single spiral or helix traversing neatly from problem to problem, but rather as (what Hart calls) a more complex and less sophisticated triple helix, mapping-out the continuous interactions and iterations between, respectively, policy problems, policy intent and policy impact through time.[32] This is shown in Figure 3.2.

Fig. 3.2   Deductive-indeterminism and the processes of planning (1): the triple helix

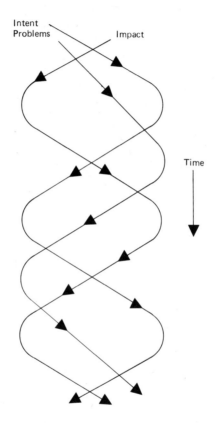

This schema needs to be taken one stage further, because quite clearly the concept of 'problem' cannot sensibly be referred to in the singular. If any one factor characterises the problems of contemporary western capitalist societies it certainly has little to do with singularity or homogeneity, but rather with heterogeneity. If this assertion is a valid one then why should not society's problems reflect and be reflected in this kaleidoscope of multifaceted and amorphous individualism? The importance of this asserted diffuseness for the processes of planning and public policy is that we cannot validly talk in terms of a 'problem' or indeed 'problems'. Rather we must refer to sets or ranges of problems — problem continuums — and to potential action spaces which face planning. From these continuums and spaces certain problem areas are purposefully selected — problem areas which are themselves competing for attention — and which are the subject of and subjected to remedial action of one form or another. [33] According to Sir Geoffrey Vickers it is this kind of selection process which characterises and indeed constitutes the processes of public planning — the problem of the multi-valued choice.[34]

Popper's original schema can be simply modified to incorporate these ideas and concepts by introducing the dual notions of 'problem continuums' and 'problem areas', as shown in Figure 3.3.

In this context $P_1$ represents the 'problem area' selected from the potentially infinite range of problems open to attack — the 'problem continuum'; TT, the 'potential solution space' selected from the potentially infinite range of tentative theories; EE, the 'elimination of error space' selected from the potentially infinite range of means and mechanisms available; and $P_2$, the 'revised problem space' emanating from the interaction between $P_1$, TT, and EE. In this revised schema, . . .p. . ., . . .tt. . ., . . .ee. . ., and . . .p. . . represent potential and latent competing alternatives outside of those selected problem areas and spaces.

These problems have been considered by Popper in a different context, that of the problem situation. But he relates it to the already-quoted observation that '. . . science begins with, and ends with problems.' In fact Popper admits to a certain inconclusiveness which can be attached to this statement:

> . . . I was always . . . worried about this summary, for every scientific problem arises, in its turn, in a theoretical context. It is soaked in theory. So I used to say that we may begin the schema at any place . . . However, I used to add that it is often from some *practical problem* that a theoretical development starts; and although any formulation of a practical problem unavoidably brings in theory, the practical problem itself may be just 'felt': it may be 'prelinguistic'; we . . . may *feel* cold or some other irritation, and this may induce us . . . to make tentative moves — perhaps theoretical moves — in order to get rid of the irritation.[35]

This leads Popper to the view that these tentative moves or adjustments (in response to a practical problem) constitute 'preconscious' formulations of theory development. Since practical problems arise relative to this adjustment process:

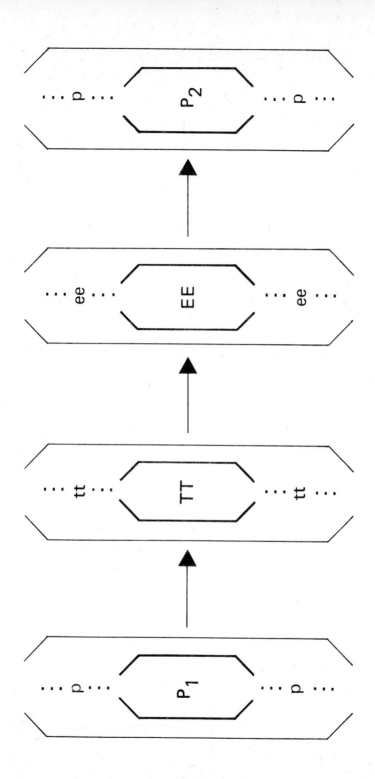

Fig. 3.3   Deductive-indeterminism and the processes of planning (2): problem continuums and problem areas

*... practical problems are, essentially, imbued with theories ... the first theories — that is, the first tentative solutions of problems — and the first problems must somehow have arisen together.* [36]

This conclusion is taken one step further by Popper: if problems and theories are developed in concert, through time, then the individual, institution (or what Popper calls) 'organic structure' which experiences and adjusts to those problems must have *also* developed in concert. This argument has some tremendous ramifications for the study of the nature and practice of the processes of planning because it implies, as Popper notes, that organic structures are theory-incorporating as well as problem-solving structures. [37]

So, far from viewing the processes of planning as the application of a series of discrete and autonomous steps, adhering to a set of orderly and rational sequences which have a beginning, a middle and an end, this deductive-indeterminist schema argues that planning is multifaceted, messy, confusing, amorphous and muddled. But more importantly, that it is a complex activity, complex in the sense that not only is it geared to problem-solving and theory-incorporating, but rather it is concerned with the manner in which these interact. In more formal terms it is charac- terised by the fusion of two important qualities of dynamics — continuous mutual interaction and constant iteration. But interaction and iteration between what? In terms of a tentative theory to account for the processes of planning, interaction and iteration between what Popper refers to as 'open' problems [38] and solutions, between conjectures and refutations, between theories and practices, between impact and intent. Treated in splendid isolation problems, conjectures, theories and impacts are largely irrelevant from the viewpoint of the process of planning. Similarly solutions, refutations, practices and intent. As ingredients of these processes they can certainly be treated as conditions for their operation, but individually they are not sufficient conditions. Each only becomes significant when considered in the context of the others, but more importantly by the processes in which they interact and iterate. [39]

This digression began with the observation that there was no satis- factory single explanation to account for the processes of planning. If these processes could be considered in terms of the philosophy of method it was argued that there were two competing schools of thought on the subject: inductive-determinism and deductive-indeterminism. The contem- porary or 'good currency' view of what constituted these processes was seen to fit more or less logically in with the ideology of rational planning, and therefore according to Popper in sympathy with the inductivedeterminists. An alternative approach, based on deductive-indeterminism, was then developed and related to the particular demands of planning. We are now in a position to pull together the various strands of this alternative approach, and so submit it as a basic organising framework for an outline of a theory to account for the (internal) processes of planning. This framework is therefore characterised by at least seven amorphous attributes:

1   it is a problem-solving framework,
2   it is also a theory-incorporating framework,
3   it is a framework which gives explicit recognition to the idea that planning is concerned with dynamics,
4   it is a framework which explicitly incorporates the idea that planning is process-oriented,
5   it is a framework which explicitly recognises that planning operates in an environment of relative if not total uncertainty,
6   it is a framework characterised by the idea that planning is concerned with the continuous and mutual interaction between problems and solutions, theory and practice, impact and intent,
7   it is a framework characterised by the idea that planning is concerned with the notion of constant iteration between problems and solutions, theory and practice, impact and intent.

### Learning, coordination and the myth of 'successful' planning

Although this framework is, potentially anyway, a useful conceptual tool for a study of the nature and practice of planning, it is still rather abstract and, some critics would say, essentially an intellectual exercise. But this would be missing a fundamental point. In fact we can argue that this framework has some interesting implications for the study of planning, but more importantly for the actual practice of planning itself.[40]

That planning is a process is a truism, but what is it a process for? From the planners viewpoint the framework which has been outlined above implicitly stresses three factors. First, that planning as an activity is concerned with the coordination of its internal component parts as well as with the coordination of exogenous elements, (for example, land use). Second, that the processes of planning are concerned with learning, and learning as much about planning itself as well as learning about the outside world. Finally, that planning qua planners are as equally concerned with learning to coordinate as to coordinate this learning.[41]

48

This raises some further interesting issues. For example in what respects is planning concerned with coordination and learning? Both concepts can be seen as further conditions necessary to the operation of planning within this deductive-indeterminist framework. But again they are not sufficient conditions. It is the third factor which holds the key to this particular 'chinese box': the relationship between coordination and learning.

The notion of learning, or rather the processes of learning, cannot validly be discussed in the singular. Popper distinguishes between three main types. The first and most fundamental, he argues, is learning as a process of discovery. This consists of what he refers to as the 'dogmatic' formation of theories or expectations, or regular behaviour, which is in turn checked by critical error elimination. The second process of learning he calls learning by imitation, and the third learning by 'repetition' or 'practising'. (Popper argues that there is no such thing as genuine repetition, but rather a change which has been brought about through error-elimination and theory-formation which results in a process which makes certain actions and reactions 'automatic.')[42] If we follow Popper in these respects, learning has to be subdivided into either learning by discovery ('true' learning), learning by imitation or learning by repetition. This has some interesting implications for the coordination component. It implies that if learning and coordination are inextricably interwoven, then learning to coordinate and coordinating learning is more than a simple dual relationship. We now have three types of learning to contend with.

In some respects the same argument applies to the problem of coordination. It too has to be considered in a plurality of contexts. Hilhorst, in the context of regional planning, suggests four kinds of coordination. These can be generalised to, firstly, coordination of the components of planning; secondly, coordination of organisational action within the processes of planning; thirdly, coordination of organisational action between the processes of planning and what is being planned; and finally, coordination of what is actually being planned.[43] This also has some interesting implications for the learning component of the processes of planning. It implies that the relationships between the two are also more complex, because we now have four types of coordination to contend with. In fact we have twelve basic relationships: three types of learning fused with four kinds of coordination. So if valid facets of the processes of planning are learning to coordinate and the coordination of learning, then we have twenty-four basic relationships to contend with (Figure 3.4):

Fig. 3.4   Learning, coordination and the processes of planning

Types of coordination

| Coordination of | | | |
|---|---|---|---|
| Components of the processes of planning | Action within the processes of planning | Action between planning and the processes of planning | Components to be planned |

Types of learning

| | Components of the processes of planning | Action within the processes of planning | Action between planning and the processes of planning | Components to be planned |
|---|---|---|---|---|
| Learning by discovery | 1 / 2 | 3 / 4 | 5 / 6 | 7 / 8 |
| Learning by imitation | 9 / 10 | 11 / 12 | 13 / 14 | 15 / 16 |
| Learning by repetition | 17 / 18 | 19 / 20 | 21 / 22 | 23 / 24 |

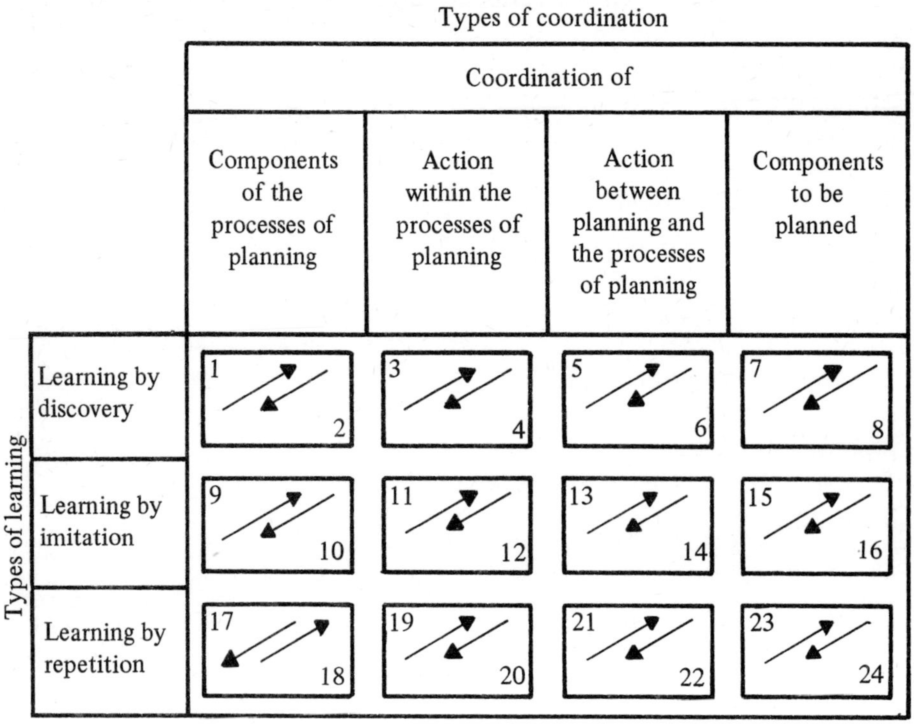

The principal implication for the practice of planning which this illustration seeks to show is that if planning is concerned with the problems and integration of learning and coordination, then it is a far from simple concern. Therefore to argue that planning is a learning process, or a process of coordination, is not sufficient. The critical factor concerns in what way is it a learning and coordination process. But this typology illustrates one further set of factors which are of no small significance for a study of the nature and practice of planning. This set concerns the interrelationship between the concepts of precision and certainty in the context of the search for 'successful' planning. [44] Three points can be made which serve to illustrate that contemporary views of planning — as searching for precision, certainty and success — are, if not misplaced, then largely irrelevant.

   The first point concerns the inference that all planning strives to be precise and certain. But are these the criteria which planning should serve and be judged by? The answer is surely in the negative. For as Popper notes: '. . . both precision and certainty are false ideals. They are impossible to attain, and therefore dangerously misleading if they are *uncritically* accepted as guides.' [45]

The second point concerns the inference that all planning strives to be successful. Is this then a better criterion than either precision or certainty? The answer again is surely in the negative. 'Successful' planning, in the sense implied here, is utopian, indeed impossible to achieve, in the sense that planned intent at time $(t-1)$ for time $(t)$ will be precisely equal to the actual outcome at time $(t)$. [46] Or as Fried notes, successful planning can only come about by comparing the degree to which the prescriptions are obeyed and the descriptions (predicted behaviours) become reality. Any deviation is ruled out because of the precision built into the plan. What this basically means is that there can be no room for so-called 'unintended consequences' associated with the proposals put forward at time $(t-1)$ that are attributable to the consequences of implementing the plan. Such a view asserts that the planner and policy-maker not only have total control over potential outcomes but also total control over the processes by which the plan is made (inputs) and implemented. Fried argues that successful planning can only come about when three fundamental propositions are fulfilled:

1  When public and private actors obey the ground rules laid down by policies and policy instruments.
2  When public and private actors maintain the commitments contained in the policies.
3  When, using their discretion, public and private actors act in accordance with the predictions associated with the policies. [47]

The key to why there can be no such thing as successful planning in the sense implied by Fried is quite simply because the picture painted is essentially a static and inflexible one. The only ground rules which can ever be substantially obeyed through time are those very generalised statements concerning morals, values and welfare. Any formal statements invite attack because of their inherently political nature and disinterest with continuously changing issues and circumstances which represent the very substance of political debate. Likewise with the idea of the maintainance of commitments through time. [48] The parallels with a vision of a static and inflexible society permeate any such notion of public planning.

But perhaps the most inflexible and arguably the most dangerous rule concerns the third of Fried's propositions: namely, that successful planning can only come about when individuals in society behave in accordance with the predictions contained in 'the plan'. In other words, it is only possible to plan successfully when 'the plan' is obeyed, maintained and actual behaviour accords with it! But by what inestimable right does such a plan have to impose itself on any society? Any such notion of successful planning smacks of élitism and autocracy, by definition.

Which brings us back full-square to our original schema: *planning can only be successful in the sense that its primary concern is with the continuous definition and redefinition of problems — wedded to action programmes of one form or another — through continuous interaction between tentative solutions and concomitant attempts to eliminate the error or dysfunction between them.*

The third point which we can make is that planning should be as much concerned with notions of changing concepts of order as much if not more than with the ordering of change itself. [49] Even more so if we are to agree with Wildavsky that we are now very much in the era of the 'messy problem' — the kind of problem which is not easily definable, which is shrouded in mystery, blurred at the edges. [50] The kind of problem which is not amenable to simple prescriptions, which changes its character as soon as remedial action is adopted. The recognition of such fundamental characteristics is clearly crucial to any proposed outline theory for public planning.

So if we are in the era of messy problems it is reasonable to postulate that any form of public planning has to match the messy nature of the real world. As Stewart argues:

> ... planning can too easily be regarded as a once and for all sequence moving logically from needs and problems identified in the environment through objectives set to policies and activities determined. *It is never as simple as that* ... planning does not have a clear starting point or a clear finishing point. It is a continuing and continuous process. Each stage is merely part of that process, which influences and is influenced by the other stages.[51] (Italics added.)

### The environment of planning

The framework of the processes of planning which we have outlined in this chapter represents the 'internal' component of planning. What has to be attempted having reached this juncture is to relate this framework to the environment within which those processes operate. With what was referred to earlier as the 'internal-external' component of planning.

In the previous chapter a relationship was established between the idea of planning and the concept of change: that planning is concerned with change, as much as with planning for change; that change itself is ubiquitous and messy, heterogeneous and not homogeneous, etc. Finally a typology of change was suggested, following Cattell, and a simple justification of planning as an institutional activity was considered 'internal' to the nature of planning itself. But quite clearly it is not sufficient to remonstrate about the need for planning to have the capacity to recognise and deal with the idea of change in a purely functional manner, *à la* Cattell. Too many questions are begged, of which arguably the most significant concerns the focus of attention as to what actually changes, and what form that change takes — social, economic, organisational, political, etc. Put another way, what constitutes the limits of planning as legitimate public activity — what Bićanić refers to as the extent of planibility, [52] the perimeter of concern of planning. [53] This is where the idea of the 'planning domain' assumes significant proportions. As Faludi notes, the concept of the environment within which planning operates: '. . . is a mental construct consisting of those objective features of a society which are of relevance to its capacity of outlining future courses of action in an efficient way.' [54]

From this interpretation it is clear that the potential perimeter of concern for planning is very wide indeed. Bićanić narrows the range somewhat by arguing that planning is synonomous with action in an 'environment' — social, political, economic and/or ecological. But more importantly, a distinguishing characteristic is that such an 'environment' is neither passive nor neutral in response to such planning, planned action or public intervention. [55] With these points in mind Faludi has developed his argument further by considering what the constituent elements of the planning domain would consist of. [56] In fact he has identified six:

1   the level and pace of development of a particular society,
2   that society's pattern of and relationships between norms and values,
3   the nature of its political system and concomitant administrative structures,
4   the institutional structure of that society,
5   any cleavages present or potentially present in that society's social structure,
6   any other specific features (common factors or significant differences) which pertain to that society — cultural characteristics.[57]

This schema, whilst not mapping-out the boundaries of the planning domain, indicates the kind of features which planning, particularly the institutionalised — and especially the public — forms, must locate, give due cognizance to, and concern itself with. But the arguably more significant factor which is implicitly at the heart of this idea of a planning domain is the dual relationship between process and change. Faludi's picture is not intended as a static image, even though it stresses structures and functions, but more a system of interlocking parts and interdependent relationships which are in turn in a state of constant flux, continuous adjustment and readjustment, assessment and reassessment, in social and political terms. In other words, with the balance between the idea of social change, broadly interpreted, and political commitment and action.

The implications for a theory of planning are clear on at least two levels: first, that by marrying the outline for a theory of the processes of planning with that of the concept of the planning domain, what emerges is a more comprehensive picture of the components which any substantive theory of planning would have to include. Second, that a crucial underpinning of such a theory would be not a full-blown theory of social change *per se* but at least an assessment of, if not a synthesis with, the relationships between public planning and ideas as to what constitutes social change.

The first implication can be illustrated quite simply. Taking the seven attributes of our framework of the processes of planning and the six elements of Faludi's planning domain, we can construct a simple two-dimensional 'contextual map',[58] or matrix of planning attributes, covering all possible combinations of the attributes of the processes of planning within the context of the environment within which it operates (see figure 3.5).[59] In fact we have a seven-by-six matrix whose elements correspond to forty-two interdependent pairs or sets of relationships.

On the basis of this schema three points can be made: first, that such a matrix represents the perimeter of concern for any study of the nature and practice of planning; second, that it provides a reasonably comprehensive picture of what is required from a full-blown theory of the processes of planning; and third, it says something about the relationships between forms of planning and types of government which operate in various kinds of society or culture, together with ideas as to the possible directions in which those governments and planning systems might evolve.[60, 61]

The second implication — that of social change — is not so easily illustrated. The problem is analogous to the earlier problems as to what constitutes theory and scientific method. The answer to those problems, as well as to the present one, is that there is no simple single explanation. Rather, a set of competing explanations, often at different levels and emphasising different qualitative and substantive points.

## Planning theory and social change

There is no unitary or universally acceptable view as to what constitutes an adequate explanation of social change. What is available is simply a set

Fig. 3.5   Matrix of planning attributes: theoretical schema and the planning domain

| Attributes of the theory for the processes of planning \ Attributes of the planning domain | Level and pace of development | Norms and values of society | The political system and its administration | The institutional structure | Social cleavages | Cultural characteristics |
|---|---|---|---|---|---|---|
| Problem-solving | *** | ** | *** | ** | *** | * |
| Theory-incorporating | *** | *** | *** | ** | *** | ** |
| Dynamic | *** | *** | ** | * | *** | ** |
| Process-oriented | *** | *** | *** | ** | *** | ** |
| Uncertainty | *** | *** | *** | * | *** | *** |
| Continuous interaction | *** | *** | ** | * | *** | ** |
| Constant iteration | *** | *** | ** | ** | *** | ** |

*** high level of interaction
 * low level of interaction

of competing theories – principally sociological – resting on different assumptions and political positions reflecting the different interests and aspirations of their respective protagonists. Two contemporary writers on social theory argue that there are basically seven broad theories of social change. Cohen, in *Modern Social Theory*, argues that it is possible to identify these seven, what he calls 'single factor', theories which attempt to explain social change solely in terms of a single or dominant factor. These are:

1  technological theory;
2  economic theory;
3  conflict theory;
4  malintegration theory;
5  adaptation theory;
6  ideational theory; and
7  cultural interaction theory.[62]

According to Dahrendorf, in *Class and Class Conflict in Industrial Society*, or more properly according to the position Dahrendorf takes, these seven theories can be abstracted from in such a way that each can be identified as broadly corresponding to one or other of two meta-theories of social change:

1  integration theory; and
2  coercion theory.[63]

Whereas Dahrendorf is principally concerned with a critique of the writings of Marx as a sociologist, he arrives at the distinction between integration and coercion as bases for theories of social change by an observation that in terms of western political thought, two views of society have stood in open conflict as to the nature and degree of social and political cohesion exhibited by different cultures. The first of these – coherence by consensus – sees society as sharing a common set of beliefs and values. The second – coherence by constraint and domination – argues that the idea of social change cannot be divorced from the idea of social order: that every society is based on the coercion of some of its members by an élite or group of others. In other words the two schools appear to be looking at a common area – that of social coherence – but argue for explanations from diametrically opposed positions – integration versus coercion. But perhaps more importantly, these alternative positions have certain political implications and moral overtones associated with them, as Dahrendorf makes quite explicit:

Unless one believes that all philosophical disputes are spurious and ultimately irrelevant, the long history of the particular dispute about the problem of social order has exposed — if not solved — what appear to be fundamental alternatives of knowledge, moral decision, and political orientation.[64]

According to Dahrendorf, the integration school (utopians) has dominated discussion and debate concerning social change and social order, with often '... unfortunate consequences'.[65]

This school, that of the structural-functionalists, and in particular Talcott Parsons, argues that order is not based on a general consensus of values, only that it may be conceived of in such terms. Around this critical assertion, four key assumptions usually follow (albeit, as Dahrendorf notes, oversimplifying and overstating the position):

1   that every society is a relatively persistent, stable structure of elements (stability);
2   that every society is a well-integrated structure comprising of these elements (integration);
3   that each of these elements has a function which contributes to the maintenance of the system as a whole (functional coordination); and
4   that every functioning social structure is based on a consensus of values among its members (consensus).[66]

The characteristics of the integration theory of social change therefore stress such concepts as persistency, stability, structure, function, maintenance, system and consensus. The 'fundamental alternatives of knowledge, moral decision, and political orientation' noted by Dahrendorf earlier are illustrated quite clearly by the *status quo* orientation (conservatism?) usually associated with and attributed to the integration approach, and need no further elaboration here. But Dahrendorf outlines one important proviso: the idea that 'stability' is not to be equated with the notion that societies are 'static', only that the processes of change which do occur are geared primarily to serve the maintenance of the system as a whole.

The coercion school (rationalists), in official opposition to the integrationists, argue in broadly similar terms to them, but from a diametrically opposed position: that social order is not based on the coercion of many by some, but rather that it may be broadly conceived of in such terms. In other words, to paraphrase Dahrendorf, both theories regard the concepts of consensus and coercion as heuristic principles rather than judgements of fact.[67]

However, like the integration argument, coercion theory is developed around the assertion that conflict and coercion are prime movers of social change, from which four key assumptions usually follow (again, oversimplifying and overstating the case):

1    that every society is continuously subjected to and the subject of processes of change (change);
2    that every society is continuously subjected to and the subject of dissent and conflict (conflict);
3    that every element in a society makes a contribution to its disintegration and change (motive force); and
4    that every society is based on the coercion of some of its members by others (coercion).[68]

The characteristic features of the coercion theory of social change therefore stress such concepts as continuity, processes, change, conflict, and disintegration. Concepts which are clearly the antithesis of those which identify the opposing school: persistency, stability, consensus, etc. According to Dahrendorf, the crucial distinction between the two is that the conflict school argue that social change and social conflict are ubiquitous in any society, but that this change has to be channelled and the conflict suppressed in the name of social order, or rather the need for social order. The 'fundamental alternatives of knowledge, moral decision, and political orientation' noted by Dahrendorf are again clearly implied, and need no further elaboration in this particular context.

Two grossly simplified and opposing, indeed competing, theories of social change: integration versus coercion theory. Is it possible to come down for one side at the expense of the other? This kind of question, according to Dahrendorf, is one of crucial significance and requires any individual concerned with social change to 'take a stand on this issue'. [69] So where exactly does Dahrendorf stand? The answer is a pragmatic, middle position — that is, neatly wedged somewhere between the two. For Dahrendorf the two opposing theories are neither mutually exclusive nor mutually compatible explanations of social change. Indeed he argues that a decision to accept or reject one or the other is neither necessary nor, more importantly, desirable. Or as he puts it:

> There are sociological problems for the explanation of which the integration theory ... provides adequate assumptions; there are other problems which can be explained only in terms of the coercion theory . . .; there are, finally, problems for which both theories appear adequate. *For sociological analysis, society is Janus-headed, and its two faces are equivalent aspects of the same reality.*[70] (Italics added.)

But Dahrendorf takes his case one stage further, not by producing a synthesis of the two theories in some dialectical fashion, but rather in the form of a dialectic argument in and of its own right:

> . . . neither of these models can be conceived as exclusively valid or applicable. They constitute complementary, rather than alternative, aspects . . . Strictly speaking both models are 'valid' or, rather, useful and necessary for sociological analysis. We cannot conceive of society unless we realise the dialectics of stability and change, integration and conflict, function and motive force, consensus and coercion. [71]

So Dahrendorf's principal argument for his middle-course position stems from the idea of viewing integration theory and coercion theory as essentially complementary. A matter of emphasis rather than fundamental choice, in a dialectical setting, where stability and change constitute a continuum from a totally static state (stability) to a state of presumably continuous revolution (change). Likewise for the concepts of integration and conflict, function and motive force, consensus and coercion. Represented in schematic form, Dahrendorf's dialectical approach could take the structure of the figure below (figure 3.6):

Fig. 3.6    Schema of social change, after Dahrendorf

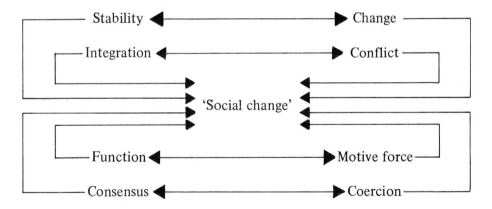

So the idea of a theory of social change is central to the very idea of public planning itself. The implications are clear: if there is to be such a thing as a theory for planning, then central to that theory will be (a) an outline of what constitutes the environment of planning, and (b) an outline of what constitutes social change. If Dahrendorf's approach is to have any utility regarding the latter point, then surely it will be as a bench mark, mapping-out the boundaries as to what constitutes the relevance of social change for public planning.

By drawing together the three broad subject areas which have characterised this chapter, it is possible to present the reader with an outline, or more appropriately, a sketch of what might constitute a more adequate theory for the nature and practice of planning, especially public planning. These three subject areas taken together are, firstly, the concept of the processes of planning ('internal'), secondly, the concept of the planning domain ('internal–external'), and finally, the concept of social change ('external'). The relationships between these three subject areas are of some significance. Quite clearly when taken together they represent an interlocking set of activities which can be labelled 'planning'. But they do not represent the *total* social system, they merely reflect it. The distinction is a useful one, and corresponds to what Shils calls the relationship between the 'total value system' and the 'central value system'. [72] Since public planning has, in this context at least, been regarded as an institutionalised activity, then clearly it can be located within the 'central value system' but concerned with the system as a whole. The result can be mapped-out with the aid of a simple diagram, representing a schema for public planning. It illustrates those kinds of area (a) with which planning is or should be concerned; (b) which any full-blown theory for planning would have to concern itself with; and (c) which might be usefully employed to assess past, present or proposed forms of public planning (see figure 3.7).

All this might appear to be at least one step removed from a study concerning the nature and practice of planning. The concept of social change is clearly important to planning, but can it not simply be left at that? Is it necessary to delve in this way into theories of social change? The answer to these questions is an unqualified 'no' to the former, and a qualified 'yes' to the latter. That planning is concerned with change is a truism, as was outlined earlier: it is neither a particularly interesting statement nor a particularly illuminating or important one, unless heavily qualified – what kind of change? What form does such change take? etc. In order to consider these kinds of qualification it is necessary to have some base from which to work – a set of assumptions or assertions, implicit or explicit, a notion of what is to be tackled and how. In other words a tentative theory as to what constitutes a basis for proposals and actions – proposals and actions which are debatable, which change as a result of the passage of time, and other actions which have some bearing on the problem(s) at hand. That this is the basis for planning has already been argued; that this is a basis for public planning also. That the process

60

Fig. 3.7   Public planning and social change

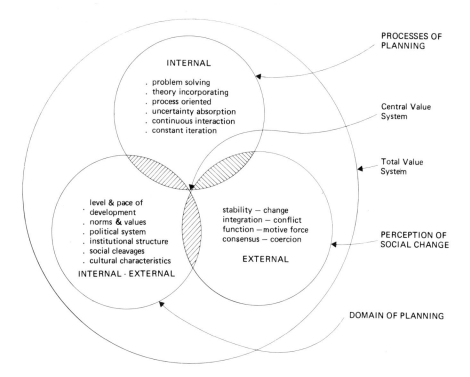

of public planning is concerned with society and the processes of change leads logically to the conclusion that underpinning any planned action is some notion, a theory, of what is social change, how it occurs, and how it can be harnessed and channelled in some or other direction. The only argument that can be put forward for a theory of social change to be included as an integral part of a book on public planning is that such a theory is implied anyway, but that it might be more useful, and hence yield greater returns, if it were to be made explicit and thus subject to open debate and constructive criticism. It is a lamentable fact that up to now there has been little attempt by individuals labelled or labelling themselves 'planners' to do just this.[73]

The other reason for delving into social change is that public planning, as presented here, has been defined as an institutionalised activity and usually tied to the purse strings and administrative arrangements of the state for its recognition and legitimation. Now this opens up a vast new field of potential analysis: if public planning is viewed in this light, then clearly it is part and parcel of the legitimate authority of the state, and therefore invested with certain powers with which it can exert and maintain not only its own authority but also that of the state itself. The parallels, with Dahrendorf's outline of a coercion theory of social change, and Shils distinction between the 'central' and 'total value system' — that public planning can be seen as a major means of accomplishing that coercion by imposing constraints and exerting authority — are only too clear. Whether this is a justifiable conclusion to reach is not an issue to be pursued here, but will be a major theme of the next chapter.

## Notes

[1]  This relationship has been suggested by Faludi, 1969, op. cit.

[2]  For alternative approaches see J. Simmie, 1974, Chapter 1; and Faludi, 1973b, op. cit., Chapter 1.

[3]  On the problems associated with differing degrees of planibility and cultural differences see J. Bray, 1970 on the UK experience; A. Catanese, 1973 on Colombia; L. Rodwin, 1969 on Guyana; and J. Friedmann, 1964 on Chile.

[4]  See for example the critical comments made by Crick, 1964, op. cit., Chapter 1; R. Sennett, 1973, Chapters 1 and 2; and Gutch, 1970.

[5]  For an excellent overview see H. Eckstein, 1961; also Rawls, 1972, op. cit., Chapter 1, especially pp. 11—54.

[6]  See Coleman, 1972, op. cit.; also Rawls, 1972, op. cit., pp. 50—4.

[7]  For a particularly gloomy account see A. Wildavsky, 1973. The title of this paper is 'If planning is everything, maybe its nothing.'

[8]  On the idea of 'social constructions of reality' see P. Berger and T. Luckmann, 1971.

[9]  Faludi, 1969, op. cit.; also Faludi, 1973a, op. cit., Part 1, Introduction.

[10]  On this kind of theory see K. Deutsch, 1971.

[11]  Faludi, 1969, op. cit.; see also Faludi, 1973b, op. cit., particularly pp. 3—5.

[12]  Deutsch, 1971, op. cit., p. 12.

[13]  On the ambiguities which result, see especially Faludi, 1973a, op. cit., Part 1, Introduction; Faludi, 1973b, op. cit., Chapter 1; Dror, 1968, op. cit., Chapter 9; J. Friedmann, 1973b, op. cit., Chapter 3; Vickers, 1965, op. cit., Chapter 10; and Rittell and Webber, 1973, op. cit.

[14]  On evidence for this 'grand conspiracy theory' approach see E. Schoettle, 1968; also Simon, 1957, particularly the introduction to the second edition.

[15]  See for example Self, 1972a, op. cit.; also Sir G. Vickers, 1970.

[16] Faludi, 1973a, op. cit., p. 1.

[17] For dissenting views see in particular Wildavsky, 1973, op. cit.; D. Braybrook and C. Lindblom, 1963; also C. Lindblom, 1959.

[18] Hart, 1974, op. cit., pp. 29–30.

[19] Faludi, 1973a, op. cit., Part 1, Introduction, especially p. 1; Dror, 1968, op. cit., Chapter 1, especially pp. 4–9.

[20] See Sir P. Medawar, 1963.

[21] Medawar, 1963, op. cit.

[22] Heavy-weight support for induction may be found in M. Friedman, 1962, with respect to the social sciences, especially economics and B. Russell, 1946, in the field of western philosophy. For dissenting views see A. Coddington, 1972, on induction in economics, and Gouldner, 1970, op. cit., on induction in the social sciences, particularly sociology.

[23] Heavy-weight support for deductive indeterminism may be found in Sir K. Popper, 1972.

[24] K. Popper, 1963, p. 67.

[25] On the concept of extrusion see Hart, 1974, op. cit., pp. 34–5.

[26] See for example K. Popper, 1959; Popper, 1963, op. cit.; and Popper, 1972, op. cit.

[27] Sir K. Popper, 1974, p. 105.

[28] On planning as a cyclic process see D. Boyce, N. Day and C. McDonald, 1970; D. Boyce, C. McDonald and A. Farhi, 1972. For dissenting views see J. Allen, 1972; Hart, 1974, op. cit.; and Hart, 1975, op. cit., especially Chapter 1.

[29] B. Magee, 1973, p. 65.

[30] Note that we are not referring solely to problems of a technical nature. Rather problems defined in the broadest possible way, of which the technical variety are but one type. Neither are we postulating that problem-solving as a facet of planning is in any way associated with the view of 'correct' or 'right' solutions, or indeed with 'successful' planning itself! See Popper, 1972, Chapter 6, also pp. 13–17; these points are taken up later in this and successive chapters.

[31] Magee, 1973, op. cit., p. 68.

[32] On this idea of helical and iterative planning, see Hart, 1974, op. cit., pp. 40–1; also Hart, 1975, op. cit., Chapter 1.

[33] On the notion of inclusion-exclusion see H. Boothroyd, 1974; also Chapter 7 of this book.

[34] On the concept of multi-valued choice see Sir G. Vickers, 1972, p. 134; for a fuller account see Sir G. Vickers, 1967; also see Vickers, 1970, Chapter 6.

[35] Popper, 1974, op. cit., p. 105.

[36] Popper, 1974, op. cit., p. 106.

[37] Popper, 1974, op. cit., p. 106.

[38] Popper, 1974, op. cit., p. 10.

[39] See Hart, 1974, op. cit., pp. 40–1.

[40] For an alternative, if not dissenting, approach see C. Cartwright, 1973; also P. Self, 1974.

[41] On public learning and coordination see D. Michael, 1973; Schon, 1971; op. cit., Chapter 5; also Vickers, 1965, op. cit., p. 80.

[42] Popper, 1974, op. cit., p. 38.

[43] J. Hilhorst, 1971, p. 148; see also Self, 1974, op. cit.

[44] For a general introduction to these problems see Wildavsky, 1973, op. cit.; also Lindblom, 1959, op. cit.

[45] Popper, 1974, op. cit., p. 17.

[46] See in particular P. Arctander, 1972; Stewart, 1971, op. cit., pp. 142–4 and Introduction; also Hart, 1974, op. cit., pp. 27–8; also T. Eddison, 1973, Chapter 2.

[47] R. Fried, 1973, p. 7.

[48] On commitment and specificity in decision-making see Levin, 1972, op. cit.

[49] This terminology belongs to Hart, 1974, op. cit., p. 27.

[50] Wildavsky introduced these concepts in the proceedings of a conference on policy-making in local government, London, June 24–5, 1974.

[51] Stewart, 1971, op. cit., p. 143.

[52] Bićanić, 1967, op. cit., p. 14 and pp. 74–5.

[53] Faludi, 1969, op. cit.

[54] Faludi, 1970, op. cit., p. 2; compare with Dror, 1963, op. cit., his Primary Facet A.

[55] See Friedmann, 1973b, op. cit., pp. 52–9; Schon, 1971, op. cit., pp. 9–30; Cartwright, 1973, op. cit.; also Grabow and Heskin, 1973.

[56] Faludi, 1970, op. cit., pp. 2–6; for an alternative approach see Dror, 1963, op. cit.; also P. Davidoff and T. Reiner, 1962, pp. 103–5.

[57] Faludi, 1970, op. cit., pp. 2–3; see also Faludi, 1973b, op. cit., Chapter 10, for a more extended treatment.

[58] On the importance of the contextual concept see H. Lasswell, 1965, especially pp. 3–28; also A. Etzione, 1968, on contextuating control.

[59] For an alternative approach see Hart, 1974, op. cit., pp. 29–41.

[60] On problems associated with this approach see R. Mayer, 1972; also Rittell and Webber, 1973, op. cit.

[61] This latter point will be taken up in the next two chapters, Chapters 4 and 5.

[62] P. Cohen, 1968, Chapter 7, especially pp. 178–203.

[63] Dahrendorf, 1959, op. cit., Chapter V.

[64] Dahrendorf, 1959, op. cit., p. 157.

[65] Dahrendorf, 1959, op. cit., p. 160.

[66] Dahrendorf, 1959, op. cit., p. 161.

[67] Dahrendorf, 1959, op. cit., p. 158.

[68] Dahrendorf, 1959, op. cit., p. 162.

[69] Dahrendorf, 1959, op. cit., p. 158.

[70] Dahrendorf, 1959, op. cit., p. 159.

[71] Dahrendorf, 1959, op. cit., p. 163; for a critique of this view see A. Giddens, 1968; also Simmie, 1974, op. cit., pp. 58–60.

[72] E. Shils, 1961.

[73] On this last point see Simmie, 1974, op. cit., Preface.

# 4 The Institutional Context

The concern of the previous two chapters has been with some of the fundamentals of public planning. The sketch for a theory of this particular form of intervention was derived from a host of assumptions and assertions, or rather a set of assertions and assumptions which can be seen as corollaries to those which prop-up what were referred to as 'good currency' ideas in public planning – the rationality model.

But this sketch is not however a corollary or the corollary to rational planning – what, after Lindblom, is referred to as 'the science of muddling through' – disjointed incrementalism.[1] Rather it is an amalgam, a moulding together, of those components which have been considered significant features of public planning in the context of a specific and alternative philosophy of method – Popperian deductive-indeterminism. As a combination of the five interconnected and interacting components and concepts of process, policy, problem-solving, theory-incorporating, and change.

We have also considered some meanings of planning and policy, their respective ingredients, and the process by which these become fused. But what we have *not* outlined in specific enough terms is the actual 'public' component – the administrative and institutional context.

## Public planning and government

In terms of the planning domain – the environment of planning mapped-out in the last chapter – it is possible to set the problem of 'public' within the context provided by the third and fourth attributes of that environment: the nature of the political system (and its administrative structures), and the institutional structuring of society. The relationship, broadly speaking, between public planning and government.[2]

In arriving at an interpretation of the nature and importance of the 'public' in this relationship we need to retrace our steps back to the beginning of Chapter Two. There a crucial distinction was introduced between formal and informal purposeful action. Also that formalised action corresponded approximately to the organised components of society, and in particular with the process of the making and implementing of decisions and policies within formal organisational structures, public and private. So what then is public planning? Paraphrasing Dror and Faludi we can present a working interpretation (approximating to a further 'good currency' idea of planning): *public planning is the formal adoption by governments and their agencies of a process of administration which attempts to decide on major guidelines for future action based on the translation of aims and objectives into public policies and concrete action programmes.*[3]

The manner in which this process is formalised and legitimated is therefore of some significance, especially since public planning extends beyond government itself to include the actions of its agencies and the officials which staff them.[4] In this context we have an immediate and direct relationship between public planning and government – in fact the two are by definition inextricably interwoven. But the relationship itself is of even greater significance; we have a situation of mutual reciprocity, where government directly controls or influences its agencies – and hence planning – and where its agencies – and hence planning – in turn influence the nature and practice of government. Government constitutes and is constituted by planning.[5]

However, the concept of government is not an abstract entity. Rather governments are made up of and staffed by individuals and groups of individuals, who in turn act out particular rôles and perform a multiplicity of different functions. From this perspective governments can be considered as social networks of authority made up of individuals, officials, coalitions and élites which are in some sense structured or organised – however loose that might be. In terms of describing and analysing these kinds of relational situation, it is useful to consider them in the context of two concepts borrowed from and employed in the sociology of organisations: the study of bureaucracy and élitism.[6]

These concepts, in particular bureaucratisation, are of relevance to a study of the nature and practice of planning because, as we argued earlier, public planning is a social activity and concerned with social change. Since bureaucratisation (in the non-pejorative Weberian sense) is an important feature of authority-dependency relationships in contemporary society, and governments and society undergo change, it therefore makes sense to relate planning to bureaucracy for two reasons: (a) because public planning is such a central feature of authority and governmental activity, and (b) government agencies are often considered to represent the most developed forms of bureaucracy. The concept of bureaucracy in the study of public planning is thus a potentially important point of entry.[7] In other words in the 'ideal-type' administration of government and public planning there tends to be:

... a series of officials, each of whose rôles is circumscribed by a written definition of his authority. These offices are arranged in a hierarchy, each successive step embracing all those beneath it. There is a set of rules and procedures within which every possible contingency is theoretically provided for. There is a 'bureau' for the safe keeping of all written records and files, it being an important part of the rationality of the system that information is written down. A clear separation is made between personal and business affairs, bolstered by a contractual method of appointment in terms of technical qualifications for office. In such an organisation authority is based in the office and commands are obeyed because the rules state that it is within the competence of a particular office to issue such commands.[8]

In terms of the individuals — the administrators and officials — who staff bureaucracies, one would expect to find a division of labour based on expertise as the principle organising characteristic in the allocation of who does what, in what manner and when. The rules on which such a principle is based, and which determines how that bureaucracy is managed, are therefore more or less stable. Indeed a knowledge of these rules is a vital and distinguishing feature of an officials acknowledged skills and accepted expertise.[9]

In fact it is not strictly permissible to treat the concept of bureaucracy in the singular. Like the concept of government itself, bureaucracy may be considered in terms of a multiplicity of individuals forming groups, coalitions, cliques and élites. Reissman, in a particularly important study of rôle conceptions in bureaucracies, argues that it is possible to identify at least four basic types: functional, specialist, service and job bureaucrats.[10] 'Functional bureaucrats' are individuals or groups with a predominantly professional and outward-looking orientation to their respective tasks. 'Specialist bureaucrats' have this professional orientation but they tend to be relatively more myopic — they identify more strongly with the bureaucracy itself and seek advancement through its career structure. 'Service bureaucrats' are those individuals and groups with a strong commitment to servicing others, particularly those outside the bureaucracy (clients), utilising routes through the lattice-like network of internal rules and powers open and available to them. Finally, 'job bureaucrats' are those who are more or less totally immersed in the structure and functioning of the bureaucracy, and in particular with a rôle conception which stresses the importance of its maintenance by ensuring adherence and commitment to those very internal rules.

The problem with the concepts of bureaucracy, bureaucrats and bureaucratisation from the point of view of public planning is that they are usually associated with a particular image of conservatism. With a certain brand of perjorative thought and action: inflexible thought, fixed attitudes and a static view of social change: what Schon refers to as 'dynamic conservatism'. [11] Contrary to Weber's 'ideal-type' of rational authority, the commonly held view associates bureaucracy with a concern for maintenance of the *status quo,* with order and stability. Planning in this bureaucratic sense, and public planning in particular, can therefore be described not solely in terms of divisions of labour, power and responsibilities, or by the presence of centres of power or élites within and between public agencies, but rather in terms of the image which bureaucracies *qua* bureaucrats have of society and the manner in which they cope with, perceive and interpret social change. In other words with the problem of ideology.

The relationships between government, its administration and planning involvement are obviously complex. Introduction of the notion of ideology extends this complexity, but in a positive manner — it is useful in attempting to explain or at least account for the way in which bureaucracies behave through time. In this sense public planning as a bureaucratic and inherently ideologically based activity ties in neatly with that general notion of ideology ('particular' and 'total') portrayed by Karl Mannheim. That is, states of mind or attitudes or 'ideas' which are at odds with reality, but which are nevertheless directed to the stability of the present or even with the restoration of the past. These so-called states of mind, attitudes or 'ideas' (mental fictions) are deemed to be a function of the individual who holds them, and of his position in the social milieu. [12] As Mannheim puts it:

> ... ruling groups can in their thinking become so intensively interest-bound to a situation that they are simply no longer able to see certain facts which would undermine their sense of domination ... the collective unconscious of certain groups obscures the real condition of society both to itself and to others and thereby stabilizes it. [13]

This process of the bending and manipulation of reality to suit certain (class) interests was also of central concern to Karl Marx. Public planning as a bureaucratic phenomenon can therefore also be described as ideological in the Marxian sense: as a process of distortion and mystification induced by bourgeois thought, and reified in practice through bureaucratisation and the process of embourgeoisment. According to the Marxian

70

concept of ideology, public planning is alienated because it ascribes to plans and planning machinery a degree of power and characteristics which rightly belongs to that of the individual. The result is that the individuals freedom and power is moved away from the control and influence of the individual to a more remote and alien level. Berger and Luckmann extend this notion of ideology by making the formal power dimension of the equation more explicit. They argue like Marx that what constitutes 'reality' cannot be functionally separated from the prevailing power superstructure. Indeed it has to be seen more as an integral and internalised component of that superstructure: 'When a particular definition of reality comes to be attached to a concrete power interest, it may be called an ideology.'[14]

This Marxian interpretation of ideology is important in one further respect for a study of the nature and practice of planning. This concerns the notion of 'false consciousness', and in particular with the manner in which public planning relates to objectivity, bias and class-interest. False consciousness, in the Marxian sense only, is one step removed from the general concept of ideology itself. In some respects it resembles the idea of 'original sin', because it too carries connotations of theological inevitability. False consciousness, according to Mannheim, is the problem of the totally distorted mind which falsifies everything which comes within its range: 'It is the awareness that our total outlook as distinguished from its details may be distorted.'[15]

The Marxian position on false consciousness then is simply that this 'total outlook' (what Marx referred to as a 'tissue of lies') is an inevitable component of bourgeois thought and action, and embedded in the very class structure of society itself. In terms of public planning this 'total outlook' is part and parcel of bureaucratisation and authority, reflecting the modes of thought and actions of bureaucrats and technicians. As such it complements the Marxian notion of ideology, but is that much more powerful: public planning is a process of mystification, reification and alienation, serving straightforward bourgeois interests — but more importantly its underlying values are bourgeois. Planners then, in the sense that they too have and pursue bourgeois interests, tend to identify with the bourgeoisie. They are part and parcel of society's superstructure of authority-dependency relationships. Therefore, a Marxist would argue, their view of society is necessarily and inevitably a distorted and selfish one. And so planners, by establishing and mobilising support for particular proposals (therefore aimed at a particular class) merely reinforce their own preconceptions, preoccupations and class interests with a distorted and distorting process of what constitutes the social construction of reality. [16] In cruder terms, with what they would prefer to see rather than what those being planned would perhaps wish, want or need. This interpretation is subtly different from the Marxian approach because it introduces an additional dimension – power. Berger and Luckmann argue that power and the exercise of power is a critical and determining feature of what Mannheim refers to as the evaluative (as against the non-evaluative) concept of ideology. [17] Their interpretation concerns the manner in which 'ideas' and knowledge are perceived by individuals, translated by them, and internalised to form particular constructions of what constitutes reality. This, they argue, is a necessarily distorted construction because the process of internalisation itself is a relatively crude device. In terms of this perception and translation, the ideological foundations are constructed when this internalisation process is part of and becomes embedded in the power structure of society. [18] Since public planning is a component of government – an arm of its authority – and bureaucratised, it follows that in the main it too is part of and embedded in the formal power structure of society.

This kind of argument is a forceful and persuasive one, and presents planners in the public arena with a major and unresolved dilemma. As Arctander neatly puts it, we need to plan but we cannot plan 'successfully' or 'properly'; for what constitutes 'success' and what is 'proper' are value-laden and political terms. [19] The point is a fundamental one because it illustrates with some clarity the value-based, debatable and tenuous set of assumptions and assertions which make up the very foundations of public planning – nothing more, nothing less. [20]

### A typology of public planning

Earlier it was stated that the relationship between public planning and government was a reciprocal one. Government determines the nature and practice of planning *qua* what is planned, and public planning *qua* agencies in turn influence the nature and practice of government. On an admittedly subjective basis we also know that in the real world types of government and ranges of intervention are about as varied as their actual number. But are there broad patterns which can be discerned from this subjective assessment, in effect between types of government and types of planning? The answer is very much in the affirmative: different types of public planning can indeed be hypothesised on the basis of this reciprocity assumption.

In fact we can begin to map-out and contrast these hypothetical styles or modes of planning by contrasting four levels of analysis. These levels, which emanate from the idea of the planning domain, range from differences in ideological content — at the broadest conceptual level — to differences in their respective administrative requirements. These four levels are:

1 ideological differences;
2 institutional differences;
3 operational differences; and
4 administrative differences.

These four levels are demonstrably interrelated, but interrelated by degree: differences in ideological content determine in part, are determined by, and reflect differences in the institutionalisation of planning; these institutional differences determine in part, are determined by, and reflect differences in the styles of the operation of planning; these operational differences determine in part, are determined by, and reflect differences in the administration of planning. Because these impacts are differential it is simpler to translate the concepts used into three broader but more meaningful *tiers*, tiers which are not mutually exclusive abstractions but which are nested. Tier I therefore incorporates tiers II and III, and tier II incorporates tier III thus:

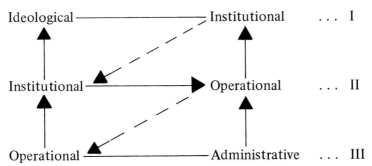

This schema, coupled with an emphasis on differences between styles of planning, enables a form of analysis to be set up which emphasises not the attributes of a potentially infinite range of planning styles, but rather one which concentrates on the extremes of that range. We can begin to map-out pure forms or 'ideal types' of alternative planning modes in terms of a continuum bounded by these contrasting forms. But before doing so, these preliminaries for the analysis may be extended one stage further. Having identified three tiers to the schema outlined above we can slot these 'ideal types' not within a single continuum but within three continuums, reflecting differences in the respective ideological-institutional, institutional-operational and operational-administrative contents.

Having prepared the format for the analysis it is now possible to identify these 'ideal types' of planning mode. One contemporary and particularly important contribution to research into planning theory has attempted to do just this.[21] Faludi has identified six varieties, or 'ideal types', from a literature review of essentially North American planning theory. These six are:

1 blueprint planning;
2 process planning;
3 rational comprehensive planning;
4 disjointed incrementalism;
5 normative planning; and
6 functional planning.[22]

But Faludi goes one stage further. He argues that each of these modes can be treated as an extreme of a continuum. He identifies six 'ideal types' so therefore formulates three continuums, or as he refers to them, dimensions of planning. These are respectively:

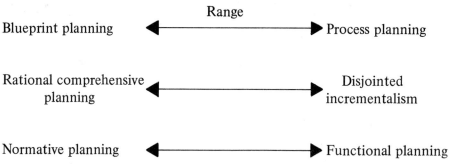

Within the terms of the framework outlined above, it is possible to reconcile these dimensions of planning with the three tiers of that schema. In fact it is possible to treat Faludi's dimensions in a similar manner to the way in which that schema was developed. Instead of regarding the three continuums as mutually exclusive abstractions, it is possible to argue that they are subtly different ways of looking at the same thing. In the manner which Faludi considers them, each continuum stresses different qualities from quite different perspectives. The first he regards as the most abstract, the third the most concrete. Implicit in his writings is the notion that there are only two 'ideal types' of planning mode: at one extreme planning as the fashioning of a blueprint, at the other planning as a continuous process. In other words there is just one substantive continuum. All other alternatives may be located somewhere between these two extremes.[23]

It is precisely at this point where the three tiers of the schema can be introduced. The first tier, stressing ideological-institutional differences, accords with and to some extent reflects Faludi's contrasting concepts of blueprint and process planning. At the most abstract level of analysis, therefore, it is possible to map-out a contrasting pair of planning styles whose differences can be described and reflected primarily in terms of their respective ideological and institutional differences.

The second tier, stressing institutional-operational differences, accords with and reflects his second dimension of rational comprehensive planning and disjointed incrementalism. At a less abstract level of analysis, therefore, it is possible to map-out these contrasting styles in terms of their respective institutional and operational differences.

Likewise with the third tier. It is possible to set Faludi's third dimension of normative and functional modes of planning within the context of their respective operational and administrative differences. Implicit in this approach is the notion that the normative and functional planning modes are nested within the rational comprehensive and disjointed incrementalism continuum. But also that this is in turn nested within the basic organising continuum: the blueprint and process planning modes:[24]

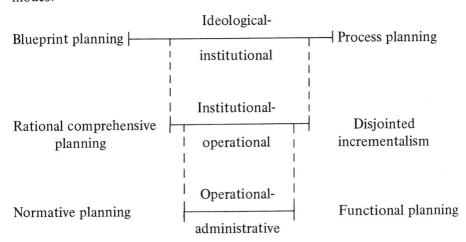

Before embarking on the analysis itself there are two additional complicating factors which need to be appended to the schema outlined above. Both concern the sketch for a theory of public planning described in the last chapter. The first is the 'internal' component of that sketch — the methodology of the processes of planning itself; the second is the contextual setting of those processes, the 'internal-external' interface — the public planning domain. The reasons for the inclusion of these two

75

components are obvious enough, for we have developed a mode of planning as an alternative to that in 'good currency'. If the schema just described has any utility then it must account and include for both of these approaches – the rationality model and the deductive alternative. So we can make an additional use of the schema by comparing this alternative formulation within the spectrum of possible alternative modes of planning from the perspective of its ideological, institutional, operational and administrative differences.

### Public planning – blueprint versus process[25]

From the perspective of ideological-institutional differences the concept of blueprint planning is self-explanatory, derived as it is from the analogy with engineering and the 'master plan'. In terms of public planning the blueprint approach starts life by a fashioning of a long-term master view of a 'desirable' (however defined) state of affairs for society. Once this ultimate 'end' has been set all that is required of authority is to supply the 'means' for its achievement, and its dual – the enforcement to ensure that the plan is implemented as was originally intended. There is no room for uncertainty. [26] In other words, to use Faludi's terminology, the image of what is to be planned is firm and static, and control over the environment is total. The principal problem for planning becomes one of coordination and manipulation – coordinating the 'means' to ensure the plans ultimate fruition, and manipulating them to ensure that the objectives are attained in the manner in which they were originally set. Blueprint planning is therefore a particularly 'mechanistic' form of planning – a technical and professional exercise in and of itself. Further, it is a 'utopian' approach – or as Mannheim puts it, a set of wish dreams which inspire collective action aimed at the entire transformation of society itself. [27] In other words the 'desired' image eventually becomes the 'actual' image, and ultimately reality itself. As Hart admirably points out, the blueprint approach is concerned solely with the ordering of change; the idea of order itself undergoing change is either considered to be irrelevant by definition or assumed away or held constant *ceteris paribus* fashion.[28]

From the perspective of preparing these kind of total plans, because of their totality they invariably suffer from very long gestation periods between the time the decision to plan is taken and when the plan is ultimately produced and implemented. A feature which can be attributed to this long lead time is that of reification. The plan itself becomes of increasing importance, gains momentum in the process, and may eventually reach an elevation of almost omnipotent proportions until it becomes almost untouchable or unmodifiable. It generates its own dynamism and importance, what has been aptly called the 'sorcerers apprentice effect': impossible to halt or hinder. An 'end' in itself rather than as a 'means' to some desirable 'end', the principle on which it started its life.[29]

Examples which approximate to the notion of the blueprint approach as a mode of total planning include major engineering schemes, such as the construction of bridges, or the design and building of dams. Examples of blueprint planning as the approach to public planning, however, include Admiral Speer's 'grand design' for the reconstruction and replanning of Germany (particularly Berlin), Le Corbusier's proposals for Chandigah, capital of the Punjab, and the Brazilian Government's commitment to the continued development of Brasilia. Examples of the 'sorcerers apprentice effect' include possibly the NASA programme and its proposals for continuing space exploration. Nearer home the so-called 'old-style' Development Plans produced under the 1947 Town and Country Planning Act, also perhaps the proposals for and later development of the 'master plans' for the British New Towns.[30]

How does blueprint planning compare with the sketch for a theory of the processes of public planning developed in the previous chapter? With regard to problem-solving it is clear that the blueprint approach is concerned with a very narrow interpretation of the concept of problems, if it considers them at all. It is theory-incorporating in an equally limited fashion. The manner in which it is dynamic is also very restricted, dealing as it does almost exclusively with the dynamics of the ordering of change. It is also clearly the antithesis of a process-orientation, and by definition dismisses or reduces the problem of uncertainty. As such the blueprint approach is not characterised by relationships between impact and intent, between continuous interaction and constant iteration between problem-setting and strategies for their solution (Figure 4.1).

From the perspective of ideological-institutional differences the concept of planning as a continuous process, process planning, is clearly the antithesis of the blueprint approach. It too is self-explanatory. But unlike blueprint planning it is an approach which attempts to adjust continuously to change, to changing conditions and circumstances, however defined. It is an inherently behavioural and totally flexible approach rather than mechanistic. Unlike the concept of the blueprint plan, process planning has no real aspirations as to what constitutes or might constitute a total, wholly desirable environment.[31] Its image of what to plan is therefore an uncertain one. It is an incomplete image, making no pretentions to understand or comprehend completely the total operation

Fig. 4.1   Blueprint planning

| | Problem-solving | Theory-incorporating | Dynamic | Process-orientation | Uncertainty | Continuous interaction | Constant iteration |
|---|---|---|---|---|---|---|---|
| Blueprint planning | * | n.a. | * | n.a. | n.a. | n.a. | n.a. |

n.a.   No association
*      Low level of association
***    High level of association


of society. Its image is restricted to what politicians, policy-makers and planners think are the key variables on which they wish to legitimately operate on in response to an issue at, say time *(t)*. At time $(t + 1)$ the planners concept of what constitutes the key variables might be different because of the perception of changed circumstances, both 'internally-externally' and 'externally'. Such a mode of planning exercises little if no control over the whole environment at any one point in time because of the problems of uncertainty. It is inherently response-oriented with considerable, if not all, emphasis on 'means' rather than 'ends'. Process planning relies heavily if not exclusively on an efficient monitoring and information base, where planners can act on or anticipate a changing set of circumstances with the minimum of time and effort. Unlike blueprint planning the process approach operates on a very short-term view of the future development of society. Its primary concern is with the function of societal pulse-taking and monitoring in the short term rather than with projecting a long-term view of a desirable end state.[32]

The priorities of the process approach are therefore very much the antithesis of those associated with blueprint planning. It is equally if not primarily interested in attempting to understand how the concept of order itself is changing rather than with simply trying to order change.

Examples of the process approach to public planning are much more difficult to find, because in terms of the ideology of public planning it is very much out on a limb. It is a 'soft', short term, and messy approach to public intervention, and as such is difficult to isolate or to readily compartmentalise. Perhaps the nearest example is the short term planning of public expenditure by central governments. For example, in the United Kingdom the combination of the triannual forecasts by the Treasury with the five-year 'rolling programme' with the annual Public Expenditure Survey Committee (PESC) reports.[33]

So how does process planning compare with the sketch for a theory of the processes of public planning developed in the previous chapter? The answer is that it accords very closely indeed, or rather may accord closely. It is or could be very much concerned with the ideas of problem-solving and theory-incorporating. It is by definition process-oriented and gives explicit recognition to the problems associated with uncertainty. It is therefore inextricably bound up with the relationships between continuous interaction and constant iteration, between impact and intent (see figure 4.2).

Fig. 4.2   Process planning

| | Problem-solving | Theory-incorporating | Dynamic | Process-orientation | Uncertainty | Continuous-interaction | Constant-iteration |
|---|---|---|---|---|---|---|---|
| Process planning | ** | ** | *** | *** | *** | *** | *** |

## Public planning — rational comprehensive versus disjointed incrementalism[34]

From the perspective of institutional-operational differences the concept of rational comprehensive planning was described in the last chapter. It is broadly a hybrid of the 'ideal-type' rationality model of decision-making as applied, in the context of public planning, to public problems. The basic idea is that its perimeter of concern should cover just about anything and everything which the planner considers of legitimate importance to include. As Faludi puts it, it is an attempt not only at overall societal guidance but also with the coordination of organisational activity to achieve that guidance. [35] But rational comprehensive planning is significantly different from blueprint planning. It is, according to an early protagonist, John Friedmann, an attempt to ensure that every component of relevance to an issue is included in the planning process in a rational and comprehensive way, and dealt with rationally and comprehensively. [36] Unlike the blueprint approach it is more concerned with the 'means' of action rather than with the formulation of 'ends', although it accords with the notion that 'ends' are a crucial component of public planning. [37] A significant difference between the two approaches is that rational comprehensive planning attempts to predict the future as it could be rather than with the forging of some desirable utopian 'end state' as it should be.

A significant feature of rational comprehensive planning is that it is geared primarily if not exclusively to the idea of goal achievement, with the attainment of goals. But more importantly, in the context of public planning at least, to the attainment of the goals of society; in other words with the 'public interest'. Rational planners argue that it is possible to obtain a consensus view of what these latent goals are, which may then be formalised as 'the public interest', and made an explicit determining feature of the process of planning itself; in other words, that society's goals may be explicitly stated and strived for through the application of systematic analysis and action which accords with the five sequential steps of the model of rational decision-making:

1   a clearly defined problem exists;
2   goals are defined and set (representing the consensus goals of society);
3   all possible alternative courses of action or strategies are explicitly identified;
4   these alternative strategies are systematically and rigorously evaluated against the goals; and
5   an optimal alternative course of action is adopted or chosen which accords with the preferences of the decision-makers. [38, 39]

This approach, which March and Simon call 'scientific management', has a number of important implications when applied to public planning. Because of its concern for coordination, rational comprehensiveness implies that the planning functions of government, and therefore government itself, should be heavily centralised rather than fragmented or federalised: that is, to ensure that the degree of comprehensiveness is maximised. Also that the activities, actions and programmes which are part and parcel of this total approach should be both derived and realised in a rational 'cold light of day' manner. There is little room for any emotive component, the emotion associated with politics and political policy-making. Rather it implies a 'scientific', 'diagnostic', almost 'clinical' approach to the understanding and manipulation of social change. Above all it is a 'technical' form of planning – a professional activity – which accords with the critical assumptions associated with the rational model. It attempts to be total, holistic, fully comprehensive, optimal, rational, innovatory, cohesive, and oriented to the long term. As a form of public planning the rational comprehensive approach is above all associated with a long term perspective of the development of society.[40]

Because this approach to planning, borrowed as it was from the extensive experience of its use in the United States, corresponds very closely to the idea of the 'normal paradigm' of planning it is not difficult to find volumes of contemporary examples. [41] In the United Kingdom it is no exaggeration to say that most major planning exercises in the public arena undertaken in the last decade (1965 to 1975) have, almost without exception, professed to the adoption of the rationality model as the basic organising device. [42] At the national level, for example, the rational comprehensive approach has been enshrined and formalised in the methodologies adopted by the Royal Commission on Local Government in England (the Redcliffe-Maud Report), the Commission into the selection of the Third London Airport (the Roskill Commission) and for the organisation and planning functions of the reorganised health and water authorities. At the regional level a good example is provided by the *Strategic Plan for the South East,* whereas at a subregional level the *Greater London Development Plan* and a pioneer of structure planning, the *South Hampshire Structure Plan,* may be taken as representative of this rational and comprehensive approach. Indeed all contemporary U.K. transport studies and plans have, without exception, adopted this basic organising methodology.[43]

So how does rational comprehensive planning compare with the sketch for a theory of the processes of planning outlined in the last chapter? The simple answer is that it does not compare very favourably. The reason is obvious, by definition, because the rationality model was used as a base for which to develop an alternative based on an alternative methodology. But the point was made earlier that this deductive alternative could not be construed as *the* corollary, for reasons which will soon become apparent.

In some respects the two methodologies are substantively different, but they do share some common ground. For example, they are both concerned with problem-solving. But there the similarity ends. For rational comprehensiveness 'a clearly defined problem exists'; for deductive-indeterminism a vital component of the whole methodology concerns the very process of identifying problems in the first place. Both approaches are theory-incorporating – they both attempt to relate practical problems to theoretical solutions and vice versa. Indeed both incorporate a particular philosophy of method. But the two approaches differ in the way in which they treat and incorporate theory. For the rational approach, theory is broadly taken as given ('end'). For the deductive alternative, theory is by no means accorded this status. Development and progress in theory is a central concern of the latter ('means').[44]

Both approaches are also process-oriented and dynamic in the sense that each is broadly responsive to changing circumstances. But the differences concern the manner in which each is treated and integrated into the respective schemas. For rational comprehensive planning allowances can be made for uncertainty; mechanisms exist within the schema to allow for basic modifications via feedback between its component parts should it become necessary. For the deductive alternative, however, uncertainty is a critical and distinguishing characteristic – it does not simply make allowances for the process and dynamics of change. Rather it sets them within a framework which accords them a certain free-standing status of being of some importance in and of their own right.

Because of its claim to comprehensiveness the rational approach does give explicit consideration to the problem of interaction between problems *qua* goals and strategies *qua* alternatives. But this interaction cannot be construed as continuous interaction. Likewise, rational comprehensive planning attempts to be iterative between goals and alternatives and their evaluation, but it is a very limited form of iteration, and certainly cannot be compared favourably with the feature of constant iteration of the deductive approach. Figure 4.3 sets out in broad terms this 'goodness of fit'.

The concept of disjointed incrementalism as a mode of public planning is very much the antithesis – a true corollary – of rational comprehensiveness. In fact the way in which it was first formulated was as a direct and full-frontal attack on the 'scientific management' approach of applying rationality and rational methodology to public problems.[45] Disjointed incrementalism – 'the science of muddling through' – after Lindblom, argues that rationality as an abstract concept is an admirable intellectual ideal. It assumes that man has infinite intellectual capacities. It is this fundamental assumption which Lindblom disputes and the basis on

Fig. 4.3    Rational comprehensive planning

| | Problem-solving | Theory-incorporating | Dynamic | Process-oriented | Uncertainty | Continuous interaction | Constant iteration |
|---|---|---|---|---|---|---|---|
| Rational comprehensive planning | * | * | * | * | * | * | * |

which he develops the alternative. Summarising Lindblom's position it is simply that, from the point of view of public planning, (a) any one individual or organisation has severely limited intellectual capacities, (b) that the quality of information is generally inadequate and costly to obtain, (c) that the idea of a consensus preference function is nothing more than a pipe-dream, (d) that problems cannot be tightly defined (rather they are 'open'), and (e) therefore, the solutions, decisions and policies proposed cannot be tightly or rigorously or rationally formulated.[46]

So what does Lindblom see as the alternative to the model of rationality? Based on these criticisms he formulates a descriptive theory, with Braybrooke, of disjointed incrementalism. The characteristics of this corollary are that choice is based not on differences between striving for utopia (goals) and utopian alternatives, but rather on incremental change at the margin (increments away from the *status quo,* and trade-off's between competing increments at the margin). This implies that the notion of identifying all possible alternatives is an absurd proposition; rather the alternatives which can be considered are restricted in number because of the lack of information, and wedded to change at the margin ('pushing forward' from the present rather than 'working back' from the future). Which means in turn that only a limited number of consequences can be considered, but at least they are well understood and can be evaluated against the (best) information available. In this kind of process — limited resources and information about problems and potential outcomes — it is possible to adjust in some continuous fashion to changing circumstances. In other words, by proceeding incrementally — by 'successive limited comparisons' — the goals themselves can be adjusted and not held constant.[47]

This then broadly describes the 'incremental' component of Braybrooke and Lindblom's thesis. But they preface it with the idea of a disjointed kind of incrementalism. The essence of the disjoint element means roughly what it implies — the almost total fragmentation of centres of planning and therefore centres of power. As Faludi points out, it means that the process of analysis and evaluation in society is taking place in a multitude of centres and at a large number of points at any one time. This reveals the two authors image of society as being fundamentally an atomistic one.[48]

There are a number of implications which need to be considered here. The first concerns Braybrooke and Lindblom's use of theory. Rational comprehensive planning is an abstract ideal, they argue, and impossible to fully implement. It is a normative theory of planning which is unworkable and therefore untenable. Disjointed incrementalism is what occurs anyway; it has certain 'natural' qualities. It is therefore a description of planning activity; by formalising it, it can be translated into a descriptive theory. But Braybrooke and Lindblom go one step further; not only is this what actually occurs but moreover it is the desirable process to adopt. In other words, they unwittingly translate it from a description of everyday life into a prescription for planning — from a descriptive into a normative theory.[49]

The manner in which disjointed incrementalism functions is also deserving of some attention. The key to the way in which decisions and policies are fashioned and implemented is through a process of bargaining, brokerage and compromise, or what Braybrooke and Lindblom call mutual partisan adjustment. Each protagonist or power élite with a particular view or interest on a particular project or policy thrashes the issue out until some agreement is reached, allowing a policy to be presented and implemented as the outcome. In other words, the holding and manipulation of power is a critical feature of disjointed incrementalism, with all the connotations which that implies. [50] So implicit in the Braybrooke and Lindblom thesis is a normative relationship between its disjointed characteristics and the distribution of power within and between competing groups: a decentralised form of government is the desirable norm because centres of power are many and dispersed (inherently 'good'), rather than few and concentrated (inherently 'bad').

So as a corollary to rational and comprehensive planning, disjointed incrementalism views the characteristics of public planning as being truly incremental, remedial, serial, exploratory, fragmented, atomistic, and oriented in a very limited way to the solving of present-oriented problems.[51]

Because disjointed incrementalism is what generally occurs in planning in practice, Braybrooke and Lindblom argue that examples of it are ubiquitous. Contemporary examples might therefore cover all those activities which function on what is generally referred to as a 'day-by-day' basis: the settling of disputes (both inter- and intra-authority, inter- and intra-organisational), the budgetary monitoring process of across-the-board organisations, etc. But perhaps the best examples are provided by the implementation of on-going policies, and in particular with the manner in which they are pursued and implemented. The criterion of importance here concerns the level of commitment given to any particular policy set, which in turn is related to its specificity. Which means the political and administrative priority with which it is accorded together with the capability of the implementing organisation to actually carry it through.[52]

So how does the concept of disjointed incrementalism compare with the sketch for a theory of the process of planning developed in the previous chapter? The answer is that in some broad respects it compares quite favourably. Where they differ is the manner in which the status of each organising concept is treated. For example, both approaches argue for a problem-solving capability, but disjointed incrementalism takes a much narrower interpretation of what constitutes the problem space and its solution. It is also theory-incorporating in an equally limited and indirect fashion — it stresses the limited amount and quality of information available, so relies implicitly on some notions of what constitutes reality by default. As a mode of planning it is inherently dynamic and responsive to change (political and exogenous), and as such treats the problem of uncertainty in a very definite and explicit manner, dealing with the problems of today and the seizing of opportunities rather than with the perpetration of 'grand designs'. But because of its disjointed and procedural concern for solving problems via political brokerage and mutual partisan adjustment, disjointed incrementalism fails to provide an adequate or satisfactory explanation of the manner in which this adjustment is resolved — for example, when and on what basis does the adjustment process reach a conclusion on an issue? As such it fails to consider the way in which problems and strategies are inextricably interwoven beyond the purely explicit political level. The 'goodness of fit' with the two concepts of continuous interaction and constant iteration is therefore also more limited than provided for by our alternative deductive account (see figure 4.4):

Fig. 4.4  Disjointed incrementalism

| | Problem-solving | Theory-incorporating | Dynamic | Process-oriented | Uncertainty | Continuous interaction | Constant iteration |
|---|---|---|---|---|---|---|---|
| Disjointed incrementalism | * | * | *** | *** | *** | * | * |

## Public planning — normative versus functional[53]

From the perspective of operational-administrative differences the concept of normative planning is a particularly interesting mode. It is above all a form of planning which, overgeneralising, is concerned not with questions such as 'given (x) will (y) occur?' but rather 'given (x), should (y) be allowed to occur?' In other words it is a form of planning which, according to Friedmann, is: '. . . chiefly concerned with the ends of action . . . The goals of normative planning are those of the system itself.'[54]

Normative planning then, as a mode of public planning, views the setting and manipulation of these goals as a function internal to the very process of planning itself. Also that decisions relating to these goals and their achievement are made 'internally'. Normative planning is concerned not with a 'value-free' approach to planning but with the very formation and fostering of values. It is therefore integrally linked and dependent on the fostering and 'internalising' of politics itself. It is as equally concerned with the derivation and setting of alternative goals ('ends') as much as with the derivation, setting and evaluation of alternative 'means'. Above all it is a 'footloose' and open kind of public planning: its canvas is very broad, it is concerned with the mobilising and institutionalising of commitment, political as well as technical. In other words, as Faludi admirably points out, the level of autonomy associated with normative planning is very great — it demands freedom to act, to instigate and to formalise its ideas and programmes. Its action space is therefore very broad. In terms of administrative requirements it is demanding of a tight and yet open and loose-knit form of organisation, where hierarchy is not as important as coordination. But above all it is a highly politicised form of public planning.[55]

Friedmann, who appears to have derived the concepts of normative and functional planning, considers two further dimensions of public planning which are of relevance to the idea of normative planning: 'allocative' and 'innovative', and 'adaptive' and 'developmental'.[56] According to Faludi, 'adaptive', 'developmental', and 'innovative' forms of planning can be interpreted as different types of normative planning. ('Allocative' planning being a form of functional planning.) The factor which Faludi argues is important in differentiating between them is autonomy: the level of autonomy and the potential of planning agencies to adopt the normative planning mode.

The 'innovative' and 'developmental' types are broadly synonymous, and by definition assume that autonomy is very high — the action space, the operational and administrative ('internal') context, is conducive to organisational innovation as well as with innovation beyond the institutional context. The concept of 'adaptive' normative planning is, as it suggests, a weaker form of public planning than its two counterparts. The level of autonomy is generally lower and so its action space is more tightly drawn, resulting in an atmosphere more conducive to adapting alternative 'means' to given 'ends' rather than innovatory change.

Contemporary examples which approximate to normative planning include most of the large-scale planning exercises undertaken in the name of the so-called 'undeveloped countries', with the assistance of the so-called 'advanced countries': in the United States, the Ford Foundation's involvement with central planning in Chile, and the Harvard-MIT Joint Centre involvement in the Ciudad Guyana Program; also, in a different context, the Tennessee Valley Authority;[57] in the United Kingdom, the attempts to initiate central economic planning in India and other Commonwealth countries. Contemporary examples within the UK context include the setting-up of the Highlands and Islands Development Board and, arguably, the attempt to establish a National Enterprise Board on similar lines to the Italian state holding company, IRI *(Istituto per la Ricostruzione Industriale)*. (The Italian state development agency, *Cassa per Mezzogiorno,* must also be included in this context.) The institutional arrangements of the New Town Development Corporations must also rank as important attempts to implement a kind of normative planning.

So how does the concept of normative planning compare with the sketch for a theory of the processes of planning outlined in the last chapter? The answer is that in many respects it compares favourably, but in others it is wholly inadequate. The problem concerns the concept of autonomy, and so it is necessary to distinguish between the 'adaptive' and 'innovative' approaches.

Both approaches do not appear to accord significantly closely with the notion of problem-solving outlined in the last chapter. 'Adaptive' normative planning comes closer to it, but it is too preoccupied with the achievement of 'ends' for a reasonable level of congruence. The notion of problem-solving clearly incorporates some element of end reduction, but not with the kind of emphasis which is the characteristic of the normative approach. The same broadly holds for the theory-incorporating component of public planning; both, whilst potentially including it, do not make it a sufficiently explicit feature of public planning. But both forms have dynamic qualities, particularly the 'innovative' variety. Both are process-oriented in a comparatively limited way and as such do not accord the problems associated with uncertainty sufficient status. Because of their rationality bias (via efficient end reduction) both approaches have limited capacities for continuous interaction and constant iteration, between problems and solutions, impact and intent (Figure 4.5).

The concept of functional planning differs substantively from its normative partner. The crucial distinction centres round the idea that as a mode of public planning the setting and manipulation of goals is not a feature or a function of the 'internal' process of planning itself. If goals or 'ends' are to be set, then they must be set and decisions about them made externally to the machinery of planning. Planning in this context is seen as primarily a functional *qua* administrative exercise: finding, coordinating and evaluating the 'means', and commenting in a 'professional' way on the implications should certain strategies be posited or adopted. Far from being a heavily politicised mode of planning, the functional approach is primarily a bureaucratic activity (in the non-Weberian pejorative sense). It pretends to be outside and beyond direct political involvement; it is, above all, a professional and technical exercise — viewing reality from a position of value neutrality. Functional planning assumes that the stability of the existing contextual elements of public planning is a key, unwritten priority. That is, stability within the administration of planning itself ('internal'), between these agencies and those individuals who are the subject of this interventionist activity ('internal-external'), and society at large ('external'). Change is only anticipated or acted upon if there is a divergence between the assumed stability of those elements *(status quo)*

Fig. 4.5    Normative planning

| | Problem-solving | Theory-incorporating | Dynamic | Process-oriented | Uncertainty | Continuous interaction | Constant iteration |
|---|---|---|---|---|---|---|---|
| Normative planning | * | * | ** | * | * | * | * |

and the actual situation of perceived instability. It assumes a 'given' order: it is not concerned with changing that order unless directed to do so by those with legitimately-regarded authority.[58]

In other words, aims and objectives (if relevant) and embryonic policies and actions are issued by precedent and/or directive from another source, having been 'handed down' or 'across' from within or outside the bureaucracy. These are assumed to be 'given' and held constant in any evaluation procedure. Functional planning then is concerned with the execution of previously defined duties, and with the coordination and articulation of the 'means' necessary to execute them. As Allison points out, this division of labour is therefore concerned with three concepts integral to the study of bureaucracy itself: options, commitment and confidence.[59]

Bureaucrats *qua* functional planners fulfill one or more of three basic roles when faced with the evaluation of an issue. What Allison refers to as 'looking down', 'looking sideways' and 'looking upward'. In the first situation − looking down − the functional planner tries to preserve flexibility until the uncertainties surrounding an issue are clarified and hopefully reduced; the planner is concerned with keeping options open. In the second situation − looking across − the functional planner is faced with the forging of a consensus or coalition favourable to a particular position on that issue; to get others committed to that particular course of action. In the third situation − looking upward − the functional planner attempts to mobilise this particular point of view in the form of professional advice; to instill confidence in politicians as to what must be done. To be capable of performing these three roles at the same time are therefore the desirable attributes associated with a functional planner. Attributes which correspond closely to what Friend, Power and Yewlett refer to as reticulist skills.[60]

Contemporary examples which accord with this notion of functional planning are numerous. One of the better examples must be day-to-day management of government by the British Civil Service — a highly professionalised, apolitical and bureaucraticised organisation of over-lapping formal and informal social networks — which has been neatly summarised by two commentators: 'The Treasury is responsible for managing the economy, departments for managing *their* subject matter.'[61]

So how does the concept of functional planning compare with the sketch for a theory of the processes of planning outlined in the previous chapter? The answer is in the main unfavourably. It is broadly concerned with a limited problem-solving capability, 'other things being equal' being the crucial assumption not shared by the deductive approach. Likewise with the theory-incorporating dimension. It is reasonably dynamic and process-oriented, responding to changing circumstances as and when necessary. But underlying these concepts is one of the *status quo* and the desirability associated with the restoring of equilibria, which is not a feature of the deductive sketch previously outlined. Functional planning recognises some of the problems associated with uncertainty, but define them in too narrow terms — primarily in the limited and limiting context of the need for keeping options open. There is also some element of continuous interaction and constant iteration between problems and solutions, impact and intent, but within purely functional (bureaucratic) horizons (Figure 4.6).

### The dimensions compared

At this stage in the proceedings we have (a) developed a schema to compare differences between types of public planning, (b) outlined three dimensions of planning, and (c) compared each dimension with the deductive sketch outlined in the last chapter. Taken together these three components provide a simple framework for the methodological evalu-ation of any form of public planning which may be identified — based on either empirical observations or derived from theoretical foundations or *a priori* assumptions.

Within the context of the sketch for a theory, however, it is possible to

Fig. 4.6    Functional planning

| | Problem-solving | Theory-incorporating | Dynamic | Process-oriented | Uncertainty | Continuous interaction | Constant iteration |
|---|---|---|---|---|---|---|---|
| Functional planning | * | * | ** | * | * | * | * |

take this analysis one stage further. Each 'ideal type' has been compared with the seven determining characteristics of that sketch. All that is required is to draw these six separate comparisons together. The picture which should emerge may then be construed as a model of the deductive-indeterminist schema outlined in terms of the conceptual boundaries of each of the three continuums, within the context of their respective ideological-institutional, institutional-operational, and operational-administrative differences (Figure 4.7).

Taking the problem-solving characteristic of the sketch first, it is clear that process planning approximates most closely with the requirements of a deductive-indeterminist approach. The other five modes all have some problem-solving capability, but of a more limited and limiting form. The same is repeated for the theory-incorporating characteristic with the exception of blueprint planning, which has no capability as such.

The two modes which correspond more closely with the notion of dynamics are process planning and disjointed incrementalism. Both normative and functional modes incorporate some element of dynamics, more so than either the rational comprehensive and blueprint approaches, but also of a more limited and limiting nature.

Similar patterns are to be discerned in comparing the process-oriented and uncertainty characteristics with each of the six modes. Process planning and disjointed incrementalism accord most closely with the demands of the deductive approach, the rational comprehensive, normative and functional modes having some limited capability. Blueprint planning bears no positive correspondence whatsoever.

Fig. 4.7  Comparison by modes of planning

| Principal characteristics of deductive schema<br>'Ideal type' modes of planning | Problem-solving | Theory-incorporating | Dynamic | Process-oriented | Uncertainty | Continuous interaction | Constant iteration |
|---|---|---|---|---|---|---|---|
| Blueprint planning | * | n.a. | * | n.a. | n.a. | n.a. | n.a. |
| Process planning | ** | ** | *** | *** | *** | *** | *** |
| Rational comprehensive planning | * | * | * | * | * | * | * |
| Disjointed incrementalism | * | * | *** | *** | *** | * | * |
| Normative planning | * | * | ** | * | * | * | * |
| Functional planning | * | * | ** | * | * | * | * |

Ideological-institutional

Institutional-operational

Operational-administrative

Similar patterns are also to be found in comparing the continuous interaction and constant iteration features. Of the six modes process planning is the only form which compares favourably, the remaining five − with the exception of the blueprint approach − having some degree of correspondence.

The deductive alternative presented in the previous chapter can therefore be set within the context of these six basic 'ideal types' of planning. According to this analysis it has characteristics which are a reflection and combination of certain qualities of each − of blueprint, process, rational comprehensive, disjointed incremental, normative and functional modes. Each occupies a significant position within the deductive schema. But, standing or falling on their own merits, each is not a sufficient condition for a deductive-oriented approach to public intervention − what may now be more appropriately referred to as responsive planning. How this synthetic schema compares with Faludi's original six-modes-as-three-dimensions may be illustrated by locating the attributes of this responsive mode (RP) within the context provided by those dimensions (Figure 4.8):

Fig. 4.8    Comparison by dimensions of planning

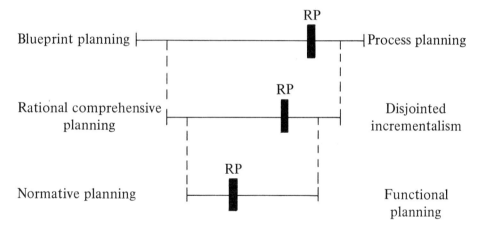

This illustration places the notion of a responsive approach to public planning within a simple comparative context of 'ideal types' of public planning. In terms of ideological-institutional differences, this responsive mode may be located closer to the process rather than blueprint end of the first continuum. At the next level down, institutional-operational differences, it approximates more to the neutral zone of the rational comprehensive and disjointed incremental dimension. In terms of operational-administrative differences it is substantively more in sympathy with the normative rather than functional mode, and so can be located closer to the normative planning end.[62]

The relevance of this simple analysis is that it has some interesting implications for a study of the nature and practice of public planning. It illustrates that planning as an institutional *qua* public activity is by no means homogeneous with respect to any single criterion or set of criteria, apart from the obvious interdependence with and juxtaposition to government. Rather it is a characteristically heterogeneous animal, stressing different emphases which more often than not are subtle and messy in nature.[63]

## Notes

[1] Lindblom, 1959, op. cit.; Braybrooke and Lindblom, 1963, op. cit.; see also the next chapter, Chapter 5.

[2] See P. Selznick, 1948 on these relationships.

[3] Compare with Faludi's and Dror's interpretations, outlined in the last chapter.

[4] For alternative approaches see D. Bell, 1964; see also J. Friedmann, 1967a.

[5] On this relationship see B. Crick, 1972, particularly pp. 44–6; also Arctander, 1972, op. cit.

[6] On bureaucracy and élites see especially Hill, 1972, op. cit.; also Silverman, 1970, op. cit.; on élites see A. Giddens, 1974; also D. MacRae, 1974 for insights into Max Weber's original formulation of bureauracy as rational authority.

[7] See Hill, 1972, op. cit., Introduction.

[8] A version of Weber's original formulation, made by D. Pugh et al., 1971, p. 22; see also Hill, 1972, op. cit., p. 16.

[9] See for example Hill, 1972, op. cit., pp. 329–41; also Etzione, 1961, op. cit., pp. 90–3; N. Beckman, 1964 considers these issues from the planners perspective.

[10] L. Reissman, 1949.

[11] Schon, 1971, op. cit., Chapter 2.

[12] K. Mannheim, 1936, pp. 49–62.

[13] Mannheim, 1936, op. cit., p. 36.

[14] Berger and Luckmann, 1971, op. cit., p. 141.

[15] Mannheim, 1936, op. cit., p. 62.

[16] On 'social constructions of reality' see Berger and Luckmann, 1971, op. cit.

[17] Mannheim, 1936, op. cit., Chapter II.

[18] See for example Berger and Luckmann, 1971, op. cit., p. 141.

[19] Arctander, 1972, op. cit.; see also P. Ylvisaker, 1961; and J. Friedmann, 1973a.

[20] See Dewey, 1927, op. cit., Chapter VI.

[21] Faludi, 1970, op. cit., pp. 3–6; Faludi, 1973b, op. cit., Part III, Chapters 7, 8, 9 and 10.

[22] For an extended discussion see Faludi, 1973b, op. cit., Chapters 7, 8 and 9. For alternative approaches see G. Beneviste, 1973, who identifies four modes of planning; also Wildavsky, 1973, op. cit.

[23] For example, see Faludi, 1973b, op. cit., p. 131.

[24] For an alternative derivation see A. Etzione, 1967.

[25] For a more comprehensive treatment see Faludi, 1973b, op. cit., Chapter 7.

[26] Compare with Fried, 1973, op. cit., p. 7.

[27] Mannheim, 1936, op. cit., Chapters II and IV.

[28] Hart, 1974, op. cit., p. 28.

[29] Compare with the idea of 'planning as future control', Wildavsky, 1973, op. cit.

[30] For a more extensive outline see Faludi, 1973b, op. cit., Chapter 7.

[31] See Arctander, 1972, op. cit.; on 'planning as a process' compare with Wildavsky, 1973, op. cit.

[32] For a more extensive outline see Faludi, 1973b, op. cit., Chapter 7.

[33] Compare with H. Heclo and A. Wildavsky, 1974, Introduction.

[34] For a more comprehensive treatment see Faludi, 1973b, op. cit., Chapter 8.

[35] Faludi, 1973b, op. cit., pp. 155–7.

[36] J. Friedmann, 1965.

[37] Compare with Dror's interpretation of planning and policy-making noted in the last chapter. Compare with the view of J. March and H. Simon, 1958, p.2, on 'scientific management'. See also Silverman, 1970, op. cit., pp. 204–6 for an illuminating critique of this approach.

[38] Compare with key 'good currency' planning texts; for example, see J. McLoughlin, 1969, pp. 94–103; P. Hall, 1974, pp. 269–77; G. Chadwick, 1971, pp. 63–9; also Sir W. Armstrong, 1970 on management in the British civil service.

[39] Compare with Hart, 1974, op. cit., pp. 29–30.

[40] For example, see Michael, 1973, op. cit., on the requirements for 'long range social planning'. Faludi, 1973b, op. cit., Epilogue, argues for a view of planning as promoting human growth – a planning society.

[41] On this all-pervading paradigm see A. Wildavsky, 1969.

[42] See for example Ministry of Housing and Local Government, 1970 — the Development Plans manual; also Department of the Environment, 1971 — the rational model as the management device for guiding the making of Development Plans.

[43] See respectively the Royal Commission on Local Government in England, 1969: the Commission on the Third London Airport, 1970; South East Joint Planning Team, 1970; Greater London Council, undated; Hampshire County Council, 1972; other examples worthy of attention are the *Strategic Plan for the North West,* North West Joint Planning Team, 1974; also the reorganisation of water services and suggestions for corporate planning (Department of the Environment, 1974a); on suggestions for the institutionalising of the rational model in Structure Planning, see R. Barras and T. Broadbent, 1975.

[44] Indeed Popper argues that deductive-indeterminism incorporates induction/empiricism in its limited and limiting form: that is, the iterations between tentative theory and error elimination, thus:

$$P_1 \longrightarrow TT \longrightarrow EE \longrightarrow P_2$$

[45] See Lindblom, 1959, op. cit.; also Braybrooke and Lindblom, 1963, op. cit.

[46] See C. Lindblom, 1965, outlined in Allison, 1971, pp. 153—4.

[47] See Faludi, 1973b, op. cit., Chapter 8, for a more comprehensive treatment.

[48] On this image of society see Faludi, 1973b, op. cit., pp. 150—4.

[49] See Faludi, 1973a, op. cit., pp. 116—120, for a brief but illuminating critique.

[50] See Faludi, 1973a, op. cit., p. 116 and p. 119. Compare with the observation made by Dahrendorf, 1959, op. cit., p. 157 (see reference 64 in Chapter 3).

[51] Compare with 'planning as adaptation and power' in Wildavsky, 1973, op. cit. For an extended treatment of disjointed incrementalism see Faludi, 1973b, op. cit., Chapter 8.

[52] On commitment and specificity see Levin, 1972, op. cit.; on political commitment, priority and capability see Hart, 1975, op. cit., Chapter 6.

[53] For a more comprehensive treatment see Faludi, 1973b, op. cit., Chapter 9.

[54] J. Friedmann, 1966—7, quoted in Faludi, 1973b, p. 172.

[55] Compare with 'planning as intention' in Wildavsky, 1973, op. cit.; see also Zeckhauser and Schaeffer, 1968, op. cit.

[56] J. Friedmann, 1967b; see also Faludi, 1973b, op. cit., p. 174.

[57] See especially the series of contributions in Rodwin, ed. 1969, op. cit.

[58] See Faludi, 1973b, op. cit., Chapter 8; also Hart, 1974, op. cit., pp. 32–5.

[59] G. Allison, 1971, p. 177; see also Hill, 1972, op. cit., pp. 101–3; see Heclo and Wildavsky, 1974, op. cit., with respect to the political administration of planning in the British Civil Service, especially pp. 360–73.

[60] Friend, Power and Yewlett, 1974, op. cit., pp. 364–72.

[61] Heclo and Wildavsky, 1974, op. cit., p. 68 and p. 76.

[62] See Faludi, 1970, op. cit., pp. 3–8, for a similar form of analysis of UK and US public planning.

[63] See in particular Hart, 1975, op. cit., Chapter 6.

# 5 The Administrative Setting

The broad relationships and interdependencies between public planning and government have already been briefly outlined. The approach taken was to treat the concept of government from the perspective of bureaucratisation − the third and fourth attributes of the planning domain. What was somewhat neglected, or rather assumed implicitly in that analysis, was recognition of the importance of differences in styles of public administration and types of political system, and their interdependent nature. In other words, with the third tier of the comparative analysis just outlined − operational-administrative differences.

**Public planning and administrative style: a macro perspective**

Relationships between administrations and political systems may be considered initially from the perspective of differences in types of political system. At the risk of considerable overgeneralisation, we can identify three basic types categorised according to whether the level of public intervention is 'considerable', 'embryonic', or 'irrelevant'. These are, respectively, autocratic political systems, 'mixed' political systems and laissez-faire political systems. The manner in which differences in administrative style 'fit' these broad types of political system corresponds to three basic types of administration geared to planning:

1   Autocratic political systems ⟶ total administrative planning.
2   'Mixed' political systems ⟶ permissive planning.
3   Laissez-faire political systems ⟶ budgetary planning.[1]

By total administrative planning we mean the manner by which public planning is geared to the 'ordering of change' primarily by diktat: direction and compulsion. Examples include the 'Stalinist' era of central planning in the Soviet Union from the 1930s to the early 1950s. This style of the administration of planning is built on the assumption that the level of autonomy (political planibility) is very high if not totally internalised. Total intervention in society, and total centralised control of the economy, are its characteristic features of legitimacy. It is considered to be more efficient in the sense that, for example, factors of production −

land, labour, capital and enterprise — can be harnessed to some desirable long-term social plan. It is therefore an administrative style which is very much in sympathy with the blueprint and normative modes of public planning.

By permissive planning we mean the administration of public planning by a process of influence and inducement. Examples include most contemporary European styles of public planning, but particularly those in the United Kingdom and France. The permissive approach seeks its legitimation through the 'public interest'. It is usually built on the assumption that the pursuit of a policy or set of policies is somehow desirable and in society's interest. For example, to achieve and maintain full employment. It attempts to supplement the workings of a primarily market-based economy. A further example is provided by the guaranteeing of commodity prices to producers of certain goods and services of primary importance, in smoothing out 'peaks' and 'troughs' associated with the 'inevitability' of the trade cycle, and hence to a continued high level of employment in the economy. The administration of public planning — in the name of government — therefore attempts to influence the behaviour of firms and individuals by offering inducements and official advice ('carrots'), backed up with some degree of compulsion, usually in the form of certain legal powers ('sticks') as a last resort. It is therefore an administrative style associated more with some aspects of disjointed incrementalism, but more importantly with the functional planning mode.

By budgetary planning we mean the administration of public planning in its minimum form, and hence legitimately regarded form. In other words, with the absolute minimum level of intervention by a government — commensurate with the problem at hand — which is considered tolerable. Its principal characteristic is therefore intervention and involvement which is essentially of an uncontroversial nature. Budgetary planning is built largely as an appendage to the private sector. Indeed it takes that sector as a model, the assumption being that governments have to 'balance their books' — planning public expenditure in the light of public revenues, and in advance of actual spending. Examples include most federal systems of government, particularly the model provided by the United States. Budgetary planning in these contexts is almost solely and exclusively concerned with the coordination of limited forms of public expenditures — primarily the field of national defence. The parallels with the process, functional and disjointed incremental modes are therefore very close.

And so in terms of the administration of public planning we have three broad types of administrative style corresponding approximately to three broad types of political system. From the comments already made about

Fig. 5.1   Public planning and administrative style

| | Blueprint planning | Process planning | Rational comprehensive planning | Disjointed incrementalism | Normative planning | Functional planning |
|---|---|---|---|---|---|---|
| Total administrative planning | *** | n.a. | * | n.a. | *** | n.a. |
| Permissive planning | n.a. | ** | ** | ** | n.a. | ** |
| Budgetary planning | n.a. | *** | * | *** | n.a. | *** |

these administrative styles it is clear that each has certain sympathies with particular styles of planning. Figure 5.1 is an attempt to illustrate these sympathies, utilising Faludi's six dimensions.

**Public planning and administrative style: a micro perspective**

The argument outlined above has been concerned with a 'macro perspective' of the relationships between public planning and administrative style. Essentially between types of political system, types of administration and types of public planning. Having forged a link at this level, a more micro perspective can be embarked upon which concerns the administrative component. This is necessary at this juncture because public planning, as we have argued, is central to the very notion of government itself. What is of interest here is therefore the more micro relationship between the administration of government and the administration of planning within government. The point is by no means academic. Because of its very broad all-meaning nature, public planning is as equally concerned with two, what may be called, dual axioms of government as government itself. These are the axioms of communication and control. Government by definition needs to communicate at two levels: at the extra governmental level (that is, government to government, government to governed, and vice versa) and intra governmentally (that is, within government itself). Governments by definition also exercise some measure of influence and control over certain facets and operations of society. Such influence and control is more often than not multiplicative, differentiated, diffused and dispersed temporally, spatially and politically in terms of mechanisms, devices and actions which government exercises to create and maintain this influence and control. The administrative component of government is therefore central to the very notion of government itself, indeed it can be argued that it represents the very heart of its operation. Two questions of crucial importance emerge from this: firstly, in what ways do the twin spearheads of communication and control interact, and secondly, what factors contribute to this interaction?

Taking the former question first, we can argue with some conviction that the link between effective communication and control is what can generally be referred to by the generic term coordination: that is, principally administrative coordination between different governments and agencies as well as coordination of action within government itself.[2] The factors which contribute to the manner in which governments cope with this interaction can in turn be outlined by considering the factors which mould the administrative operation of government. Paraphrasing Self, to explore some of the factors which determine and influence the internal organisation of government and to settle how administrative functions are allocated, performed and coordinated.[3]

It is generally regarded that the functions of government (including planning) cannot be allocated according to any neatly ordered set of axioms or principles.[4,5] Nevertheless, it is possible and indeed desirable that certain principles be used as organising devices, as tools of analysis as to how a particular organisation works and how it might perhaps be improved. At a minimum it is possible to argue that functions can be allocated in one of two ways:

1  according to the groups to be served (user-oriented); or
2  according to the type of service to be provided (service-oriented).

But this does not get us very far; it is too broad a classification. Most writers on administrative theory accept and extend this approach to the allocation of functions by identifying four competing (as Self refers to them) principles of organisation. These are:

102

1   the purpose to be served;
2   the processes employed;
3   the person(s) or thing(s) dealt with; and
4   the area covered.[6]

Whether or not one or more of these competing principles is dominant or should dominate is a debate which will not be pursued here, suffice to say that, depending on the nature of the administrative task, all four are equal contenders. But from the perspective of public planning we can say that all four principles are of fundamental importance to a study of the nature and practice of planning in its administrative context. By adopting this pragmatic approach it can be argued that if the allocation of functions between government departments and agencies is not to be decided or organised according to any particular set of accepted and unquestionable principles, then is the inference such that functions are decided as part and parcel of the broader formal and informal political processes of government itself? That functions, rather than being the subject of rational analysis, are 'carved-up' according to the competing interests and broad political undercurrents which are characteristics of contemporary government?[7] According to Self:

> In general, this is a fair conclusion, so long as politics is broadly understood as including the views of officials, professional groups, clients, etc. (In this way) The governmental system and factors of political management *determines* the general contours of administrative structure.[8]

In terms of the competing interests and broad political undercurrents within the structure of government, Self continues:

> ... It is naturally at the highest levels that the allocation of functions becomes most political. As one moves down the structure of a department or agency, organization is much more determined by factors of functional convenience. However, administrative style and tradition play a considerable part as well, for example, over the reconciliation of (interdepartmental disputes).[9]

Generalising from these interpretations, it can be said that the allocation of functions between government, government departments and their agencies, and hence the organisation and administration of planning — based on the dual notions of competing interests and political undercurrents — involves the resolution of three interrelated issues:

1   the perceived importance of a particular function;

2 the manner in which the different functions can be organised; and
3 the nature and type of centralised control to be exercised and which is deemed desirable.[10]

A principal problem in attempting to resolve these three issues, and therefore of central concern to the notion of public planning (within the context of the four competing principles of organisation) is that by according preference to one more often than not results in a form of 'positive discrimination' against the others — a negation of the importance of the remainder. Therefore in the process of attempting to develop and accord priorities and preferences within the constraints and opportunities imposed by this discrimination, government is constantly engaged and concerned with 'trading-off' the benefits of according preferences to one particular course of action against other alternative sets. In other words, in promoting one set of preferences above others, the others become automatically demoted. The implications of this interpretation for the administration of public planning are obvious. Functions are not abstract entities. They are organised, influenced and implemented by — in the case of public planning — public agencies. As was pointed out earlier these agencies are also not abstract entities. Rather they are staffed by individuals (officials) and groups of individuals (cliques). In the administrative context, by according preferences to particular functions over others means in effect attributing differential levels of bureaucratic status to individuals and groups within a particular agency. But, more importantly, by according differentials in bureaucratic status between public agencies.

This process of bureaucratic 'positive discrimination' means that these agencies are in effect in situations of intra-agency and interagency competition: agency versus agency, department versus department, etc. A problem with this situation is that this competitive element may not be one which accords with the notion of homeostasis. Neither may it be endowed with steady-state or entropic qualities. In other words, in the process of allocating functions between agencies and within them situations might arise where too great a level of competition is engendered. Or its corollary — too little a level of competition. In terms of the administration of public planning a situation could occur where, to put it crudely, too much planning could be generated (the 'sledge-hammer to crack a nut' syndrome). Or indeed its corollary — too little planning (the 'drop in the ocean' syndrome).

In this kind of 'trade-off' situation there is a serious conflict of interests. Indeed it is a problem for which the notion of 'trade-off' analysis was originally developed — within the framework of welfare economics. This conflict concerns the dual notions of efficiency and equity. In an administrative context, between 'bureaucratic efficiency' and 'administrative coordination'. Between notions of efficiency – in performing and discharging organisational functions – and coordination – in the degree of participation and coordination to be exercised and tolerated – between competing departments and agencies performing similar administrative functions. This conflict has some profound implications for a study of the nature and practice of public planning.

## Bureaucratic efficiency and administrative coordination

At the risk of overgeneralising, 'bureaucratic efficiency' is an integral feature associated with the discharge of administrative functions. The classic administrative view is that a department or agency is 'efficient' if the time taken to reach a decision or process an application, over which it has authority, is minimised. The kind of administrative style which corresponds to this minimising-criterion of 'efficiency' is based on a 'vertical' organisational structure – the pure hierarchy. The task of making a decision, processing an application or request, is divided up into neat and often discrete administrative sequences. Formal messages pass up and down fairly rigid channels of communication based on the principle of the division of labour. This hierarchy corresponds closely to the Weberian model of the structure of rational authority – the pure-form bureaucracy (Figure 5.2).

At the risk of exaggerating the generalisation, the concept of 'administrative coordination' is very much the antithesis of 'bureaucratic efficiency'. The organising criterion is not the minimisation of processing time but rather the maximisation of information diffusion and coordination of action. It is concerned therefore with liaison between departments and agencies, with the comprehensive coordination of interdepartmental and interagency decisions, and with ensuring that functions are not duplicated unnecessarily or indeed left out. In other words, with the notion of what may be called administrative equity.

The kind of administrative style which corresponds to this maximising-criterion is based on a 'horizontal' organisational structure. The demands associated with this administrative style are severe: a loose-knit format, little or no hierarchy, a high degree of accessibility to all other individuals and agencies with an interest in the decision area. If a division of labour is a facet of this lattice structure, then it is based on the notion of what Schon refers to as 'pools of competence'. [11] This polyarchy corresponds

106

Fig. 5.2    The criterion of bureaucratic efficiency

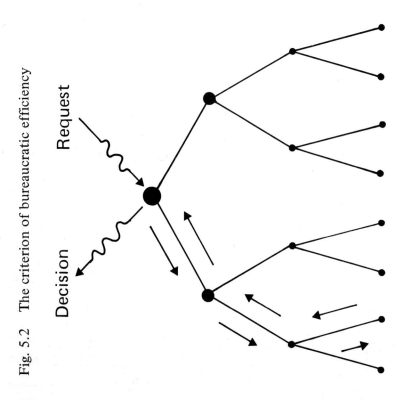

Fig. 5.3 The criterion of administrative coordination

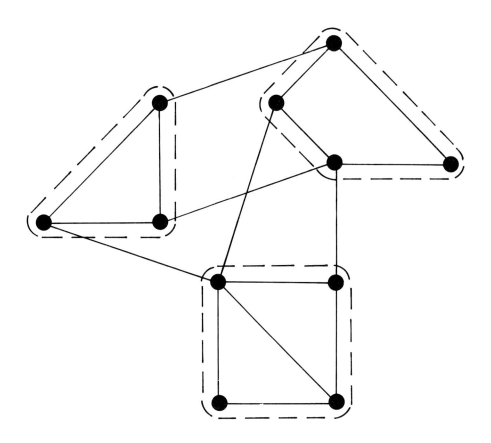

to the democratic model of the structure of authority — the pure-form participatory model (Figure 5.3).

Clearly the notions of 'administrative coordination' and 'bureaucratic efficiency' are extreme 'ideal type' examples. It is doubtful whether any administrative style would be wholly representative of either one or the other model. It is more likely that any organisation — hypothetical or in reality — would portray certain elements of each of these pure-form models. In which case it is possible to construct a further continuum, or dimension, staffed at one end by the efficiency criterion and at the other by the equity criterion—coordination. Between tight hierarchical structures with rigid channels for communication and open participatory lattices with loose and undefinable channels for communication.

And so we have our conflict, efficiency versus equity: between 'bureaucratic efficiency' and 'administrative coordination'. Any attempt to introduce or strengthen one will, in certain respects, mean a relative dilution or diminution of the other — other things being equal. On the one hand departments and agencies attempt to discharge their individual functions as efficiently as possible, whereas on the other there is a need for these functions to be coordinated. In this kind of situation efficiency and coordination cannot both be maximised. Rather it is a problem of the level of efficiency limiting the degree of coordination, and the level of coordination limiting the degree of efficiency.

This conflict, involving as it does a 'trade-off' between efficiency and equity, raises some important questions which are in the main outside the scope of this particular book. Perhaps the most critical of these concerns the need for fleshing-out the meanings of these two concepts. Taken together, 'bureaucratic efficiency' and 'administrative coordination' are not abstract concepts but integrally bound-up with the notions of power and authority, and in particular with the derivation, manipulation and distribution of political power and authority in government and society. [12] In terms of public planning, this means the balance between political power and political authority, and its manipulation and distribution, within and between those agencies concerned with planning. But more importantly with the way in which the pattern of power and authority relations can be interpreted as determinants of the very levels of efficiency and coordination.

According to the Weberian concept of power, Dahrendorf argues that it is the probability of an individual within a social relationship being in a position to implement a course of action in the face of opposition, regardless of the foundations on which that probability rests. The Weberian concept of authority, however, is something radically different: the probability that a substantive command will be assimilated and obeyed by a given group of individuals. [13] The difference is significant: '. . . Whereas power is essentially tied to the personality of individuals, authority is always associated with social positions or roles.'[14]

From the perspective of public planning *qua* bureaucracy, Dahrendorf argues that the concept of authority is an all-important variable, especially when considered within the context of a conflict theory of social change. He makes five assertions which, he argues, reinforce its importance:

(1) Authority relations are always relations of super- and subordination. (2) Where there are authority relations, the superordinate element is socially expected to control, by orders and commands, warnings and prohibitions, the behavior of the subordinate element. (3) Such expectations attach to relatively permanent social positions

rather than to the character of individuals; they are in this sense legitimate. (4) By virtue of this fact, they always involve specification of the persons subject to control and of the spheres within which control is permissible. Authority, as distinct from power, is never a relation of generalized control over others. (5) Authority being a legitimate relation, non-compliance with authoritative commands can be sanctioned; it is indeed one of the functions of the legal system (and of course of quasi-legal customs and norms) to support the effective exercise of legitimate authority.[15]

Dahrendorf therefore presents a persuasive case for a study of conflict theory which involves the notion of authority as a vital ingredient. But the interesting feature of this idea from the viewpoint of public planning concerns the other side of the equation. Authority assumes, indeed presupposes, subordination — in other words dependency. A concern of public planning is therefore not simply with authority or dependency, but with authority-dependency relationships also. To complicate matters further there are three broad levels to this concern: (a) 'internally' — that is, the pattern of authority, dependency, and authority-dependency relations within the administration of public planning; (b) 'internally-externally' — that is, the pattern of authority, dependency, and authority-dependency relations between the administration of public planning and its actual intervention within the planning domain; and (c) 'externally' — that is, the pattern of authority, dependency, and authority-dependency relations within society as a whole.

The parallels with the idea of bureaucratisation outlined earlier are therefore intense and immediate. According to the Weberian concepts of authority and bureaucracy, the latter tends to monopolise political authority. This monopoly is at its zenith in the context of demands for expertise and specialised knowledge. It is also clearly strengthened by the very characteristics of bureaucracy itself: status, tenure, professional ethos, etc. But, as Dahrendorf notes, this makes for something of a paradox. For if bureaucrats have this ubiquitous monopoly of authority, and they exercise it in the kind of manner outlined at the beginning of the last chapter, then why is it that they are not the ruling élite? The solution is simple: the bureaucracy may be all-powerful but it is unable to determine how that power should be used.[16] In other words, paraphrasing Dahrendorf, this monopoly of authority is a mere potential — it is unrealised and unrealisable because it is impossible to attain. Why this should be the case is a digression worthy of attention, because it has a considerable bearing on a study of the administrative component of public planning.

As Dahrendorf indicates, both Weber and Bendix have gone some way to explain this potential rather than realised facet of bureaucracies. The explanation in turn cuts right to the heart of the subject matter outlined in this chapter: the relationships and interdependency between government (the state) and public planning (its administration). To return to Dahrendorf:

> ... The indispensability of bureaucracies for the administration of the modern state (i.e., the very basis of their authority) has led to the development of a professional ethos, the dominant values of which are duty, service and loyalty – in other words, values of subordination, not of autonomous domination.[17]

And so back to the paradox: bureaucrats are not the ruling élite because they are dependent on the ruling élite. It is a monopoly of authority unaccompanied by a substantive interest in that authority. They are therefore concerned not with questions about 'what' authority, but rather with 'how' that authority is exercised.

Dahrendorf again:

> Their latent interest aims at the maintenance of what exists; but what it is that exists is not decided by bureaucracies, but *given to them*. ... their authority is borrowed or delegated authority (from) outside the orbit of bureaucracy. Although all commands are channeled, specified, perhaps adapted and even modified by bureaucracies, these commands originate from outside their hierarchy ... conceived and formulated elsewhere and by others. [18] (Italics added.)

The picture which emerges is therefore neither as neat nor as concise as the canvas with which we embarked on this analysis – notions of 'bureaucratic efficiency' and 'administrative coordination'. Rather it is a messy and confusing picture. But this would be missing a point of fundamental importance. Both 'bureaucratic efficiency' and 'administrative coordination' are concise, tight concepts. Indeed they describe with some power the formal structural configuration of the administration of public planning. But they do not exhaust the universe of discourse on the subject. Efficiency and coordination are vital explanatory variables, but they do not account for a sufficient explanation of administrative style. By introducing the notions of power, and in particular authority, into the equation – the informal structural configuration – we have the outline for a model at once more powerful and revealing. So can we not fuse these two dual notions – formal and informal – into one? Efficiency and coordination with power and authority relations? The answer is in the

110

affirmative, and corresponds roughly to what has been called the typology of cliques.

On the assumption that the informal power structure can be radically different from the power structure illustrated by formal hierarchies, Dalton has formulated a three-fold typology to describe the structure of cliques: random, horizontal and vertical. [19] Random cliques are those overlapping networks of informal power relationships which cut across barriers associated with differences in status or function. The most obvious examples are links developed by personal friendships and contact (Figure 5.4a). Although they may not be particularly significant from the viewpoint of the formally structured administration, they may — as Hill points out — contribute to the general state of solidarity or conflict, commitment or dissension, within and between administrations. [20] Horizontal cliques are also overlapping networks of informal power relationships which cross functional boundaries, but which are more horizontal than random. They represent social groups within and between administrations which are roughly of the same level of status. The most obvious examples are links developed between individuals with similar expertise, background or training — 'the professions', trade unions, etc. As such they may be either aggressive, neutral or defensive (Figure 5.4b). Vertical cliques are arguably the most significant of the three types from the perspective of overlapping informal power networks. They are essentially channels of communication from 'top' to 'bottom', and vice versa. Dalton argues that these vertical cliques can assume one of two formats: symbiotic or parasitic cliques. Parasitic vertical cliques are those where networks of relationships are based on some element of exploitation. An immediate example concerns an authority-dependency kind of relationship based on friendship between the authority and a subordinate. This relationship, as Hill notes, is then exploited in two ways — on the part of authority as an informal source of information (and hence control of subordinates), and on the part of subordinates as a means of gaining personal advantage. [21] Symbiotic vertical cliques, according to Dalton, are perhaps the most fundamental and important of all clique-type networks. They involve links and relationships based on 'exchange': exchange of information, consultation, commitment, loyalty, support, etc. They are networks of informal power relationships which parallel but not necessarily be congruent with the very structure of formal hierarchies. In the context of the administration of organisations they can assume proportions of crucial significance, especially when decisions about commitments have to be taken (Figure 5.4c). For as Hill lucidly explains:

Fig. 5.4    Dalton's typology of cliques

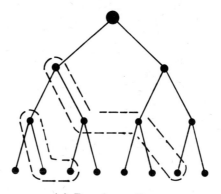

(a) Random cliques

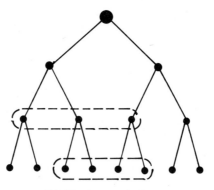

(b) Horizontal cliques

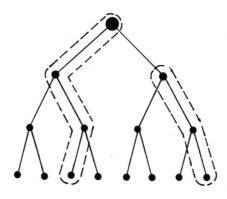

(c) Vertical cliques

... When decisions have to be made, the key consultations and exchanges of information often occur rather more through the informal channels provided by symbiotic cliques than through the formal channels.[22]

The implications of clique formation for the administration of public planning are self-evident. Firstly, in the same way as a plan does not represent the process by which it was forged, the formal power structure (represented more often than not by neatly defined organisation charts) may not correspond to the actual power structure (represented by informal cliques). Dalton suggests six reasons why there may not be a one-to-one correspondence, and why informal power structures may emerge: (a) problems associated with different personalities, (b) the process by which cliques are formed, (c) ambiguities associated with the definition of rôles, (d) ambiguities associated with the responsibilities of assistants, and in particular young protégés, (e) special relationships of certain individuals with the 'centre', and (f) the influence of status associated with external groups (for example links with a professional institute, etc.).

Secondly, the relationship between the formal and informal power structures, and in particular with the notions of 'bureaucratic efficiency' and 'administrative coordination'. One interesting conclusion which emerges from the literature concerning informal power structures is the general impression that these groups will emerge irrespective of formal power structures – that is, predominantly hierarchical or lateral. Translating the formal power structure into the formal administrative structure of organisations implies that the exercise is a largely irrelevant one because it bears little resemblance to the 'real' administrative structure. This 'real' structure of informal power is to be found in the sum of relationships between random, horizontal (aggressive, neutral, defensive) and vertical (parasitic, symbiotic) cliques.

This leads to a third, and perhaps the most relevant, implication from the perspective of public planning. This concerns in particular the way in which informal lattice structures influence the process by which decisions and public policies are forged and implemented. The illustration is a simple one, based on a particularly interesting piece of research undertaken by two American political scientists – Pressman and Wildavsky. They were concerned with this intertwining of political with administrative problems within the context of informal power networks, public policy and the magnitude of 'decision points' needed for 'successful' implementation. [23] They compared two broad components of the administration of public policy: (a) the level of internal agreement associated with a particular policy, and (b) the number of 'clearances' (essentially the number of 'thumbs' in any particular policy 'pie') which it has to pass before it can be implemented. They considered four arbitrarily-determined levels of agreement and then proceeded to calculate the probabilities of successful implementation after 70 'clearances' (Figure 5.5):

Fig. 5.5   The implementation problem

| Probability of agreement on each clearance point (%) | Probability of success after 70 clearances | No. of agreements that reduce probability below 50 per cent |
|---|---|---|
| 80 | 0·000000125 | 4 |
| 90 | 0·000644 | 7 |
| 95 | 0·00395 | 14 |
| 99 | 0·489 | 68 |

Source: Pressman and Wildavsky, 1973

This illustration serves to show that even with an 80 per cent level of internal agreement, the probability of a policy being implemented in its original form is negligible if more than four 'clearances' are demanded! Even at the 99 per cent level, the probability of success is less than an evens chance if more than sixty-eight 'clearances' are involved. The implications are all too clear, especially since Pressman and Wildavsky argue that a seventy 'clearance' decision is fairly trivial. (They suggest between four and five hundred as representative of a more average policy decision involving internal clearances.) Perhaps we may concur with Hill then when he states that:

> ... it is important to draw attention to a specific weakness of much work in this field. This is a failure to deal properly with the power dimension in organizations. Inevitably linked with this is a lack of emphasis upon *conflict,* a tendency to exaggerate consensus, particularly with regard to (organizational) goals.[24]

**Public planning and administrative style: the United Kingdom**

Having outlined the importance of the administrative component of public planning we can begin to make some observations about administrative style and its organisation within the context of an example which can be taken to reflect 'current best practice' — that of the United Kingdom.

To say that government in the United Kingdom is highly centralised is perhaps another simple truism. But this leaves many important questions unanswered: for example, in what way is it centralised? How is it structured? How does the formal structure differ from informal networks of power? What importance is attached to the formal as against the informal attitude to public planning? etc. These kind of questions need some examination, especially since one of the principal objectives of this book is to assess the nature and importance of regional planning *qua* public planning in the United Kingdom. An obvious point of entry into this administrative maze is to consider the first of these basic questions: In what way is British government centralised?

The first point which can be made is that the British style of government is highly centralised, with respect to both its political and administrative organisation. British political administration, in spite of persistent calls for devolution, remains largely impervious to suggestions that, at the level of formulating and implementing national policies and programmes, power should be anywhere but at the centre — in the hands of a non-federalised style of government. Since we have argued elsewhere that the political and administrative components of government are inextricably interwoven, it therefore follows that the administrative organisation parallels the political administration. In other words, the style and nature of the administration reflects and is reflected in the structure of political-government relations. British administrative organisation is therefore highly centralised with respect to the formulation and implementation of national policies and programmes.

The second point which can be made concerns this idea of national policies and the manner in which they are implemented. This 'top-down' approach is but one characteristic — if perhaps the one of most significance. It is mirrored and modified by a configuration of local centres of political administration, working from the 'bottom-up' — local government. A relationship of interest here concerns the balance between what can be called policy content and implementation capability, within the context of the actual and potential impact which central and local political administrations have and attempt to achieve (Figure 5.6).

British central government ('top-down' planning) can be seen as being concerned with the formulation, setting and implementation of policies and programmes which have a national impact. But within this fundamental rôle is concealed the balance between the components of policy

Fig. 5.6  Policy content and implementation capability in the UK

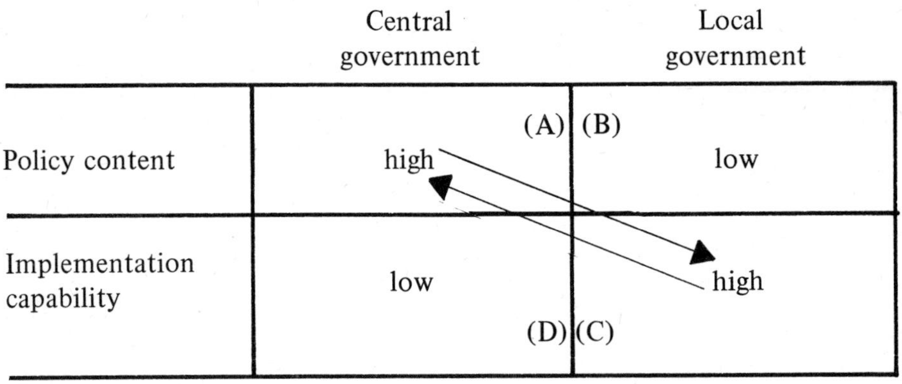

| | Central government | Local government |
|---|---|---|
| Policy content | (A) high | (B) low |
| Implementation capability | (D) low | (C) high |

formulation and setting (intent) and physical implementation (impact). These tasks are clearly of gargantuan proportions. And so successive governments in the UK have attempted to exercise authority over both intent and impact. But because of the enormity of the task they have been actively concerned with the development and fostering of agencies and organisations whose primary responsibilities are to physically implement the policy proposals of central government. In other words, these agencies have been evolved to discharge functions and physically implement policies handed to them by central government in the name of central government. So in terms of policy content and implementation capability, central governments principal task is with the formulation and setting of policies. Policy content is therefore very high (A). Central government strives for a significant implementation capability, but can only achieve it by indirect means, by endowing other organisations with power and authority. Direct implementation capability is therefore very low (D).

British local government ('bottom-up' planning) can also be seen as concerned with the formulation, setting and implementation of policies and programmes, but with those which have a more local and localised impact. But the balance between these three components, and between impact and intent, is far from equal. The reasons are straightforward. The manner in which a local government can set and formulate policy is potentially as large as that of central government itself. But in reality the picture is very different. Local government by definition is concerned with a local area, albeit with problems probably specific or peculiar to that area. But its ability to intervene is subject to any number of severe constraints, which can be conveniently categorised under the labels of 'authority to act' and 'financial' constraints. In other words, local government more often than not has the potential but very rarely the sufficient means to act.

In terms of the simple typology illustrated in Figure 5.6, it is therefore clear that local government is characterised by a relatively low level of 'policy content' *vis-à-vis* the national context (B), but with a high potential 'implementation capability' (C). In other words, the 'bottom-up' approach is very much a mirror image of the 'top-down'. On the one hand central government scores highly on 'policy content' and low on 'implementation capability', whereas local government scores highly on the latter and low on the former. The common denominator in trying to reconcile central government policy with central government implementation is therefore local government ('bottom-up' planning) and the endowment of public agencies with central government functions ('top-down' planning). Local government therefore assumes a rôle of discharging many of central governments functions which are delegated to it, for example, by statute. The 'periphery', in the form of local government, becomes an agent of the 'centre'. In the UK, since most local government activity is concerned with implementing central government policies, it is more fitting to refer to them by their proper name – local authorities. Arms of the 'centre' with a democratic face. The high potential of local government with respect to both 'policy content' and 'implementation capability' is therefore partially realised – but at no small cost. The 'authority to act' and 'financial' constraints are still very much apparent, but in a different guise. In some respects it corresponds to a supra-vertical clique – a primarily exploitative relationship for both parties. Central government effectively guides local government by controlling, in many respects, the only two variables that matter – the purse strings and the statutory authority. Central government develops relationships with local authorities, and then uses those relationships as an informal source of information. (What is sometimes euphemistically called 'an ear at the grass-roots level.') The information thus gained can then be utilised as a further control device on the freedom of local authorities to pursue their own ends. But this kind of parasitic network also works the other way around. Local authorities can make use of those very relationships as a means of obtaining local advantage from, or preferential treatment by, the 'centre'. (What has euphemistically been referred to as 'an ear in Whitehall'.)

A third point which can be made about British political administration follows on from this last point – that of centre/periphery relationships. The agencies which central government has evolved to develop this 'implementation capability' have not all been directed at local authorities (a primarily historical development). Rather a number of quasi-government institutions have been set-up, usually with respect to specific functions. Examples include the nationalised industries – in the fields of steel production, rail transport, certain other modes of transport (notably air, coach, bus, road freight and ports) and, latterly, certain firms in the airspace industry (notably Rolls-Royce (1971) Ltd.). Besides these publicly owned or controlled industries there are also the public utilities – power and energy, communications, health, water, etc. [25] A contemporary administrative innovation in this context has been the setting up of an embryo development agency for the Highlands and Islands of Scotland – the Highlands and Islands Development Board. All of these agencies have been organised primarily as platforms from which central government policies can be physically implemented at a subnational scale. As such they have considerable powers at their disposal, powers vested in them by statute as agents of the centre.

In terms of the formal structure of British political administration at the centre, it is clear that, as Heclo and Wildavsky point out, there are three principal components:

> ... 1) a *Cabinet* of Ministers, subdivided into ministerial committees which are mirrored by comparable committees of civil servants; 2) *three central groups* – the Treasury ...; Civil Service Department ...; and Cabinet Office ...; and 3) ... *ten operating departments,* some of which (such as the Department of Health and Social Security) spend ten or more times the amount spent by smaller ministries.[26] (Italics added.)

What is of interest here, in the context of public planning and administrative style, is the relationship between these three components, the style in which the major departments conduct their affairs, and the nature of the public planning function within and between these departments.

One way in which the relationships between Cabinet, (essentially) the Treasury, and the major operating departments can be illustrated is to consider the authority-dependency relations and how they are conducted. In particular in the context of one of the key variables associated with the rôle of implementation – the budgeting function. How are public funds allocated to the twenty or so departments of central government, particularly the ten operating departments? One potentially useful approach which can be adopted is to make use of the framework spelt out in the middle of the last chapter: the framework combining the three tiers of analysis (ideological-institutional, institutional-operational, operational-administrative differences) with Faludi's three dimensions of public planning (blueprint versus process, rational comprehensive versus disjointed incrementalism, normative versus functional). But before we embark on this particular course of action it may be useful to outline a brief description of the process by which the allocation procedure takes place. A particularly useful description has been provided by Heclo and Wildavsky, in diagrammatic form (Figure 5.7).[27]

On the assumption that Heclo and Wildavsky have adequately caught the key relationships in the internal budgetary process, how does their outline compare with the framework of analysis which we have developed? In terms of 'ideological-institutional' differences, does the allocation procedure conform with either the blueprint or the process modes? The answer is of course that it corresponds perfectly to neither. Rather it is a mixture, or rather combination, of both types. But at the risk of over-generalising it is possible to argue that because of the relatively short time horizons involved it approximates closer to the process end. The Treasury has a fairly tightly defined image of the economic environment and rôle (in terms of financial commitments) which it sees for each operating department. Likewise with each operating department. In this sense both the Treasury and the departments views are more to the blueprint end. But the pressures which can be exerted are considerable and sufficient to make the allocation process resemble a negotiable exercise. The net result is clearly a movement away from the blueprint approach on the part of both the Treasury and the departments concerned toward the process end:

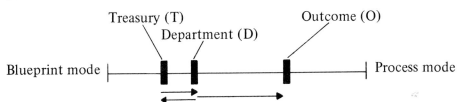

In terms of 'institutional-operational' differences the same kind of picture emerges. Both the Treasury and the departments concerned pre-sumably have some long term 'ideal' notion as to their respective allocations ('means') *vis-à-vis* the 'ends' which each aspires to achieve. In this respect they conform very roughly with the rationality thesis. But what about when each department has to approach the Treasury and negotiate for their allocation? Does the picture still resemble the rational compre-hensive model? The answer must clearly be in the negative. Heclo and Wildavsky make references to concepts like 'negotiate', 'bargain', 'bilateral', 'appeals', and 'bids'. Are these terms typically associated with the rational allocation of scarce resources between competing administrative uses? The answer again has to be in the negative. Coupled with the short-time horizons

119

Fig. 5.7　The internal allocation of public funds in the UK

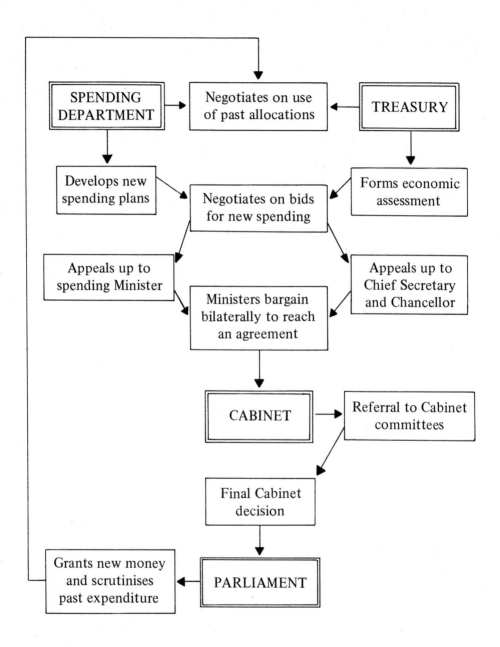

Source: Heclo and Wildavsky, 1974

involved (typically annual allocations attached to five-year rolling programmes) it is clear that the process is far from the rational mode, and
more in sympathy with disjointed incrementalism: short-time horizons,
adjustments at the margin, imperfect knowledge, uncertainty, etc., etc. Or
as Heclo and Wildavsky describe it:

> ... We asked how (the Minister) knew what his proper share was.
> 'There were', he said, 'two and only two objective criteria. One,
> what had happened before. What was our share of total government
> expenditure last year? Are we doing as well this year? Two, what is
> the rate of growth of the department compared with the rate shown
> by others?' (As they remark elsewhere) ... incrementalism to the
> $n^{th}$ power.[28]

In terms of rational-comprehensive versus disjointed incrementalism, the
picture which emerges can be illustrated thus:

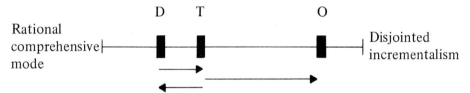

With respect to 'operational-administrative' differences, how does the
process of budgeting compare with the normative and functional modes?
There are two levels which need to be disentangled. First, how are the
spending plans of departments initially prepared, and second, how are
they finalised with respect to Treasury involvement? The first is fairly
clear. Departmental spending plans are formulated within the framework
of central government policies ('ends') – corresponding to the functional
mode. These 'ends' are therefore treated as more or less given, and the
problem is to consider appropriate alternative 'means'. Combined with the
evidence available about the nature and value-neutral position of the
British Civil Service this conclusion is more than reinforced.[29] As the
management consultancy group of the Fulton Commission reported, there
are four broad areas which characterise the tasks of civil servants:
(a) formulation of policy under political direction; (b) creating the
'machinery' for implementation of policy; (c) operation of the administrative machine; and (d) accountability to Parliament and the public.[30]
The second question is not so straightforward since it assumes that
spending plans have been prepared. These are subject to internal nego-
tiation with the Treasury. In effect a conflict situation arises – department against department (in this case the Treasury). The situation is

therefore one where both normative and functional modes are applicable. Normative, because individual Ministers and the Cabinet are involved; functional because the organisational framework within which these negotiations take place are primarily of a functional nature. So not only the 'means' are brought into this conflict situation but the 'ends' also — with the result that it is quite probable that in the ensueing spectacle the 'ends' (policies) themselves might be subject to modification. As Heclo and Wildavsky admirably point out:

> To ask 'how shall public money be spent' and 'what should government do' are kindred, though not identical questions. Decisions about public expenditure shade imperceptibly into decisions about public policy and subtlely still into judgements on the general welfare of society.[31]

In terms of the distinction between normative and functional modes the kind of picture which emerges can be illustrated as follows:

In a similar manner to the treatment of the analysis of the deductive responsive mode in the previous chapter (Figure 4.8), these three comparisons may be brought together to form a synthesis of the relationships between Cabinet, the Treasury and operating departments (Figure 5.8).[32]

It is perhaps important to stress that this series of illustrations can only act as a hypothetical guide through the formal-informal administrative maze. But they are illustrative of the heterogeneity which surrounds and permeates a study of the administration of public planning, related to the British experience. All too often these relationships are either held constant or considered homogeneous with respect to administrative style in the planning literature.[33]

The second and third points of interest — administrative style of departments in British political administration, and the nature of their respective planning functions — may be considered in tandem. From the perspective of public planning functions, evidence indicates that the administration is biased strongly toward the idea of 'bureaucratic efficiency' rather than 'administrative coordination'. The formal structuring of departments shows that priority is accorded to the discharge of functions and in the provision of services. The very titles and organisational arrangements of departments reinforces this evidence. For example, departments of 'trade',

Fig. 5.8    The internal allocation function – a comparison by modes

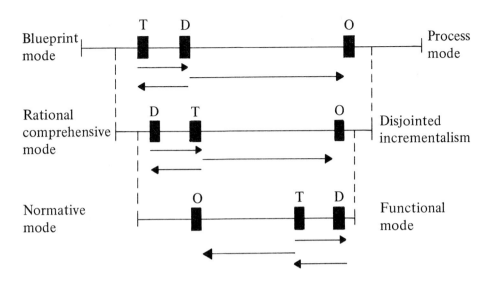

'industry', 'employment', 'health', 'social security', 'defence', etc. The only departments which do not fit this mould are the respective Offices for Scotland and Wales. These two 'umbrella' organisations are the nearest thing in British political administration to where the idea of coordination is relatively formalised if not pronounced. But, like the setting-up of the Highlands and Islands Development Board, Scotland and Wales – as well as Northern Ireland – have invariably been the seed-bed for British administrative innovation.[34]

Of the twenty or so major departments of government it is possible to identify ten major spending departments (at 1975): Education and Science, Employment, Health and Social Security, Environment, Industry, Defence, Posts and Telecommunications, Trade, Scottish and Welsh Offices. All have specific and formalised planning functions. As an example the largest of these – not in terms of spending power – is the Department of the Environment, encompassing as it does three separate Ministries: respectively, the Ministry for Planning and Local Government, Ministry of Transport, and Ministry for Housing and Construction. Included under each are, respectively, twenty-two and thirty-eight separate sub-units. Responsibilities range from urban policy, ancient monuments, new towns, regional strategies, urban and passenger transport, local government, London, etc. (all under Planning and Local Government). Likewise, ports, railways, freight, environment, road safety, water engineering, highways, etc. (all under Transport). Likewise, housing research, quantity surveying, housing development, estate management, the Transport and Road Research Laboratory, etc. (all under Housing and Construction).[35]

With respect to the explicit planning functions of these major departments, it is possible to identify four with such functions which are not major spending departments (Treasury, Cabinet Office, Home Office, and Energy), and ten which are both. At the same time it is possible to broadly identify ten significantly different forms of public planning. These are:

1   public expenditure planning;
2   defence planning;
3   regional development planning;
4   transport planning;
5   communications planning;
6   land use planning;
7   social planning;
8   education planning;
9   manpower planning; and
10  energy planning.

The problem is that there is not a neat one-to-one correspondence between departments with planning functions and types of public planning. Rather the situation is rent with confusion — illustrating the functional efficiency criterion of the allocation of functions and not the broader tasks which demand high levels of coordination. This descriptive confusion can be reduced by resorting to a simple tabulation of types of department against types of public planning (Figure 5.9).[36]

This tabulation shows that there are at least forty-nine different ways in which formal departmental involvement in planning interacts with different types of public planning in the UK. A truly formidable set of arrays, illustrating perhaps the incredibly complex task for formal 'administrative coordination'. The asterisks merely indicate some positive association, political commitment, statutory responsibility and administrative involvement in formal or informal planning of one or more of ten basic forms. They do not indicate strengths or the magnitude of relationships. But quite clearly each of these ten basic forms are broadly functional in character rather than embedded in a kind of problem-oriented framework — for example, capital investment planning, income planning, etc. Each is also a service-oriented rather than process-, person(s)/thing(s)-, or area-oriented function. For example, presumably the planning of regional development, transport, and land use are pretty much concerned with

Fig. 5.9  Department involvement and planning functions, United Kingdom

| Forms of public planning | Treasury | Cabinet Office‡ | Energy | Home Office | Dept. of Industry† | Dept. of Environment | Dept. of Employment | Ministry of Posts and Telecommunications | Dept. of Health and Social Security | Ministry of Defence | Dept. of Education and Science | Dept. of Trade† | Welsh Office | Scottish Office | Planning involvement |
|---|---|---|---|---|---|---|---|---|---|---|---|---|---|---|---|
| Public expenditure | * | * | | | | | | | | | | | | | 2 |
| Defence | * | ? | | * | * | * | | * | | * | | | | | 6 |
| Regional development | * | ? | | | * | * | * | | | | | * | * | * | 7 |
| Transport | * | ? | | | * | * | | | | | | * | * | * | 6 |
| Communications | * | ? | | | | | | * | | * | | * | | | 4 |
| Land use | * | ? | | | | * | | | | | | | * | * | 4 |
| Social | * | ? | | * | | | | | * | | | | * | * | 5 |
| Education | * | ? | | | | | | | | | * | | * | * | 4 |
| Manpower | * | ? | | | | | * | | | | * | | * | * | 5 |
| Energy | * | ? | * | | | | | | | * | | * | * | * | 6 |
| Departmental involvement | 10 | 1? | 1 | 2 | 3 | 4 | 2 | 2 | 1 | 3 | 2 | 4 | 7 | 7 | 49 |

MAJOR SPENDING DEPT'S (columns: Home Office through Scottish Office)

Government departments with explicit planning functions

† The Departments of Trade and Industry are linked in certain respects, e.g. they share accounting, legal and establishment functions
‡ Principally the Central Policy Review Staff

125

similar kinds of problem – the physical spatial organisation of society. Clearly there are different emphases within each, and yet one can identify three functionally separate and administratively distinct departments which are substantially involved – not including the involvement of either the Scottish or Welsh Offices. There are two further general points which can be made concerning this tabulation. The first concerns departmental involvement in planning. Notwithstanding the Scottish and Welsh Offices the award for most involvement is shared by the Department of the Environment (defence, regional development, transport and land use planning) and the Department of Trade (regional development, transport, communications, and energy planning). With respect to involvement in planning by different departments, regional development planning takes the award for the most involvement – seven separate departments (Treasury, Industry, Environment, Employment, Trade, Scottish and Welsh Offices).

To conclude, the picture which emerges from this very cursory analysis – as applied to the UK experience – is one which emphasises both the complexities and the simplicities of administration, and the concomitant strengths and weaknesses associated with the administration of public planning itself. In particular to draw attention to the idea that rationality, formal organisational structures and bureaucratic efficiency – which stress the gains to be reaped from consensus, authority, and the 'natural' division of labour – are value-laden terms which have served mainly to confuse the study of political administration. As Michael Hill admirably sums-up:

> ... there seems to be a continuing tendency ... to assume that the adoption of certain kinds of formal procedures *necessarily produces* efficiency ... three mistakes are made: first, it is assumed that organizational ends are normally clearly specified and understood so that the adoption of efficient means *guarantees* the efficient attainment of ends; second, efficiency itself is treated as an unambiguous concept which ... it is not; and third, the simplifications which are involved in giving formal procedures an internal logic are overlooked.[37] (Italics added.)

### Notes

[1] This terminology has been suggested by Faludi, 1969, op. cit.

[2] This schema, 'communication : co-ordination : control', has been suggested by Hart, 1975, op. cit. See also Self, 1974, op. cit.

[3] P. Self, 1972b, Chapters 1 and 2, especially p. 55.

4 The following treatment leans heavily on Self, 1972b, op. cit., pp. 55−61.

5 For example, see Simon, 1957, op. cit., p. 44; for a dissenting view see L. Urwick, 1947, for eight such principles.

6 Self, 1972b, op. cit., p. 55.

7 On the implications of political factorisation see Hart, 1974, op. cit., pp. 32−5. For a more clinical treatment see Stewart, 1971, Introduction.

8 Self, 1972b, op. cit., p. 60.

9 Self, 1972b, op. cit., p. 63.

10 Self, 1972b, op. cit., p. 61; compare with Hart, 1974, op. cit., pp. 38−40.

11 Schon, 1971, op. cit., pp. 173−4.

12 On power and authority see in particular Dahrendorf, 1959, op. cit., pp. 165−7.

13 Dahrendorf, 1959, op. cit., pp. 166−7.

14 Dahrendorf, 1959, op. cit., p. 166.

15 Dahrendorf, 1959, op. cit., pp. 166−7.

16 On bureaucratic impotence see R. Bendix, 1952, p. 129.

17 Dahrendorf, 1959, op. cit., p. 299.

18 Dahrendorf, 1959, op. cit., p. 300.

19 M. Dalton, 1959, especially Chapter 3.

20 Hill, 1972, op. cit., p. 48.

21 Hill, 1972, op. cit., p. 51.

22 Hill, 1972, op. cit., p. 51.

23 J. Pressman and A. Wildavsky, 1973, pp. 102−10.

24 Hill, 1972, op. cit., p. 32; see also Silverman, 1970, op. cit., Chapter 6.

25 For example, on planning in a public utility in the UK see C. Mills, 1974; on planning in education in the UK see Sir W. Pile, 1974; on social planning in the UK see J. Bennington and P. Skelton, 1972. On a comparison between US and UK attempts at social planning see P. Marris and M. Rein, 1967.

26 Heclo and Wildavsky, 1974, op. cit., p. 4; compare with Armstrong, 1970, op. cit., on the 'official' view.

27 Heclo and Wildavsky, 1974, op. cit., p. 5.

28 Heclo and Wildavsky, 1974, op. cit., p. 27 and p. 238.

29 On the supposed value-neutrality of British civil servants, see J. Garrett, 1972, especially Chapters 1 and 2. Garrett was a member of the management consultancy group to the Fulton Committee.

30 See Garrett, 1972, op. cit., Chapter 2; and especially Committee on the Civil Service, 1968, Volume II, para 303.

31 Heclo and Wildavsky, 1974, op. cit., p. 264.

[32] Compare with the views on the need for rational decision-making of the ex-head of the British Civil Service, Armstrong, 1970, op. cit., based on the eight principles of management suggested by Urwick, 1947, op. cit.

[33] For example, see McLoughlin, 1969, op. cit.; Chadwick, 1971, op. cit.; Hall, 1974, op. cit.; F. Chapin, Jr., 1965. It is perhaps of interest to note that Faludi, 1973b, op. cit., originally proposed these dimensions, together with the attributes of the planning environment, as the basis for a comparative piece of empirical research.

[34] For example, the proposals for setting-up Welsh and Scottish development agencies. The exception has to be the setting-up in 1971 of the Central Policy Review Staff (CPRS), the ex-Rothschild 'think tank', at the elbow of the Prime Minister, and now chaired by Sir Kenneth Berrill. Perhaps a notable exception too. See Heclo and Wildavsky, 1974, op. cit., for an 'outside' assessment.

[35] A useful entry point into the administrative maze of the political administration of central government in the UK is provided by the Civil Service Commission (1972) concerning government departments and their work; also Civil Service Department (1974) concerning up-to-the-minute administrative changes in ministerial appointments and responsibilities; also senior staff appointments. Heclo and Wildavsky, 1974, op. cit., pp. 1–10, paint a particularly useful introduction to this maze, which has to date largely escaped the attention of British political scientists.

[36] Compiled from the reports of the Civil Service Department, 1974, op. cit., and the Civil Service Commission, 1972, op. cit.

[37] Hill, 1972, op. cit., pp. 15–16.

# 6 Regional Planning as Public Planning

The concern of the book thus far has been with a critical examination of the nature of public planning. But its purview is also with something labelled regional planning. Is the inference to be drawn from this that regional planning is simply one facet of the generic umbrella of public planning? The question is by no means trivial, as the weight accorded to the first five chapters should indicate. But the answer is nevertheless broadly in the affirmative: it is possible to see regional planning as a facet of public planning. However, for a study of the nature and practice of planning this simple affirmation is of little direct importance. The more vital questions concern its general relevance. For example, in what way is it a facet of public planning? What are its distinguishing characteristics as a specific field of study? It is with these kinds of relational question which will be the subject of this and the following chapter.

## The idea of regional planning

Two points of immediate and general relevance can be made. The first is the simple observation that there is indeed such a thing as regional planning. A significant number of contemporary governments, for example, make provisions for and endorse departments and agencies with arrays of commitments, directives and authority labelled 'regional planning'. The second is a little weightier in terms of substantive content but − as we shall see − is equally pragmatic. It is simply that regional planning is explicitly concerned with space: with the spatial relationships of activities, their arrangements in space, and hence their spatial and aspatial characteristics.

Clearly this does not take us very far. Governments appear to have machinery for and some commitment to regional planning, and regional planning is in turn concerned with space. *But governments are also the principal protagonists of public planning.* In other words we have regional planning and public planning. Are they the same kind of thing? Are the ideas, concepts and theories which are applicable to public planning − as outlined in the previous chapters − of direct relevance to regional planning?

The assumption implicit in what follows is that, broadly speaking, the two are synonymous, at least with respect to their underlying methodologies. The significant differences occur in the manner in which regional planning emphasises and makes explicit certain aspects which are perhaps of a more general and implicit nature in public planning *per se*. But an assertion such as this, dressed up as an assumption, is no substitute or synonym for what is obviously a question of fundamental importance: what makes regional planning so distinct from public planning?

A useful point of entry is with the very concept of regional planning itself. In the outline concerning the administrative context of public planning the point was made that there were effectively two substantive components to the formulation and implementation of policies and action programmes — policy content and implementation capability. In the UK setting these were translated into political administrations operating at a national and local level. Implicit in this outline was therefore some notion of space. But more importantly a configuration of spatial relationships between different political administrations (national/local/local) and within the context of the central political administration of public planning as a whole. Implicit in this configuration is a difference in emphasis, a difference in what might be called the *scale* of the respective 'policy content' and 'implementation capability' tasks of central and local administrations. So, differences in 'policy content', 'implementation capability', 'space' and 'scale'. Where does regional planning fit into this schema? One answer is that it fits somewhere in between national and local levels. In terms of the political administration of public planning, between central and local governments.

This then may go some way to account for the administrative component. But what of the methodological component? The key words here are 'space' and 'scale', within the context provided by the differing emphases between national and local levels of, respectively, 'policy content' and 'implementation capability'. In terms of the 'top-down' approach to public planning, regional planning may be seen as both a political and an administrative vehicle which guides the translation of national policies into local action programmes. In terms of the 'bottom-up' approach regional planning may be seen as a platform and framework on which local governments may hang their respective programmes. In terms of informal power networks — especially symbiotic vertical cliques — regional planning may also be seen as the vehicle by which national policies and information of relevance to their formulation are collated, formalised, articulated and — most importantly — coordinated and mobilised from the national to the local levels. From the 'bottom-up' regional planning may also provide the informal communications channels to the 'centre' necessary to the instigation and/or continuation of central commitment to problems and issues associated with the 'periphery'. In these contexts regional planning acts as a filter and a sounding-board for both the 'centre' and the 'periphery'.

Regional planning – politically, administratively and methodologically – cannot be seen as either an exclusively technical exercise or a free-standing and autonomous administrative machine. It is not and cannot be considered an 'end' in and of itself. Rather it is a 'means' – and arguably a politically significant means – concerned with the influence and manipulation of power and political influence within and between central and local political administrations.

### The 'good currency' idea of regional planning

The relationship between 'top-down' and 'bottom-up' approaches to the implementation aspects of public policy vis-à-vis regional planning has been outlined by Peter Self (in the context of the political and administrative components) and subsequently developed by Peter Hall (in the context of the technical problems of regional planning).[1] But Hall's approach – emphasising as it does the methodological/technical dimension – has resulted in a diminution, if not dilution, of many of the key aspects of the political/methodological dimension which concerned Self. What follows here is an attempt to reaffirm Self's original position, whilst at the same time employing the notions suggested by Hall.

The Self/Hall approach to the problem of the regional dimension of public planning is to take a surgeons knife to the interrelationships between the 'policy content' and 'implementation capability' components of the respective national and local tiers. Self refers respectively to the 'national contribution' and the 'regional contribution'. The former stresses involvement by the 'centre', the latter by the 'periphery'. 'Top-down' meets 'bottom-up' at some intermediate regional level of government. Hall crystallises these differences in emphasis, labelling the 'top-down' approach national/regional planning and the 'bottom-up', regional/local planning.

Both authors emphasise the importance played by the scale of public intervention and the nature of the tasks involved. For planning at the national/regional level the common denominator is the task of implementing national policy, combined with the scale of the problem which the 'centre' faces in trying to mobilise the necessary resources (qualitative and quantitative; political and physical). By definition this mobilisation task is at some subnational or regional level. For planning at the regional/local level the common denominator is provided by the task of giving national policy a specifically localised dimension, combined with the scale of the problem which the 'periphery' faces. In this context the 'periphery' is faced with primarily functional problems associated with the coordination and mobilisation of expertise – the direct implementation problem. By definition this task is at some supralocal or regional level: the 'periphery' in this context is made up of a configuration of one or more local political administrations. The common denominator for both national/regional and regional/local approaches to the policy-implementation problem is therefore essentially administrative: giving national policies a subnational dimension, and local policies a supralocal dimension. The common dimension is therefore the regional perspective – 'national-down-to-regional' and 'local-up-to-regional'. Both emphasise the spatial element of public planning at primarily national and local levels. So the identification and integration of the spatial dimension of public planning is to be found alive and well in the guise of regional planning. The spatial element is therefore a necessary and critical condition of and for public planning. But it is not necessarily the critical or necessary condition which it is often made out to be.

Having briefly outlined the political/methodological approach to regional planning proposed by Self, it is necessary to note the way in which Hall modifies it and has, to some extent, helped to make the resultant methodological/technical emphasis a feature of contemporary regional planning practice. Hall's stress, and subsequent modifications, may therefore be identified as another example of an 'idea in good currency' *vis-à-vis* 'current best practice' in regional planning at the national/regional level.

To Peter Hall the idea of national/regional planning is of fundamental importance to the 'success' of regional planning. But he treats it more as a weapon in the general armoury of intervention by central government. It is 'top-down' planning in the sense implied by Self. But its principal concern is with a much narrower conception – the addition of a regional dimension to national economic policy. As Hall puts it, national/regional planning is:

> ... the planning of *public investment* and the *guiding* of private investment through negative and positive inducements . . .[2] (Italics added.)

He makes a number of additional qualifications: first, it is a process of steering economic growth away from certain regions and into others;

second, it is concerned with the allocation of national investment down to some aggregate regional level; and third, with the problem of allocating these national totals among regions.[3]

The problem with Hall's interpretation is that it masks a basic conceptual confusion. On the one hand he refers to the historical development of successive central governments attitudes to regional planning in the UK, and draws the inference that this has been national/regional planning. The inference is therefore a *descriptive* one. On the other hand he implicitly abstracts from this description certain key technical features, and then proceeds to endow them with explicit prescriptive qualities: to this is what national/regional planning *should* be. The inference is a translation from a positive technical description to a normative political prescription, with no intervening critical assessment of the utility of that particular style of public planning as compared with potential competitors.

With the conceptual equipment provided in the previous two chapters it is a relatively simple matter to outline Hall's position *vis-à-vis* this methodological/technical approach to regional planning. In fact because his proposals correspond closely to what happens anyway, most of the analysis of UK public planning provided in the last two chapters is of direct relevance. For example, in terms of 'ideological-institutional' differences the political administration associated with Hall's notion of national/regional planning is relatively more blueprint than process oriented. In terms of 'institutional-operational' differences his notion is an explicit plea for a rational comprehensive approach to be the cornerstone of regional planning – as he remarks elsewhere.[4] But it is perhaps at the level of 'operational-administrative' differences that his position crystallises and can be most readily analysed. The key concepts which Hall makes use of in his categorisation of national/regional planning are 'guiding', 'inducements', 'steering', 'allocation down to', 'allocate among', etc. Do these concepts correspond more to the characteristics of the normative or the functional planning modes? If the conceptual schema outlined in the last two chapters adequately captures the strengths and weaknesses of different modes and styles of public planning, it is clear that Hall's approach is much more in sympathy with the idea of functional rather than normative planning. That is, the objectives of action have been broadly mapped out (policy, 'ends'); the problem is therefore one of carrying-out those objectives through action programmes (implementation, 'means') (see Figure 6.1 later).

The political environment within which Hall sets out his idea of national/regional planning may also be readily identified. The key concepts which he makes use of here are 'public investment', 'guiding', 'negative and positive inducements', 'economic growth', etc. These are all concepts which may be associated with the idea of permissive planning. The political context is therefore a 'mixed' political system: public planning *qua* regional planning at the national/regional level as a process of influence and inducement. In this setting the tasks and range of government intervention is concerned more or less exclusively with supplementing the workings of a primarily market-based economy — hence the stress on economic concepts and economic policies (for example, economic growth).

So much for the differences in emphasis which Self and Hall make at the national/regional level of regional planning. But national/regional planning has a dual — regional/local planning. Are there similar differences in emphasis between Self and Hall here? The answer is that the two authors are much more in sympathy, possibly reflecting the conceptual problems associated with the very identification of this level of planning.

The 'good currency' idea of regional planning at the regional/local level is again admirably illustrated by Peter Hall. He sees it as complimentary to, but also the logical antithesis of, national/regional planning. It too is of fundamental importance because it provides the 'bottom-up' thrust necessary for 'successful' planning. But unlike its corollary the regional/local approach is concerned with the building-up and integrating of public planning into a supra-urban configuration — the problem of planning the city region. As Hall puts it, regional/local planning is primarily:

> ... planning for what we can call the relationships between the region and the parts of the region; ... it deals with the mainly *physical disposition* of investments within the particular region.[5] (Italics added.)

A number of qualifications are made: first, it is a dual process — one strand emphasises investment allocation, the other the physical coordination of that investment; second, it is a hybrid form of public planning, combining as it does components of the economics of location with the physical problems of land use and aesthetic urban design; and third, its objectives are primarily social and ameliorative.[6]

A brief analysis can be made of the Hall/Self position with respect to regional/local planning in similar fashion to the assessment of national/regional planning. Utilising the conceptual equipment built up in the previous two chapters it is possible to set this concept of regional/local planning into that schema. For example, at the level of 'ideological/institutional' differences it is possible to argue that this style of supra-urban planning is broadly in sympathy with a more blueprint approach, since it is concerned, as Hall puts it, with the physical disposition of investment. In terms of 'institutional-ideological' differences, Hall again stresses the unquestionable attributes of a rational and comprehensive methodology — the need for a rational comprehensive approach as the cornerstone of this type of regional planning. At the level of 'operational-administrative' differences, the emphasis shifts subtlely closer toward the normative end of the normative-functional continuum than planning at the national/regional level. The logic is straightforward. Although there is emphasis on aspects of allocation in order to meet policy objectives ('means' reduction) it is not the sole emphasis. Hall's interpretation is marginally broader since it includes social and aesthetic aspects of public planning. He also sees some capability — however limited — for local governments to concern themselves with the interpretation of policy, some interaction between 'policy-content' and 'implementation-capability,' therefore some 'means'/'ends' interaction. Nevertheless it corresponds more to the functional approach (Figure 6.1).[7]

Fig. 6.1   National/regional and regional/local planning, after Peter Hall

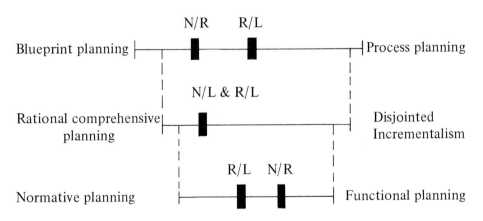

We are now in a position to return to the question posed at the beginning of the chapter — what makes regional planning so distinct from public planning? We have made a case for regional planning, albeit indirectly, and outlined a 'good currency' approach to the idea of regional planning — following Self, but particularly Hall. Four basic concepts have been put forward, each concerned with some aspect or other of the relationships and differentiation between the 'policy content' and 'implementation capability' of, respectively, national and local political administrations ('centre' and 'periphery'). These are the concepts of scale and space — within the context of national/regional and regional/local planning. Each of these is concerned with the dynamic qualities of public planning. In other words they are components or ingredients of the process of one particular strand of public planning – regional planning. They are also heavily interdependent concepts, each being dependent in some way on the others. But most importantly of all they are concepts which help the distinguishing of regional planning from other forms of public planning and intervention. In terms of the sketch for a theory of public planning, outlined in Chapter Three, these four concepts must be appended to that schema. In other words, the basic organising attributes of the process of a regional form of public planning would need to incorporate the following eleven concepts:

1   a problem-solving framework;
2   a theory-incorporating framework;
3   recognition of dynamics;
4   a process-oriented emphasis;
5   recognition of uncertainty;
6   continuous and mutual interaction between problems and solutions, intent and impact;
7   constant iteration between problems and solutions, intent and impact;
8   recognition of scale;
9   recognition of space;
10  a national/regional dimension; and
11  a regional/local dimension.

This methodology, based on the notion of a responsive approach, is therefore concerned with what we have labelled the 'internal' component of public planning, but at a regional level. Implicit in this account – and illustrated by the word 'level' in the last sentence – is some notion of the processes of public planning and its concomitant political administration. In effect we have outlined two broad processes of a regional form of public planning (national/regional; regional/local) and yet three levels at which it appears to operate: national, subnational/supra-urban, and local. By collapsing the subnational and supra-urban levels we arrive, somewhat indirectly, at a regional level. From this perspective – viewing regional planning as one strand of public planning, a regional strand – it is possible to fashion a pragmatic interpretation of this form of planning. *Regional planning then may be seen as the dual and simultaneous processes of public planning at an intermediate level between national and local political administrations.* At the national level it is an attempt to add a subnational 'thrust' to public policy, to ensure its translation and ultimate implementation. At the local level it is an attempt to add a supra-urban dimension to the mobilising and implementation of national policy and ultimately with the solution of local problems.

However there are two qualifications which need to be made. The first concerns the differences between these two types of regional planning. National/regional planning is, by definition, concerned more with the way in which public policy is 'regionalised'. The assumption is that there is not just one region but rather a plurality or set of regions. National/regional planning is therefore concerned not only with the translation of public policy into a regional context, but with the mobilising and balancing of national commitment and action between regions. What might be better referred to as the 'interregional' component of public planning.

Regional/local planning, with its emphasis on the implementation aspects of public policy, is also concerned with the way in which that policy is translated within a regional context. But unlike the national/regional approach it is concerned more with the mobilising and balancing of local commitment and action – within the context provided by national policy guidelines – within that particular region. What might be better referred to as the 'intraregional' component of public planning.

The second qualification concerns the way in which Self's concepts, and in particular Hall's later developments, have been utilised in this chapter. Earlier we separated the descriptive from the conceptual element of their interpretations of regional planning. Doubts have been cast on the case made by Hall of the national/regional idea, and a brief consideration made of Hall's position with respect to Faludi's three dimensions of planning. But these doubts concerned a confusion between the elements of descriptive analysis and prescriptive proposals. The use of the concepts themselves have remained untouched. So in a critique of Hall we have not fallen into the euphemistic trap of 'throwing the baby out with the bath water'. Hopefully we have saved the 'baby' – in the form of Hall's tighter interpretation of Self's original concepts of national/regional and regional/local planning – and dispensed with the muddy 'water', in the form of Hall's prescriptive interpretations.

### Regional problems and problem regions

Having established a conceptual base for a study of public planning at the regional level, and considered some of the 'ideas in good currency' with respect to it, we can now proceed to a more rigorous interpretation. A useful starting point is from the perspective of a consideration of 'regional problems' and 'problem regions'. This can be approached at two levels.

First, by continuing with the 'ideas in good currency' approach, and second, from a more conceptual and hence abstract form of analysis.

'Ideas in good currency', with respect to the notions of regional problems and problem regions, cannot legitimately be divorced from the experience of public planning at the regional scale. Four broad themes can be identified. The first is that in practice regional planning has historical roots of a prolific and prestigious nature. For example, Leonardo da Vinci is reputed to have prepared a 'regional plan' for the diverting of the river Arno in 1503, a strategic military operation of massive proportions designed to sever the water supply to key towns in Northern Italy. Also the gargantuan Tennessee river basin scheme, constituted by Congress in 1933 under the auspices of the largely autonomous Tennessee Valley Authority. This was a (disjointed) 'regional plan', covering 41000 square miles, the principal objective of which was to control and harness the flood waters from the Appallachians.[8] A more contemporary example is provided by the Ciudad Guayana programme in Venezuela, undertaken under the auspices of the Harvard-MIT Joint Center in the 1960s. Here the problem was one of large-scale 'regionalised' urban-industrialisation of a 'remote frontier region'. A key feature of this programme was with the idea of institution building as much as with the physical location of public investments.[9]

The second theme which can be identified concerns the orientation of the practice of regional planning. Until the middle 'fifties, at the risk of overgeneralising, regional planning was concerned more or less solely with explicit single-objective, large-scale development projects. For example, the TVA scheme − a clearly-defined and specific problem (flood water) with a clearly-defined and specific objective (to control it). From this period onward there was an identifiable shift toward explicit multiple-objective, large-scale development projects. For example, the Guyana Program − loosely-defined and messy problems (industrialisation) with a set of loosely-defined and interrelated objectives (to promote and accelerate it).[10]

The third theme concerns different meanings which have been given to the contemporary practice of regional planning. We have already mentioned the idea of subnational and supra-urban planning as public planning at the regional level. In the United Kingdom these have been variously labelled as 'regional policy', 'subregional planning', 'city region planning', 'regional strategic planning', and 'regional development programming'.[11] Despite − or perhaps inspite of − these different labels it is nevertheless a remarkable feature of contemporary UK regional planning practice that both the formats and substantive content of each of these approaches have changed little over the past two decades. It is also possible to reach similar conclusions about any two or more regional planning studies which were prepared at approximately similar times. Their formats and content are so remarkably similar — the obsession with the rational methodology being one example — that it is tempting to draw a parallel here with that old cliché: 'Only the names and titles have been changed . . .' [12] However, implicit in each of these studies, via the documents which have provided the tangible evidence for these assertions, has been some distinctive approach to regional planning which can be reduced to a particular functional style of regional planning. In fact the functional style employed is usually to be found interposed between the words 'regional' and 'planning'. The kinds of public planning which have been pursued in the UK and the United States at the regional level have been one or other of, for example, regional resource planning, regional economic planning, regional land use planning, or regional development planning.

Examples of regional resource planning include the river basin approach commonplace in the US and the planning of water utilisation in the UK under the reorganised regional water authorities. Other examples include the regionalised production and administration of the gas and electricity authorities. Examples of regional economic planning include all of those programmes which proposed explicit economic policies to achieve an explicit set of economic objectives at a regional level — the largely administratively autonomous industrial development strand of UK regional policy is a good example. Land use planning at the regional level is perhaps the most familiar and identifiable style of regional planning in both the UK and the US. Examples include most of the British regional studies and strategies produced in the 'sixties, including the brief love affair with subregional or city-regional planning. Also the plethora of US studies in the 'sixties which involved planning at the supra-urban level. [13]

The fourth style — the notion of regional development planning — must include all those examples of a multi-programme approach which have attempted to achieve an explicitly multiple set of objectives. One of the best examples must be that provided by the aforementioned Guyana Program — a US/Venezuelan cross-cultural attempt at a truly regional development form of public planning. The sole UK examples are provided by central government's regional development policy (although administratively fragmented) and the relatively autonomous activities of the Highlands and Islands Development Board. Clearly in this contemporary context regional development planning can be thought of as an amalgam of two or more of either resource, economic or land use planning.

The fourth theme which can be identified concerns the contemporary basis, the assumptions, on which regional planning — as one form of public intervention — has in the main been grounded. Two grounds can be established, one subnational the other supra-urban. As outlined earlier, at the national/regional level the principal basis for regional planning — couched in the shape of a diagnostic justification — has been in the form of a trilogy of assumptions: (a) that a country 'suffers' from some form of spatial imbalance which calls for attention from central government; (b) that the national rate of economic growth may be spurred by promoting discriminatory policies between regions; and (c) that public expenditure and in particular the problems associated with the provision of major public investments — transport, housing, etc. — requires some knowledge of the needs of particular areas and the coordination of that provision between regions. [14] The contemporary history of national/regional planning is therefore littered with the problems associated with primarily economic issues concerning economic policies and economic variables.

Its dual — regional/local planning — has clearly had a very different set of emphases, which Self and Hall have admirably outlined for the UK — and which we considered earlier. Here the emphases have been much less economic-oriented and concerned more with the spatial configurations and aesthetic qualities of land use — existing and proposed — at the supra-urban level. Here the principal basis for regional planning has also usually been couched in the form of a trilogy of assumptions: (a) that a market solution to the spatial juxtaposition of land uses results in a less than desirable physical environment within a particular region which calls for attention from primarily local but also central governments; (b) that a regions rate of 'development' (not necessarily economic) may be spurred by promoting discriminatory policies within its boundaries; and (c) that the complex problems and scale associated with the provision of major public investments — transport, housing, etc. — within a region requires a coordination of activities at a level beyond that of any one local area, because the problems 'spill over' and affect others. [15]

The justifications for regional planning, of one form or another, have therefore been based implicitly on one or more of the four notions grounded in welfare economics outlined in the second chapter: (a) the provision of public or collective goods; (b) the presence — existing or potential — of externalities; (c) the problems or potential problems attributable to indivisibilities; and/or (d) for the sake of general public welfare. In other words, what we have referred to here as regional planning has been concerned with the manner in which these four notions have interacted and been given a spatial, or geographical, dimension. For example, we have seen that national/regional planning has been justified in the UK in terms of the provision of major public investments (public

140

goods) within the context of general public welfare (rate of national economic growth). We have also seen that regional/local planning has been justified on similar grounds: the scale of public investments needed (indivisibilities) and the 'spill-over' effects associated with them (externalities).

This then accounts for much of the 'good currency' approach to public planning at the regional level. But implicit in this account has been the concept of what constitutes the regional level. That is, some explicit notion of what is meant by a region. The approach which has underpinned the contemporary practice of regional planning has relied almost exclusively on the geographical definition of space, and formalised in the idea of the geographical region. However, this concept has in turn been the subject of a subtle modification in one of two directions: first, at the national/regional level, with its emphasis on 'imbalance' between geographically-defined regions; and second, at the regional/local level, by the idea that the influence, and therefore strength, of 'spatial interaction' extends beyond, but decreases with, distance from urban centres. These relationships between 'imbalance' and 'spatial interaction' have been modified in regional planning practice as a typology of geographical regions concerned with different kinds of regional 'problem'. This typology consists of:

1   where one or more geographically-defined regions are considered to be underdeveloped in relation to other regions and the country as a whole;
2   where one or more geographically-defined regions are deemed to be depressed, according to some accepted and acceptable criterion;
3   where one or more geographically-defined regions are considered to be congested.[16]

The idea of an underdeveloped region is largely self-explanatory. According to Anatol Kuklinski, of the Regional Development Group at the UNRISD:

In underdeveloped regions, different barriers hamper the regions from participating in the modern processes of urban and industrial development which change the structure of the economy and the society of a given country. Southern Italy and Southern Yugoslavia could be mentioned as regions of this type.[17]

The idea of a depressed region is likewise self-explanatory. As Kuklinski observes:

In contrast to underdeveloped regions, depressed regions are areas developed during the first industrial revolution. In this case, economic

141

and social depression is brought about by the difficulty of replacing declining industries (coal, steel, cotton, etc.) by modern, quickly growing industries (electronics, chemicals, metal, etc.) Frequently quoted examples are the Pittsburgh region and Southern Belgium.[18]

The idea of a congested region is also pretty much self-explanatory. Following Kuklinski again:

> Overcongested regions are areas in which the economic growth has reached a scale in a given time that is bigger than the optimal from the point of view of internal environmental conditions of the over-congested region and the development of other regions of the country. London, Paris and Budapest can be mentioned as examples of overcongested regions.[19]

The 'action space', the cornerstone and *raison d'être* of contemporary 'good currency' approaches to regional planning practice, has therefore evolved around the use of one particular concept of space — the geographical region — within the context of three kinds of problem region, defined in turn in terms of 'imbalance' and/or 'spatial interaction'. The principal questions which must be asked of this approach is whether or not it represents the only and best approach which may be adopted to tackle the problem of public planning at the regional level. For example, are there other and perhaps more meaningful concepts of space and region which are of relevance to regional planning? Is the dual notion of 'imbalance' and 'spatial interaction' the sole criterion which should be taken to assess and justify involvement by the state in subnational affairs? Are the concepts of underdevelopment, depression and congestion the only valid criteria by which to identify and categorise problems which can be 'regionalised'? In other words, does this 'good currency' approach to regional planning exhaust the universe of discourse on the subject of regional planning practice? It is with these questions in mind that we embark on the latter part of this chapter.

In fact these kinds of question, it is maintained here, cut right to the heart of the idea of regional planning itself. Note that the questions do not necessarily mean that we search for the 'best' solution as to what constitutes space, region and regional planning. Rather, they imply that there just may be other equally if not more valid accounts and explanations of key concepts which may be important to regional planning practice. It is the contention here that the most critical of these concerns the way in which regional planning organises itself, from the contextual setting within which it fits, its perception of what it is supposed to be

142

doing, and how it is setting about accomplishing those tasks. This contention therefore cannot be neatly divorced from an analysis of the rôle of regional planning itself. Having argued a case for public planning in the first five chapters, also that regional planning can be seen as one strand of public planning, it makes sense to use that conceptual framework to embark on this analysis – and hence to develop an alternative approach wedded to that framework.

The starting point for this departure is to be found in two simple notions which lay at the very heart of the 'good currency' approach. The first of these concerns what may be called the spatial problems of public policy within a particular country or nation-state. The second is the notion of the problem region. The former stresses the idea that public policy consists of more than the formulation and making of a policy decision (intent). Rather, an equal if not more important strand is the manner in which that policy is translated and implemented (impact). Public planning at the regional level can be seen as one vehicle for this dual process of formulating and implementing public policy – as was noted earlier, the matching of 'policy content' with 'implementation capability'. This is therefore a broader and yet narrower interpretation of the idea of spatial policy problems associated with the 'good currency' approach. [20] It incorporates the political and administrative components of public planning as primary organising devices, as a *sine qua non* of regional planning. Implicit in this idea is the dilution and diminution of the status of problems defined solely within and in terms of geographical space. A more important notion of space in this context is what may be called political space.

'Political space' is also an important facet of the second notion – the problem region. Implicit in the 'good currency' approach is the idea that problem regions are essentially geographical regions within which are located geographically space-specific problems. These problems may not necessarily be determined by geographical space, but nevertheless they can be defined in locational and geographical space-specific terms. This has represented the approach of successive generations of geographers, crystallised in the idea that so-called 'natural geographical regions' could be identified if only agreement could be reached on the right criteria to be used. To some extent this almost ideological treatment of physical space has led to at least two quite serious and deleterious consequences for regional planning practice. Firstly, because attention has been paid almost exclusively, if not reverently, to the concept of geographical space, work on other possibly more fundamental notions of space – for example, economic space – has been the subject of serious neglect. Secondly, this reverence for geographical space has led to the rather more important unfortunate consequence of being accorded a significant status, in regional planning terms, by those concerned with planning who began to view geographical space as the determinant, a prime mover, of societal behaviour. In fact it is possible to argue that regional planning practice has merely represented a modification of the early geographer's grapplings with the descriptive-positivist idea of the search for 'natural' regions. It did not take long before a prescriptive-normative component became tacked on to the end as geographers became increasingly involved with regional planning. This normative thrust stressed the importance and need for an orderly geographical arrangement associated with the symmetry of structures and functions of societal activities within physical terms as the primary organising device — and hence to an implicit ideology of stability in the social spatial structure *vis-à-vis* the societal use of buildings and land.[21]

This, what may be referred to as the 'traditional' approach to the relationship between the concept of region and regional planning, was structured in a supremely simple and elegant manner. At the risk of oversimplifying, social behaviour, however viewed — social, economic, temporal — was manifestly determined and in some respects caused by physical structures (Figure 6.2).

These relationships were translated into and formally subsumed within the 'traditional' approach to regional planning, not only in how society was perceived to be structured but in how society should be structured. Positive description to normative prescription in one simple and apparently logical transformation. Such a proposition has rightly been called into question by many contemporary writers. For example, as Friedmann notes, a region is a time-space continuum — so why invest it with deterministic and Euclidean properties?[22]

But this should not be construed as implying that physical space is of no importance — only that it can never assume the mantle of prime determinant. This notion of physical space therefore joins other notions of space on a comparable basis (Figure 6.3).

What this contemporary idea of space implies is that societal activities, however viewed — socially, economically, temporally, physically — interact in a continuum of a multiplicity of different types of space — social space, economic space, temporal space, physical space, what Perroux rather aptly describes as abstract topological space. There are therefore as many kinds of space as there are constituent facets of abstract or concrete societal relations.[23] However, for the purposes of this book, and its concern for regional planning, we shall distinguish between these topological

144

Fig. 6.2    The regional concept – traditional

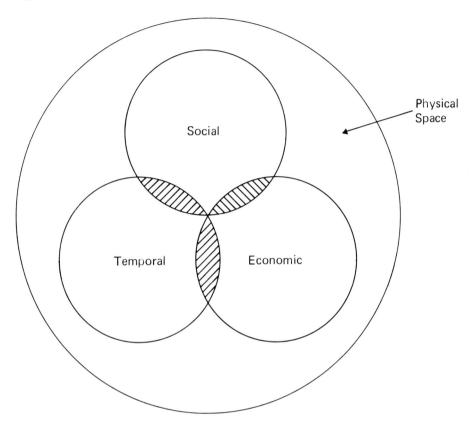

spaces by according a higher status to one of these constituent facets –
that of politics and its administration. One of the themes of this volume
which has been consistently stressed is that of the inherently political
nature of public planning, of which regional planning may be seen as one
vital strand. The arena within which public planning operates is the
political arena – in other words, political space is that notion of space
within which the political administration of public planning operates (the
'centre') but more importantly is seen to operate (the 'periphery'). It is
with the relationships between social space, economic space and temporal
space, within the organising context of political space, which will be taken
as the meaning of 'space' for the remainder of this volume, unless otherwise specified.

Therefore if we accept that there may be some utility in this concept of
'political space' – which, we have concluded can include geographical
space – then this brings into question the whole notion of problem

Fig. 6.3    The regional concept — contemporary

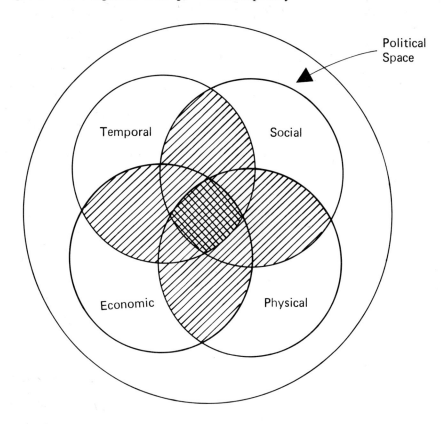

regions as defined in geographical terms. If this is the case then two
fundamental and interrelated issues are raised:

1    Who defines a region as a problem region?
2    How do particular regions emerge as problem regions?

Both of these questions concern the way in which problem regions are
perceived as being problems in the first place. Kuklinski has provided a
three-fold typology of problem region, whose roots are grounded in geographical space. But the way in which he describes underdeveloped, depressed and congested regions are more or less divorced from any notion
of geographical space as the prime criterion of their identification. Rather,
he refers to, respectively, 'barriers', 'processes of development', 'economic
and social depression', 'internal environmental conditions', etc. The framework on which he hangs these terms is the notion of geographical space

but the determinants of those problems which he identifies have little to do with it.

The 'good currency' approach to regional planning practice argues primarily from the geographical perspective of problem regions, which are seen as either underdeveloped or depressed or congested. But in reality it is reasonable to assert that these three categories of problem region are by no means as clear-cut or as unitary as might at first appear. For like every concept we have outlined so far, Kuklinski's typology is an attempt to generalise and simplify the real world to a level which is comprehensible to and manipulatable by those concerned with the crystallisation and implementation of public policy. In practice it is rarely possible to identify a black-and-white case of either an underdeveloped region or a depressed region or a congested region. All regions, however defined, tend to exhibit symptoms which accord roughly with Kuklinski's typology, however mild or chronic (politically, socially, economically, etc.) those might be. [24] This is expressed in diagrammatic form in figure 6.4.

Fig. 6.4   The idea of problem regions

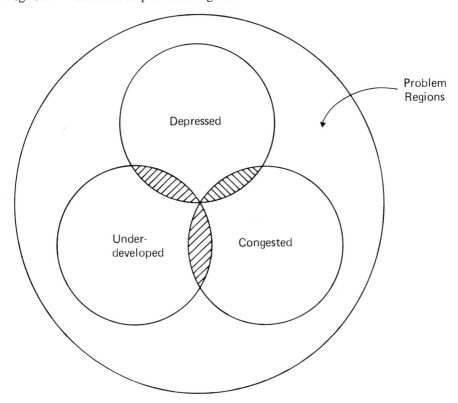

This diagram illustrates interactions between the three concepts of problem region, but it does not indicate differences in the scale or magnitude of those problems. This can be tackled in a fairly pragmatic manner. Instead of attempting to assess scale in a quantitative sense — which is the generally accepted 'good currency' approach (for example, regional unemployment estimates) — it can be approached more qualitatively. In so doing we again reinforce the view that there is not necessarily a 'right' or 'wrong' approach which can be adopted; no case of neat distinctions or tight black-or-white definitions. Rather, subtle shades of grey are its distinguishing characteristics. In other words, the suggestion is being made that problem regions are essentially political problems, and thus demanding of politically-oriented solutions.

On this basis *any and all regions are problem regions of one form or another*. And so we depart from the 'good currency' approach in one further respect — that of the notion of what constitutes a 'problem'. The schema developed by Popper, and outlined in Chapter Three, is what is meant by a problem in this particular context: the positive seeking and grasping of opportunities, as well as the more obvious negative remedial kind. According to this perspective the concern of regional planning *vis-à-vis* problem regions is with relationships between the perception of political problems, the political priority accorded to them, and the administrative capability necessary for their resolution — within the context of the three-fold typology of problem regions outlined earlier.

On the assumption that all regions are problem regions, and regional planning problems are primarily political, a case can be presented that the differential political status of problem regions is the determining criterion by which the scale and magnitude of their respective problems may be more usefully assessed. This concept of political status, and in particular differentials in political status, can be articulated within the context of a dual continuum. In fact it is possible to identify a range of problem regions according to differentials in political status, between what may be referred to at one extreme as 'mild symptoms' and at the other 'chronic symptoms', and 'high' and 'low' political status. Any region, however defined, is therefore capable of being located somewhere along this dual continuum:

Mild symptoms                                           Chronic symptoms

∞ ←——————       Range       ——————→ ∞

Low political status                                 High political status

For illustrative purposes this continuum can be taken one stage further by conceptually separating the differentials in symptoms between problem regions from differentials in their respective political status (Figure 6.5). Thus problem regions exhibiting chronic symptoms may be associated with high political status, and vice versa, problem regions exhibiting milder symptoms may be associated with correspondingly lower levels of political status.

Fig. 6.5   Problem regions and political status (1)

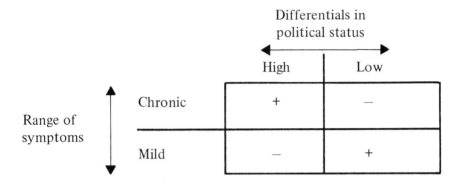

But 'problem regions' in this context have been treated in the singular, although we have already made it explicit that three broad kinds of problem region can be distinguished. The notions of underdeveloped, depressed and congested region must therefore be integrated with the notions of range of symptoms and differentials in political status. A simple division into two dual continuums – one per type of problem region – would not suffice because of the degree of interaction which we have postulated occurs between them. What is needed to illustrate this more complex set of relationships is to fuse the concept of the dual continuum outlined above with the schema presented in Figure 6.4. This may be achieved, for the sake of a simple example, by (a) dividing the range of symptoms and differentials in political status into, say, an arbitrary three-fold classification, and (b) to superimpose this classification on each of the three types of problem region. We have therefore derived a set of nested problems for each type of problem region (Figure 6.6), within the context of a set of nested problem regions (Figure 6.7):

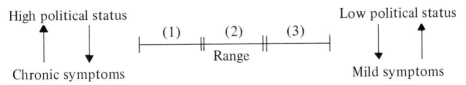

149

Fig. 6.6  Problem regions and political status (2)

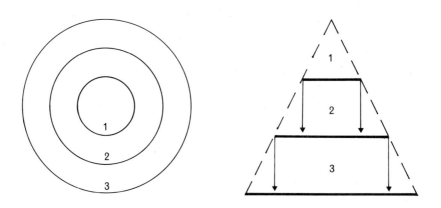

This latter diagram illustrates two important facets of relationships between problem regions and regional problems which public planning at the
regional scale has to continuously grapple with. First, we cannot consider
the concept of *a* problem region as a valid concept from the perspective of
regional planning practice. Any region is likely to exhibit problems of
underdevelopment, depression and/or congestion through time. *All regions are therefore problem regions by definition.* The emphases will
obviously differ, but nevertheless each emphasis will be there in some
discernible form – however marginal that might be perceived. The distinguishing characteristics for regional planning purposes will be the level
of the symptoms of each together with their accompanying and corresponding political status. Second, that the sum of the three kinds of
problem region do not add up to what may be called regional problems.
Regional problems cannot usefully be divorced from the idea of problem
regions, and vice versa. But which comes first, the identification of problem regions or regional problems? Identification of the symptoms or the
endowment of political status? And so we arrive back at square one, to
the two questions which were posed at the beginning of this excursion
into the idea of problem regions: who defines a region as a problem
region? and, how do particular regions emerge as problem regions? That is,
at what stage along the dual continuum – between mild and chronic
symptoms, and low and high political status – does the problem region
enter the critical area? This is clearly of no small importance to the study
of the nature and practice of planning itself because, as was argued in
Chapter Three, problem-solving is one of the most crucial aspects of a

150

Fig. 6.7   Problem regions and regional problems

A . . . . . Underdeveloped
B . . . . . Depressed
C . . . . . Congested

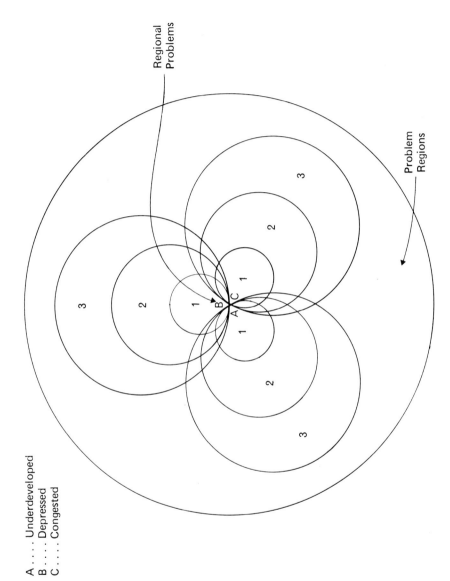

Regional
Problems

Problem
Regions

responsive approach to public planning. To be in a better position to tackle these questions we need to turn attention to the problem of what constitutes a problem and in particular how such problems emerge into the public arena.

## Public planning and the emergence of political problems

There are a number of interrelated themes which concern public planning which need to be explored in this context: the kinds of problem with which public planning is concerned; the forms of control and control mechanism which public planning is concerned with; the learning qualities of public planning; and the ways in which uncertainty and ambiguity impinge on the processes of planning.

The first of these themes concerns the idea that few if any of the kinds of problem with which public planning is more often than not faced are unique and which require total, definable, immediate and unquestionable action on the part of government. [25] Rather they are more often than not piecemeal, messy, debatable, and arbitrary. In other words, they are essentially and inherently problems of a primarily political nature.

The second theme concerns the way in which the mechanisms of control and regulation are employed within the machinery of public planning. Public planning, we have argued, is concerned with — and the concern of — social change and hence with the nature of society itself. On the one hand the prerogative of the public planner is with what Hart calls the 'ordering of change', whereas on the other it is concerned with the understanding of 'changing concepts of order'. Planning is therefore very much concerned with the dual notions of control and regulation. [26] Building on the deductive approach outlined in Chapter Three, it is possible to view the operation of public planning as consisting of what Vickers calls the relationships between the organising processes of predicting and correcting by experience, processes which continuously weld the problem-setting nature of planning with problem-solving expertise — and learning about relationships between the two. [27] In other words, with Popper's approach to the idea of the elimination of error — what Ross Ashby refers to in a different context as the cybernetic approach to error-controlled regulation. [28] Ashby's concepts have been outlined in the context of public planning by McLoughlin (Figure 6.8). [29]

McLoughlin differentiates between two components of public planning — 'internal' and 'external'. The latter consists of the 'real world' and 'disturbances' within it; the former of four sub-components — a 'model of

152

Fig. 6.8    Error-controlled regulation and public planning (1)

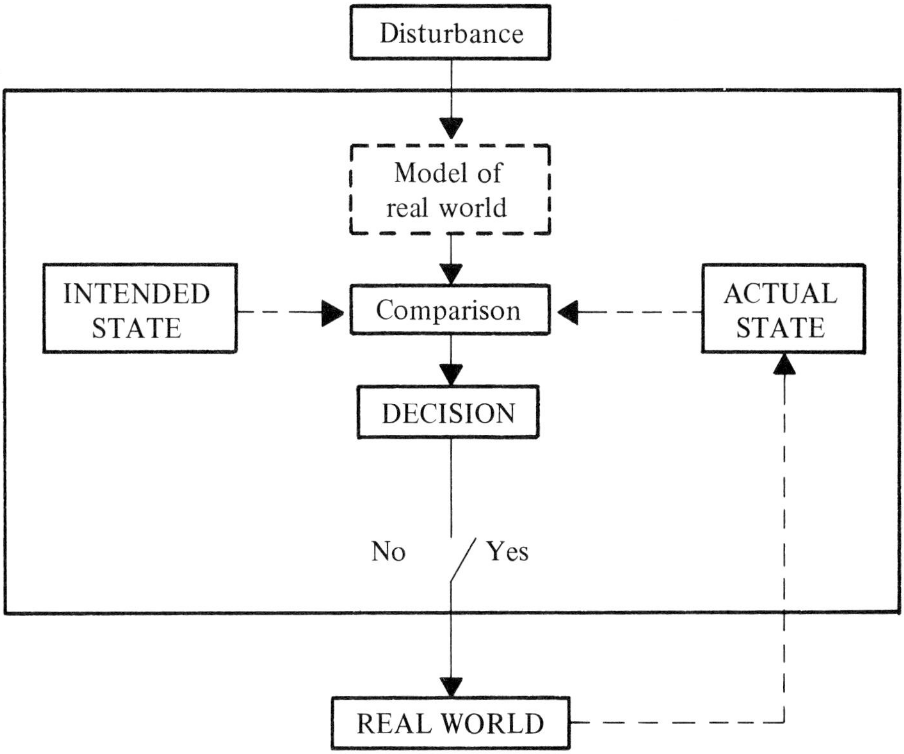

Source: McLoughlin, 1969

the real world', some notion of an 'intended state' for the real world, an assessment of the 'actual state' of affairs, and some 'decision' sequence based on comparisons of actual with intended. As a result of some 'disturbance' in the 'real world', the key attributes of this dysfunction are fed into a 'model'. Within the context of this 'model' the 'intended state' is compared with the 'actual state'. On the basis of that comparison 'decisions' are taken, and presumably implemented, and the results fed-back into the 'internal' component of the planning process. McLoughlin's idea of the control mechanism in public planning is therefore a particularly interesting one. But it is a wholly rigid and mechanistic schema, both in terms of its basic organising structure and its idea of process as a sequence of comparative statics. The only procedural component in his diagram is the box labelled 'decision', which is in itself revealing because it says nothing about the processes of deciding *per se*. That is, who is doing the deciding,

153

in what manner are decisions being made, and on what legitimate pretext? Following Vickers illustrating and incisive critique of the cybernetic approach to the process of the making of public policy, this is not to dismiss McLoughlin's schema out of hand. [30] Rather it suggests that his approach, embedded as it is in cybernetics, is neither a particularly useful nor an illuminating one for our specific purposes. However, it is possible to develop a potentially more satisfactory schema of error-controlled regulation, based on some of McLoughlin's ideas and concepts, which is capable of being extended into a potentially more satisfactory framework for an outline of a theory for public planning. It builds on the foundations of deductive methodology but incorporates some of the ideas proposed by Vickers — particularly his notions of tacit values and appreciative judgement. [31] The starting point for this schema is illustrated by Figure 6.9:

Fig. 6.9    Error-controlled regulation and public planning (2)

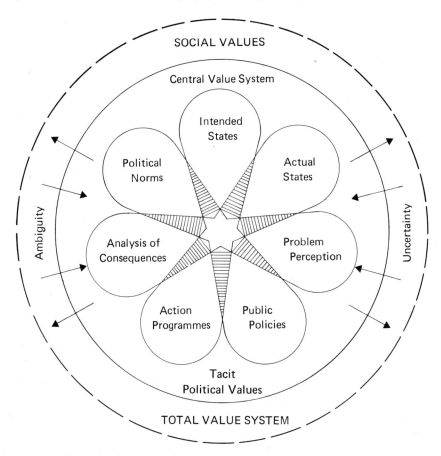

This schema incorporates most, if not all, of the organising concepts of public planning which were outlined in Chapter Three. The 'internal' component is represented by Shil's notion of the central value system; the 'internal-external' component is based on Faludi's construction of the planning environment; and the 'external' component is represented by Shil's notion of the total value system. Relationships between the 'centre' and the 'periphery' are perceived, modified, distorted and to some extent controlled within the terms of the all-pervading notions of uncertainty and ambiguity. The concern of public planning in this context is therefore with the total contextual setting of public planning *vis-à-vis* societal relations. This form of error-controlled regulation is therefore a central, if not the central, concern of public planning, and vice versa.[32]

The 'internal' component — what we have referred to as the operational/administrative requirements of the process of public planning — consists of seven interlocking, interacting and iterating ingredients: political norms, intended state, actual state, problem perception, public policies, action programmes, and analysis of consequences. These are not distinct or mutually exclusive elements or black boxes which can be connected by neat lines illustrating simple cause-effect relationships. Rather this schema is inextricably bound-up with proposals for a deductive methodology of the processes of planning, as outlined in Chapter Three. As such each ingredient needs to be considered within the context of each of the others.

The 'internal' component therefore needs to be set within the context of the 'internal-external' component — what we have referred to as the institutional/operational requirements of the processes of public planning. This domain consists of the central value system, in this case reflected in and reflected by the tacit political values underpinning public planning, and the relationships between the 'centre' and the total value system — the 'periphery'. On the one hand these tacit political values determine and are determined in part by the total value system (the 'external' component — the 'ideological/institutional requirements') and the 'centres' perceptions of and attempts to influence them. In other words it is part of the continuous attempt to internalise this total value system, and as such is subject to the problems associated with uncertainty and ambiguity about what constitutes reality 'out there'. On the other hand these tacit political values determine and are determined in part by the 'internal' component of public planning — the demands associated with its operation and administration. The tacit political values are therefore translated into and a translation of the technical planibility concept — the fundamental expertise necessary to implement the processes of planning itself.

These notions of 'control' are therefore distinctly different from those commonly associated with the use of that term in the cybernetics approach to error-controlled regulation. Rather it accords more closely with the context provided by Popper of plastic control — levels of control mechanism which are intermediate between total control and no control. The idea that control is an all-or-nothing, black-or-white situation is therefore misplaced and misleading. It recognises that in most situations control by one 'organism' over another is more likely than not to be a relational, fragmented and polycentric form of control at a level which is substantially lower than 100 per cent. Or as Watkins concludes:

> In cases of plastic control there is a certain give and take between that part or aspect of the system which is more controlling than controlled and those parts which are more controlled than controlling.[33]

Watkins also provides a summary of the deductivist context within which this particular notion of less than total control fits — a context which admirably describes the framework for public planning which has been outlined here. He bases this summary on three overlapping suppositions:

> (1) An organism comprises a complex of plastic controls. (2) An organism is a polycentric system in which controls operate simultaneously at various levels, and in which a control may shift from one locus to another ... (3) Despite this polycentricity, we can roughly distinguish an organisms *central* control-system (which may itself have a polycentric structure) from its executive or 'motor' parts. As an acknowledgement of this, we might call an organism a quasi-hierarchical system of plastic controls.[34]

In the public planning context, therefore, what is meant by control is something less than total centralised authority over a totally dependent periphery. Indeed perhaps the terminology is basically at fault here, for what is meant or implied is clearly something softer and more open than total control — what is referred to as influence, and in particular political influence, is perhaps a more meaningful and relevant concept. If this is a valid proposition to make, then the implications for public planning are worthy of some consideration.

If planning is rather less concerned with direct control and more concerned with political influence, then a primary rôle for public planning has to be with the perception, moulding, fostering, development, mobilisation and, ultimately, implementation of political influence — and the consequences of political influence — within the context provided by legitimate intervention in the form of public policies and public action programmes. In other words, a central concern for public planning has to be with policy leverage – the exercise and systematic manipulation and moulding of political influence of disparate forms, found at different levels and in different quarters, to the related problems of proposing public policies, disposing of authority to ensure their ultimate implementation (intent), and to assess their effectuation (impact). Or as Wedgewood-Oppenheim et al. stress:

> ... this activity offers an opportunity to help to bridge the gap between intent on the one hand, and impact on the other ... continuous and systematic feedback would not be a regrettable interruption of the planning process, but a central and integral component. In this way future *anticipation* of events leading to (political) commitment could be balanced by adaptation based on recent *experience.* [35]

In this sense public planning may be seen as a crucial and significant component of the political process itself. We have already made note of Crick's interpretation of the political process *vis-à-vis* the rôle of government: that of the balancing and reconciliation of conflicting interests. We have also noted that this is a rôle which is both evaluative and predictive. So implicit in this schema of error-controlled regulation is a model of the political process itself. This model consists of three principal interfaces – the 'internal' component (the processes of the forging of public policy and the mobilising of action programmes), the 'internal-external' component (the interaction between (a) the perception of problems and their translation into the 'internal' political processes, and (b) the forging of prescriptions to those problems and their translation into 'external' action programmes); and the 'external' component (society writ large, what may be called, grossly oversimplifying, one particular political construction of what constitutes reality). We may therefore concur with Vickers' interpretation of the nature of the political process as we have implied it here:

> ... to produce, from confusion of conflicting and competing views, a stream of policy *sufficiently coherent* to realise one of all the possible combinations of achievement, *sufficiently flexible* to allow rival claims a renewed hearing, and *sufficiently controlled* to keep within the total resources available ... (It) is commonly supposed that policy problems have, at least in theory, a 'best' solution ... to choose 'rationally' between alternative policies ... Policy making is not like playing chess (where) the rules of the game are defined and are not alterable ... (In) managing human affairs at any level ..., the *nature* of success and the rules of the game are what have to be decided. [36] (Italics added)

But the concern of this part of the book is with public planning. Is it to be assumed then that we are treating the processes of public planning synonymously with political processes? The answer must clearly be in the affirmative, but with one subtle deviation. In fact we may concur with part of Dror's observations on the differences between public planning and policy-making, outlined in Chapter Two. To reiterate: 'Sometimes planning is a major means of policymaking, characterised by being relatively more structured, explicit and systematic, and by presuming to be more rational.'[37]

On the basis of the proposals put forward in Chapter Three and this chapter, we can agree with Dror that public planning can be a major means of policy-making; that it is relatively more structured, explicit and systematic. But that is as far as the similarity and congruence goes. We part company with the observation that planning is essentially the making of policy. This can represent only one side of the equation — implementation is *as* important, if not more so. Also that the idea of the rational approach, as Dror implies it, is but one of a range of competing methodologies. Perhaps the only really significant difference between the political process and public planning can be described quite simply as a difference in formality: public planning presumes to be more formal.

The third theme which can be identified stems out of the last point — the matching of a perception of the 'actual state' of affairs with an image of an 'intended state'. Obviously this matching process occurs through time. In other words it is dynamic and, in the context provided by the schema, presumably responsive to changing conditions, assumptions, political demands and outcomes. Implicit in these two notions is some idea of reality and order, but more importantly how they are in turn changing — the evaluative and predictive elements of the 'internal' component *vis-à-vis* the 'external' component. [38] A critical feature of public planning is therefore with this process of comparing actual with intended. But this is not a sufficient condition. Reality, as we have argued, is not a static concept, where desired intent at time $(t)$ can be translated totally into actual impact at time $(t+1)$. Figure 6.10 illustrates this dichotomy.

There are two facets to this diagram, one illustrating the basic approach to the 'good currency' idea of public planning, the other illustrating why this approach — wedded as it is to a notion of 'successful' planning — can be nothing more than a simple illusion.

At time $(t)$, which we shall assume is the present, public planning holds an image of reality — reality $_t$. This image is projected to some future date — reality $_t \longrightarrow t+1$. On the basis of this projection, and with what is deemed desirable, the image of the present is fashioned into a statement

Fig. 6.10   The dynamics of public planning

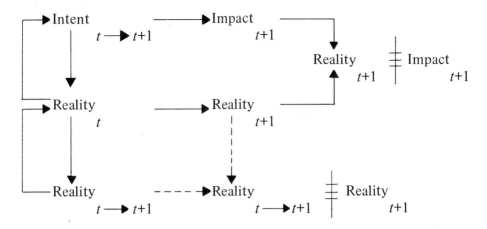

of intent for the future – intent $_t \longrightarrow _{t+1}$. The package of intent is then mobilised and implemented, the assumption being that intent for time $(t+1)$ will eventually become forged into reality – impact at time $(t+1)$. The illusion associated with this naïve proposition concerns what is happening to the image of reality in the meantime. The 'good currency' approach 'assumes' that any change in reality will be attributable to the measures proposed in the intent package. In other words impact will match intent on a one-to-one basis, albeit with some allowance for leads and lags. But is reality only fashioned by the package of intent? Is it not conceivable that, as Fried noted, unless the image of the total value system was totally understood and more importantly controlled by the 'centre', there might be some forms of change which may not have been predicted and which might 'upset' the key notions implicit in the planned package of intent? In other words, that the image of a predicted desirable reality may be at considerable variance to the image of reality when time $(t+1)$ eventually arrives. If this is the case, and there is no substantive reason to suggest otherwise, then the hoped-for impact at time $(t+1)$ will also be at some variance to the perceived reality at time $(t+1)$. The ramifications are therefore clear. To use Hart's terminology, public planning cannot solely be concerned with the process of translating planned intent into planned impact through time (what he refers to as the 'ordering of change' part of the equation). It has also, and if not more importantly, to be concerned with understanding how reality itself is changing (what he refers to as the understanding of 'changing order'). On this basis the notion of public planning presented here can be viewed as a rather different and contrasting animal to the 'good currency' approach. Public planning is concerned more than simply with the eradication of mismatch between intent and impact. Rather it emphasises the idea that public planning is as equally concerned with at least an understanding of why mismatch occurs in the first place.

This process, of comparing 'actual' with 'intended' and — as McLoughlin began to illustrate — 'unintended', is therefore a continuous and iterative process. Searching for mismatch also teaches those concerned with public planning something new about the nature of the problem or set of problems which are being subjected to public scrutiny, public policy and public (planned) intervention. In other words it indicates a measure of the relative effectiveness of those policies and action programmes, together with an assessment of the intended and unintended side-effects or consequences — potential or actual — associated with that action — potential or actual. [39] Public planning is therefore, as Schon illustrates, concerned with a learning situation, with learning from this iterative experience, and hence from its mistakes. [40] For example, of misplaced emphasis or importance, and of changing circumstances which may make certain components of public policy irrelevant or redundant. When, as Wedgewood-Oppenheim et al. stress, these components have lost their original meaning or are simply unobtainable. [41] But most importantly by being responsive to the circumstances associated with the dual problems of uncertainty and ambiguity which — it is tempting to add, inevitably — surrounds and permeates public planning.[42]

The fourth and final theme concerns these notions of uncertainty and ambiguity. Firstly, public planning is by definition future-oriented, involving consideration and estimates of future levels of activity. But the future is also by definition uncertain and ambiguous — social, economic, political, institutional, administrative, technological, etc. Secondly, the very concepts of uncertainty and ambiguity are neither discrete nor homogeneous concepts. Rather each covers a multiplicity of different forms. Friend and Jessop — later modified in Friend, Power and Yewlett — have identified three kinds of uncertainty:

1   uncertainties attached to the perception of what constitutes the environment outside the political administration of public planning (UE — uncertainties about the operating environment);
2   uncertainties attached to the future intentions of decision-makers in related fields of choice within the political administration of public planning regarding future options (UR — uncertainties about related choices); and

3   uncertainties attached to the nature, perception and impact of value judgements used by decision-makers in the political administration of public planning (UV — uncertainties of policy).[43]

The importance attached to the explicit identification and interpretation of uncertainty is matched by the need to identify and interpret in equally explicit terms the degrees of ambiguity associated with the processes of public planning. Like uncertainty, ambiguity permeates its every facet: in the form of the perception and communication of ideas and concepts, in the formulation of policies and action programmes, in the implementation of policy involving different actors and public agencies, in the assessment of policy outcomes, and in the impact of policy proposals and policy changes on the administration and organisation of public planning itself. The three basic forms of uncertainty outlined by Friend and Jessop may be usefully extended to incorporate these different kinds of ambiguity:

1   ambiguities attached to the perception of what constitutes the environment outside the political administration of public planning (AE — ambiguities about the operating environment);
2   ambiguities attached to the future intentions of decision-makers in related fields of choice within the political administration of public planning regarding future options (AR — ambiguities about related choices); and
3   ambiguities attached to the nature, perception and impact of value-judgements used by decision-makers in the political administration of public planning (AV — ambiguities of policy).

Uncertainties and ambiguities are therefore facets which continuously pervade and impinge upon the very nature and practice of public planning. So strategies which attempt to make reductions in the levels of uncertainty and ambiguity are often central features of 'good currency' practice. But can they be reduced to acceptable if not minimal levels? It is the contention here that the kind of strategies usually employed in attempts to reduce uncertainty and ambiguity are misplaced if not also illusory. The reasoning is straightforward. 'Good currency' approaches to public planning cannot be neatly divorced from the idea of social change and attempts to manipulate and engineer that change. But, as we have argued, this 'ordering of change' is only one side of the equation. What it neglects are the processes of change — 'changing concepts of order' — which are either not the subject of legitimate control by the political administration of public planning or, more importantly, beyond direct or indirect control. In other words, unless it is possible to plan wholly in the blueprint mould then the problems of uncertainties and ambiguities have a certain inevitability attached to them. According to the 'good currency' approach, actions to reduce them usually involve one or more of three broad administrative strategies: (a) to develop better methods and techniques to ensure a better quality of information massing and analysis, the assumption being that 'successful' planning can be equated with more research and quality of information, therefore reducing the uncertainties and ambiguities which surround the operating environment (UE and AE); (b) to extend the coverage and degree of control, the assumption being that 'successful' planning can be equated to the addition, and hence coordination, of a few more key variables, therefore reducing the uncertainties and ambiguities which surround related policy choices (UR and AR); (c) to make explicit the preference function of policy-makers by formalising the decision-making structure, the assumption being that 'successful' planning can be equated to a clearer and more detailed specification of policies, therefore reducing the uncertainties and ambiguities which surround policy (UV and AV).[44]

All three strategies are based on rather dubious assumptions, the most important of which concerns relationships between 'ordering change' and 'changing concepts of order'. Each strategy is more or less exclusively concerned with the former, arguably simpler, part of the equation – the problem of ordering change. The results manifest themselves in very familiar pleas. For example: *'if only* we had more time', '. . . better information', '. . . better techniques', '. . . more resources', '. . . greater control', etc. But time for what? Information on what? Techniques to aid in what tasks? On what would the additional resources be employed? Additional controls over what? What is the subject of serious neglect concerns not so much improvements in the quality of methods, techniques or whatever of 'ordering change' but rather improvements in our understanding of 'changing concepts of order' – of understanding the processes of social change itself. Unless social change is better understood, and made an explicit feature of the processes and practices of public planning, uncertainty and ambiguity have a certain inevitability attached to them. Strategies for their reduction, so long as they are myopically embedded in the 'good currency' idea of planning as primarily the 'ordering of change', can therefore be nothing more than illusory. Or as Wedgewood-Oppenheim et al. conclude:

> . . . however well exposed are the assumptions on which the plan is based the biggest assumption of all and the one with the most far-reaching implications for the planning process, is that all factors not referred to in the plan are either *irrelevant* to the plan or that they will remain *constant.*[45] (italics added)

162

If uncertainty and ambiguity reduction is so inextricably bound-up with the understanding of social change, but that understanding remains at a fairly crude level, is it possible that there might be a more rewarding alternative? An affirmative answer is provided by Popper, at the methodological level, and Dror, at the level of policy-making. For Popper, as was outlined in Chapter Three, uncertainty – and implicitly, ambiguity – is a critical distinguishing feature of a deductive indeterminist methodology. In other words, the notion of error-elimination recognises and proposes strategies to absorb uncertainty and the problems associated with the kinds of uncertainty outlined by Friend and Jessop. For Dror the critical distinguishing feature is precisely this idea of the absorption of uncertainty. It can only usefully be tackled, rather than reduced, by, firstly, explicitly recognising it as a problem which extends beyond the boundaries of 'hard' data and formalised organisational structures. [46] Dror's interpretation may also be similarly extended to the problem of ambiguity – that of ambiguity absorption. In other words both uncertainty and ambiguity – and the manner in which they are treated – are factors which determine the practice of public planning. As such they cannot be treated in 'good currency' terms simply as undesirable side-effects or inevitable spin-off's of attempts to plan 'successfully'. It is this fundamental assumption of 'successful' planning, which lies at the very heart of the 'good currency' approaches, which is questionable.

These four themes – the kinds of problem with which public planning is concerned, the idea of control and control mechanisms, the qualities of public learning, and uncertainty and ambiguity – can be combined and utilised to provide a framework which may indicate how problems emerge into the public arena. The critical, and to some extent determining, variables are those of uncertainty and ambiguity – in particular the institutional perception of uncertainty coupled with the degree of ambiguity surrounding relationships between planned intent, policy implementation, and policy impact. With reference to the schema illustrated in Figure 6.9, an argument can be presented which asserts that problems emerge in one or more of at least six ways:

1   by a structural change in the prevailing set of social values constituting the 'total value system';
2   by a structural change in the prevailing set of tacit political values constituting the 'central value system', and hence a change in the prevailing set of political norms;
3   by a non-perceived mismatch between planned 'intent' and its eventual translation into actual 'impact';

4 by a misperception of what constitutes the 'actual state', and hence its impact on the perception of what constitutes the problem;

5 by a set of policies which, as prescriptive devices, are unworkable, impossible to implement, or which cannot be 'tuned' or assessed; and

6 by an action programme which is either too massive (the 'sledge hammer to crack a nut' syndrome) or too miniscule (the 'drop in the ocean' syndrome) to have a desired level of impact.[47]

Clearly each of these six broad areas is neither a unique nor a mutually exclusive way in which a problem may arise. They only serve to indicate the subtle differences in emphasis which characterise the kind of problems with which public planning is more often than not faced. In this respect it is important to stress once more the 'contextual setting' of these six areas: (a) the all-pervading rôles of uncertainty (UE, UR, UV) and ambiguity (AE, AR, AV); (b) the perception of planning problems as largely and inherently political problems; and (c) the location of public planning at the 'centre' of the total value system, a facet of the central value system.

Six broadly different ways in which problems may emerge into the public arena have therefore been considered. But the notion of 'problem' has been treated as a singular and homogeneous concept — which clearly it is not. So we need to focus attention on what we understand by the term 'problem', and in particular with the kind of problem which constitutes a problem for public planning.

A useful typology of problems, or problem encounters as he refers to them, has been developed by Steiss. [48] He argues that problems cannot be separated from the uncertainty which surrounds them. Indeed it is this uncertainty which is the starting point for the analysis of problem situations. Steiss asserts that the first questions which have to be asked are: is this kind of situation a symptom of a fundamental disorder, a problem, or simply a stray event? Is the problem encounter truly unique or is it one which occurs frequently? Furthermore, does the situation represent a problem which is merely one part of a broader generic problem which has not emerged in this manner before, or is it simply a different version of part of a broader generic problem which has already been identified? According to Steiss this kind of approach distinguishes between four types of fundamental problem encounter:

1 the first occurrence of a generic problem;

2 a recurrent generic problem;

3 a non-recurrent generic problem; and

4 a truly unique problem.

These four types can be structured according to three criteria based on the response necessary to meet those situations: (a) the frequency of occurrence of the problem (high to low), (b) the availability of expertise to identify and tackle the problem (high to low), and (c) the nature of the response (adaptive to innovative). The resulting typology is illustrated in diagrammatic form in figure 6.11:

Fig. 6.11   Typology of problem encounters, after Steiss

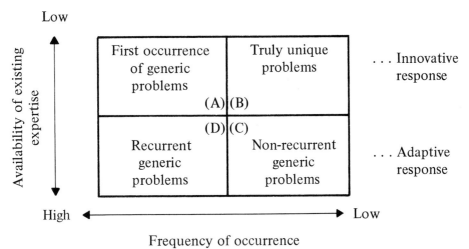

Source: Steiss, 1972

It is clear from this illustration that it is not possible to treat the concepts of problem or solution as homogeneous concepts. At this fairly abstract level we have distinguished between four broadly different kinds of problem — each requiring a substantively different approach to its solution. In fact it is possible to generalise what kind of solution is required for each kind of problem encounter. For example, in situations where the problem is 'new' — the first occurrence of a generic problem (A) or a truly unique problem (B) — the availability of existing expertise is more limited than for situations where the problem is 'old' — a recurrent (D) or non-recurrent generic problem (C). For the latter it is reasonable to suppose that existing procedures and methods might be of direct relevance, albeit with some minor or adaptive modification. In these problem encounter situations it might simply suffice to make a more adaptive response. For the former it is reasonable to suppose that existing procedures

165

and methods will not be of much relevance, even if they were revised or adapted substantially. In these problem encounter situations what is required is the establishment of new procedures and methods, in other words a more innovative response is demanded. Or as Steiss puts it:

> General rules, policies or principles can usually be developed or adapted to deal with generic situations. Once (a) policy has been found, all manifestations of the same generic situation can be handled fairly pragmatically through the *adaptation* of the (policy) to the concrete circumstances of the situation, that is, through *adaptive* decision-making. The unique problem and the first (occurrence) of a generic problem frequently require greater innovation to arrive at a successful solution.[49]

Any situation involving demands for public planning, and hence the mobilising and articulation of a public problem, may be considered within the context of these four types of problem encounter. But it has already been stressed that problems emerge into the political arena in combinations of one or more of at least six ways. This finding, if it correctly interprets the situation, has some interesting implications for the study of the nature and practice of public planning. First, if it is reasonable to conclude that neither the concept of problem encounter nor the concept of public problem can be treated in the singular, then the kinds of problem with which public planning is concerned are therefore a combination of one or more or all of twenty-four possible types at any one point in time — with the concomitant demands on the availability of expertise related to the nature of the response required. These combinations can be illustrated in tabular form, indicating the relative complexity involved with the adoption of a problem-oriented approach to public planning (Figure 6.12).

Secondly, the importance attached to a careful identification, consideration and specification of the problem at issue. As Steiss notes:

> Vague statements . . . lead to vague methods, and success is doubtful. The more a (problem) is extensionalised, the better the classification, and the greater the promise of a successful solution.[50]

> By far the most common mistake . . . is to treat a *generic problem* as if it were a series of unique events. The other extreme, treating every problem incrementally . . . (treating a unique event as if it were just another example of the old problem to which the old rule should be applied) can have equally negative results.[51]

166

Fig. 6.12    Problem encounters and the emergence of political problems

| | First occurrence of generic problems | Truly unique problems | Recurrent generic problems | Non-recurrent problems |
|---|---|---|---|---|
| Structural change in total value system | Frequency of occurrence *high*, availability of existing expertise *low*, *innovative* response demanded | Frequency of occurrence *low*, availability of existing expertise *low*, *innovative* response demanded | Frequency of occurrence *high*, availability of existing expertise *high*, *adaptive* response demanded | Frequency of occurrence *low*, availability of existing expertise *high*, *adaptive* response demanded |
| Structural change in political norms | | | | |
| Mismatch between intent and impact | | | | |
| Misperception of actual state | | | | |
| Misspecification of policies | | | | |
| Misspecification of action programmes | | | | |

Thirdly, the kind of problems with which public planning is concerned are therefore characterised by a tremendous degree of overlap — between cause and effect, effect and cause, between problems and solutions, solutions and problems. These characteristics have been neatly summed up by Stewart as being dominated by:

1   their complexity and interdependence: planning problems are not separate but interrelated, both in the ways in which they are perceived and the manner in which they are dealt with;

2   their dynamic character: planning problems are not static but change and develop over time, both with respect to the ways in which they can be perceived and the manner in which they can be dealt with;

3   their varying scale: planning problems have a number of dimensions — temporal, political, spatial, administrative, historical, technical, etc.; and

4   our general lack of knowledge: perception of planning problems is necessarily imperfect; we can only offer prescriptions and solutions with some understanding of the uncertainty (and ambiguity) which surrounds problems and solutions alike.[52]

This complex state of affairs may be briefly summarised with reference to a schema developed by Hart to account for what he argues is critical to the successful operationalisation of public planning. In this context public planning reflects the interaction of three key factors:

1   the conception on the part of the political administration of public planning as to what constitutes the configuration of underlying order (for example, urban, regional, economic, etc.) and how it is changing;

2   the capability of the political administration to respond to a situation where that configuration is perceived to be in a state of disconnexion; and

3   the priority which the political administration accords to the remedying of that state of disconnexion.[53]

## Notes

[1]   Hall, 1970, op. cit., p. 20; P. Self, 1964, pp. 8–10; see also J. Alden and R. Morgan, 1974, p. 312, for an alternative view.

[2]   Hall, 1970, op. cit., p. 32.

[3]   See Hall, 1970, op. cit., p. 21.

[4]   See Hall, 1970, op. cit., pp. 10–12.

[5]   Hall, 1970, op. cit., p. 32.

[6]   See Hall, 1970, op. cit., pp. 20–4.

[7]   The analysis of the political environment of regional/local planning is similar to that outlined for national/regional planning; that is, a permissive style of planning — a mixture of influence, inducement and limited controls.

[8]   On the TVA see M. Derthick, 1974, pp. 18–45; also Friedmann, 1973b, p. 5.

[9]   See the contributions in Rodwin (ed.), 1969, op. cit.; especially J. Friedmann, 1969.

[10] See in particular A. Hirschman, 1958; especially Hirschman, 1967, op. cit.; also Rodwin (ed.), 1969, op. cit.

[11] For a chronology of UK regional studies, strategies, etc. see the CoI report on regional development, Central Office of Information, 1974, pp. 53–54.

[12] For example, compare the 1963 white papers for the North East (Secretary of State for Industry, Trade and Regional Development, 1963) and Central Scotland (Scottish Development Department, 1963); compare 'Opportunity in the East Midlands' with 'Yorkshire and Humberside Regional Strategy' (East Midlands REPC, 1969; Yorkshire and Humberside REPC, 1970). Compare with Wildavsky's comments on US experience, Wildavsky, 1969, op. cit., and Wildavsky, 1973, op. cit.

[13] See T. Cowling and G. Steeley, 1973 on UK subregional planning; Boyce et al., 1970, op. cit., and Boyce et al., 1972, op. cit., on the US equivalent.

[14] See for example the report by the Trade and Industry Sub-Committee on regional development incentives in the UK (House of Commons, 1973); G. Cameron, 1968, for a British commentary on US experience; also Hall, 1970, op. cit., particularly Chapter 3.

[15] See Hall, 1970, op. cit., pp. 10–32; also the DoE Circular on the preparation of Structure Plans (Department of the Environment, 1974b).

[16] This particular classification is to be found in A. Kuklinski, 1970, p. 269; compare with M. Broady (ed.), 1973 on 'marginal regions'; also J. Friedmann and W. Alonso, 1963, Introduction, especially pp. 3–4: metropolitan, development axes, and depressed regions.

[17] Kuklinski, 1970, op. cit., p. 269.

[18] Kuklinski, 1970, op. cit., p. 270.

[19] Kuklinski, 1970, op. cit., p. 270.

[20] For a 'good currency' interpretation see Alden and Morgan, 1974, op. cit., especially Chapter 9.

[21] For example, see Harvey, 1973, op. cit., Chapter 1; this schizophrenic state punctuates the pioneering work of B. MacKaye, 1928 – a paradox compared with many of his concluding comments:

> it is not for (the planner) to 'make the country,' but it is for him to know the country and the trenchant flows that are taking place upon it. He must not scheme, he must reveal . . . His job is not to wage war – nor stress an argument: it is to 'wage' a determined visualization. (p. 227).

[22] See for example Friedmann, 1969, op. cit., Chapter 7, especially p. 151; also Harvey, 1973, op. cit., pp. 27–36.

[23] F. Perroux, 1950, quoted in H. Brookfield, 1975, pp. 90–3.

[24] See Broady (ed.), 1973, op. cit.; also the review by J. Rhodes, 1972.

[25] Obvious exceptions include conditions of impending war or other catastrophe – short-run factors affecting the very future continuance of a society or culture.

[26] See Vickers, 1965, op. cit., Chapter 1; also Vickers, 1970, op. cit.

[27] See for example Sir G. Vickers, 1973; also Sir G. Vickers, 1974a. Alternative approaches have been suggested by Hart, 1975, op. cit.; also Schon, 1971, op. cit., Chapters 5 and 6; Stewart, 1971, op. cit.; Eddison, 1973, op. cit., refers to these relationships as impact, interaction, and learning.

[28] W. Ashby, 1956.

[29] McLoughlin, 1969, op. cit., pp. 84–9, especially p. 86.

[30] Vickers, 1970, op. cit., Chapter 5; also Vickers, 1965, op. cit., Chapter 2, especially pp. 36–42.

[31] On 'tacit values' see Vickers, 1973, op. cit.; on 'appreciative judgement' see Vickers, 1965, op. cit., Chapter 4, pp. 70–3; on their interconnection see Sir G. Vickers, 1974b, pp. 9–11.

[32] On five different kinds of control see Vickers, 1973, op. cit., especially p. 111; also Shils, 1961, op. cit., on the centre/periphery relationship.

[33] J. Watkins, 1974, p. 389.

[34] Watkins, 1974, op. cit., p. 389.

[35] Wedgewood-Oppenheim et al., 1975, op. cit., p. 3 and p. 61.

[36] Vickers, 1974b, op. cit., pp. 6–8.

[37] Dror, 1968, op. cit., p. 17.

[38] On intent-impact relations see Hart, 1974, op. cit., pp. 27–29; also Hart, 1975, op. cit., Chapter 1 and 6.

[39] See Vickers, 1974b, op. cit.; Hirschman, 1967, op. cit,, Chapter 1, particularly his concept of the 'hiding hand'; on a more conceptual plane see especially Popper, 1963, op. cit., p. 342.

[40] Schon, 1971, op. cit., Chapter 5, pp. 116–79.

[41] Wedgewood-Oppenheim et al., 1975, op. cit., p. 60.

[42] In this context Y. Dror, 1974, makes an interesting distinction between learning and misplaced learning from experience. The latter occurs because of a naive view of policy-making as that concerned with the setting of precedents coupled with a static view of the planning domain. He argues that policy-makers need to displace such subjective notions of certainty with a more objective notion of uncertainty of the kinds suggested by Friend and Jessop, 1969, op. cit., and outlined below.

[43] Friend and Jessop, 1969, op. cit., pp. 88–9; extentionalised in Friend, Power and Yewlett, 1974, op. cit., pp. 30–5.

[44] See Friend and Jessop, 1969, op. cit., pp. 95–7.

[45] Wedgewood-Oppenheim et al., 1975, op. cit., p. 15.

[46] Dror, 1974, op. cit.

[47] Dror, 1974, op. cit., argues that this is the problem of 'critical mass'. If the degree of political commitment, resources, organisational capability, and political action is too great the result may be over-reaction. Conversely, if too miniscule the result may be under-reaction.

[48] A. Steiss, 1972.

[49] Steiss, 1972, op. cit., pp. 128–9.

[50] Steiss, 1972, op. cit., pp. 128–9.

[51] Steiss, 1972, op. cit., pp. 128–9.

[52] J. Stewart, 1974, pp. 2–3.

[53] Hart, 1975, op. cit., Chapter 6; compare with the concepts of importance, organisation, and control suggested by Self, 1972b, op. cit., (see note 10 in the last chapter).

# 7 Regional Planning: A Responsive Approach

This excursion into relationships between regional planning as public planning and the emergence of political problems has inevitably covered a very wide canvas. It has meant a concentration of attention on a select number of key variables – for example, the kinds of problem with which public planning is concerned, notions of control and influence, ideas on public learning, and the importance attached to uncertainty and ambiguity absorption. Implicit in this excursion has been the methodological framework for public planning outlined in Chapter Three. These additional key variables may now be formally appended to that framework to construct a paradigm for the practice of public planning, which may then be extensionalised to form a sketch for a theory of the nature and practice of regional planning, based on the notion of responsiveness.

## A paradigm for public planning: a problematic approach

The building blocks for this proposed paradigm consist of an attempt at a synthetic treatment of those concepts and schema developed in previous chapters with the schema proposed and employed by Boothroyd. In certain respects the work by Boothroyd concerns very similar problems to the kind which have been emphasised in this book. But his arena of concern is substantively different from theories about the political administration of public and regional planning; his arena is the theory and practice of operational research. The two areas of mutual interest are in both cases the distinguishing characteristics, the respective cores, of planning and operations research: (a) the need for an alternative to inductive determinist methodology, and (b) the need for a deductive action-orientation approach in the form of action programmes. The distinguishing characteristics of Boothroyd's approach concern the manner in which four key attributes – theories, proposals, actions and consequences – are structured and given an interdependent meaning. This structure is provided by the idea of action programmes, and the process – the essence of the articulation and mobilising of action – is provided by the notion of articulate reflection.[1] By 'action programmes' Boothroyd means:

... the actions that happen, the theories the actors have about their actions, and the proposals that are made into, within, and out of the action programme ... 'programme' is used with the idea of a continuing process which has an association with human actors ... stability and modifiability ... (It) includes not only the development of theories over time but also the development of proposals and the development of actions ... Action programmes can be born, expand, wither, change direction, revivify, and die.[2]

By 'articulate reflection' — reflective intervention, reflection before action — he argues that:

There are several components ...:
— a set of concepts of possible actions,
— a set of theories about how actions might lead to consequences,
— a set of proposals about which actions and theories and consequences are to be considered and how they are to be regarded.[3]

Boothroyd then presents an heuristic model of 'reflection before action' based on these attributes, which in turn are based on a set of thirteen suppositions, propositions and assumptions:

1   active theories are drawn from a potentially infinite set of latent theories;
2   these theories depend in turn on an infinite cascade of supporting theories;
3   'articulate reflection' includes the act of including and excluding theories from the active set;
4   active proposals are drawn from a potentially infinite range of latent proposals;
5   these proposals depend in turn on an infinite cascade network of supporting proposals;
6   'articulate reflection' includes the act of including and excluding proposals from the active set;
7   actively considered actions are drawn from a potentially infinite set of actions;
8   'articulate reflection' includes the act of including and excluding actions from the active set;
9   'articulate reflection' includes the act of articulating the relation of active theories and active proposals to actions in the action set;
10  these actions lead in turn to a potentially infinite range of consequences — intended and unintended;

174

11 conceptualisation of the consequences of an action is necessarily incomplete;

12 'articulate reflection' includes the act of including and excluding conceptualisable consequences from the actively considered range of consequences;

13 'articulate reflection' includes the act of articulating the relation of active theories, active proposals and active actions to the range of actively considered consequences.[4]

This model of 'reflection before action' as being inherently problematic is summarised by Boothroyd as a perspective which:

> ... is therefore not a fairly tidy one of systems and subsystems, but a somewhat untidier one of action programmes nested and overlapping at all levels of aggregation and disaggregation, with interrelationships in which the degree of consistency between programmes is a matter for discovery, and with changes the important ones of which are discontinuous and represent a greater or lesser upheaval in the theories and proposals.[5]

The manner in which these suppositions have been structured by Boothroyd — that is, between selected and excluded theories, between selected and excluded proposals, between selected and excluded actions, and between selected and excluded consequences — is illustrated in the following diagram (p. 176) (Figure 7.1).

This schema is embedded, indeed immersed, in a problem-oriented, deductive-indeterminist approach directed at the process and practice of operational research. But it is a sufficiently generalised model to be applicable to societal problem solving *per se*. By fusing the notion of 'reflection before action' with the outline for a theory of the processes of public planning developed in Chapter Three — plus the schema for error-controlled regulation developed in the last chapter — we have the foundations for the proposed paradigm for public planning.

For this paradigm the seven 'internal' attributes of the sketch presented in Chapter Three will be taken as axiomatic, together with the six 'internal-external' attributes of the planning domain and the four 'external' dual attributes of social change. Similarly with the seven 'internal' characteristics of the core of the central value system, together with the three 'internal-external' characteristics of the core-periphery interface of the 'central value system', and the one 'external' characteristic of the periphery — the 'total value system'. Likewise with the four distinguishing characteristics and the thirteen suppositions of the 'articulate reflection' schema just

Fig. 7.1  Boothroyd's model of reflection before action[6]

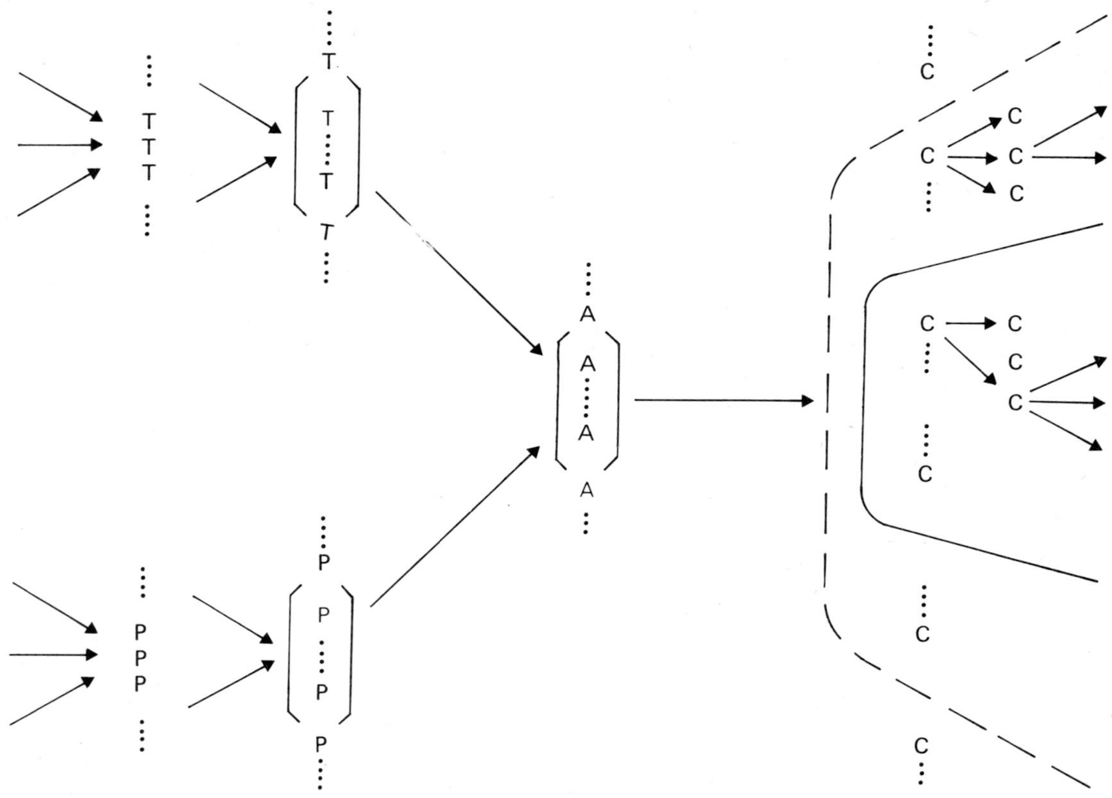

T . . . theories;  P . . . proposals;  A . . . actions;  C . . . consequences

presented. This amorphous collection may be synthesised according to the three facets made use of previously. These consist of the three differentiated contextual settings of public planning based on Shil's notion of centre-periphery relationships: 'internal', 'internal-external', and 'external' settings. This attempt at a synthesis may be illustrated in diagrammatic form (Figure 7.2):

Fig. 7.2   Paradigm for public planning – organising framework

### TOTAL VALUE SYSTEM

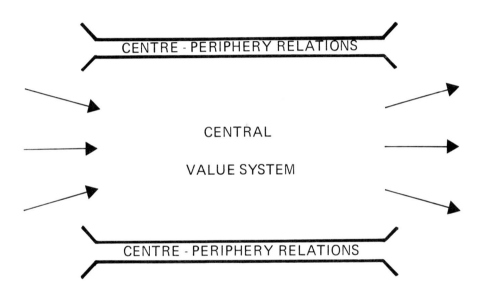

### TOTAL VALUE SYSTEM

This presents the basic organising framework for the proposed paradigm, indicating the fundamental 'centre-periphery' relationships. This diagram may be utilised to map-out the interdependencies of the paradigm more fully (Figure 7.3).

This latter diagram constitutes the proposed structure of the paradigm for public planning, based on a deductive-indeterminist problem-solving methodology – what was referred to earlier as the responsive mode of planning. It is also a methodology which stresses the idea of public planning

177

Fig. 7.3    Paradigm for public planning

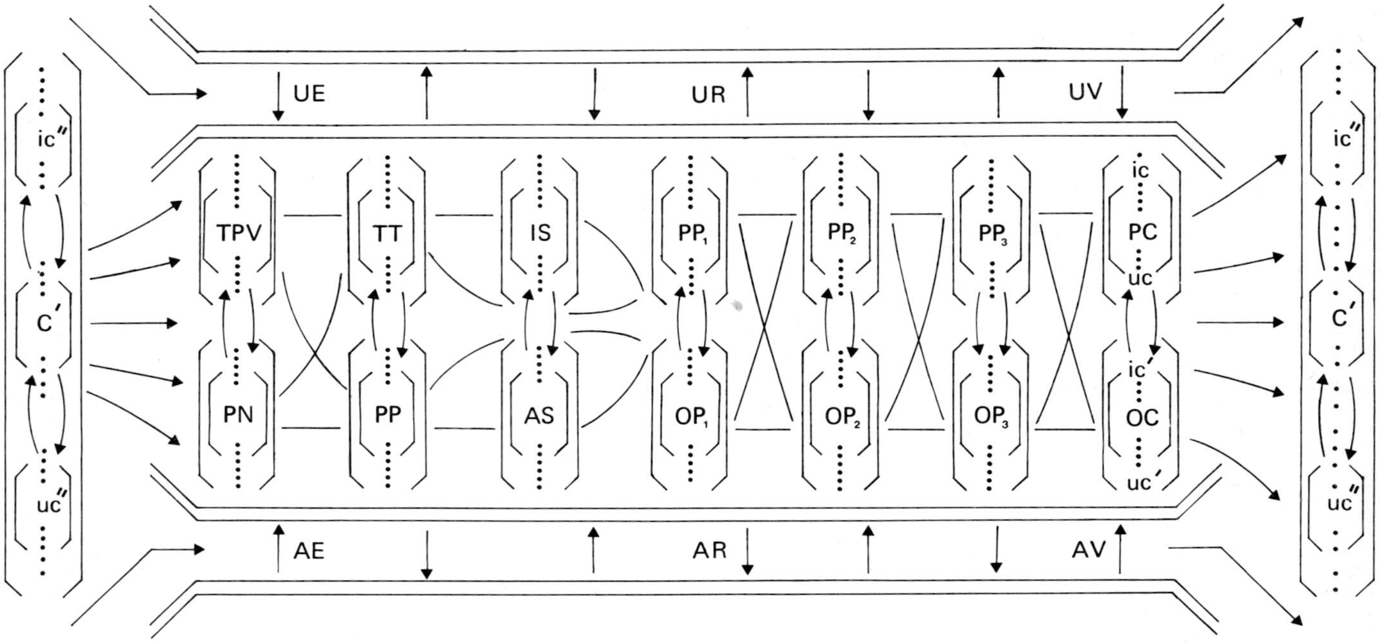

as a fundamental and distinguishing component of political administration itself, embedded as it is in the moulding, manipulation and leverage of political influence. But above all it is a paradigm wedded to action and interaction in the formulation of public policy (intent) and its corollary, implementation (impact).

Of the three components of this paradigm it is the 'internal' component which emphasises most strongly the uncertain and ambiguous nature of public planning. The fact that the political administration's perceptions and constructions of reality (the 'external' component) is necessarily an incomplete one means that it is not possible to include or 'internalise' everything of relevance to any problem situation. By definition, theories, proposals, actions and consequences are in competition for selection, which means that most are excluded by design or by ignorance or by a combination of both. Hence Boothroyd's useful distinction between 'active' and 'latent' sets — which corresponds to the distinction between 'problem continuums' and 'problem areas' made in Chapter Three — by the operation of what may be called the inclusion-exclusion principle of selective perception in public planning.

There are effectively fifteen substantive characteristics of this 'inclusion-exclusion' facet which together constitute the attributes of this 'internal' component of the paradigm, together with nine primary interdependencies which operationalise the schema. These may be considered as a formal statement consisting of seventy-five basic propositions structured as a set of thirty-six relational suppositions. Taken together these may be treated as an abstract formalisation of the ideas contained in this and the previous six chapters.

1   Tacit political values (TPV) are drawn from a potentially infinite set of competing latent political values of the central value system.
    1.1   These values depend in turn on an infinite cascade of supporting values constituting the total value system.
    1.2   The political administration of public planning includes the action of including and excluding political values from the tacit set (political space).

2   Active political norms (PN) are drawn from a potentially infinite set of competing latent political norms of the central value system.
    2.1   These norms depend in turn on an infinite cascade of supporting norms.
    2.2   The political administration of public planning includes the action of including and excluding political norms from the active set (political leverage).

3   The political administration of public planning includes the act of articulating the relation of tacit political values to active political norms, and vice versa, to actions in the problem space – tentative theories, policy proposals, intended state, and actual state (problem articulation).

4   Active tentative theories (TT) are drawn from a potentially infinite set of competing latent tentative theories *vis-à-vis* the social construction of reality.
   4.1   These theories depend in turn on an infinite cascade of supporting theories as to what constitutes the social construction of reality.
   4.2   The political administration of public planning includes the action of including and excluding tentative theories from the active set.

5   Active policy proposals (PP) are drawn from a potentially infinite set of competing latent policy proposals.
   5.1   These proposals depend in turn on an infinite cascade of supporting policy proposals.
   5.2   The political administration of public planning includes the action of including and excluding policy proposals from the active set.

6   The political administration of public planning includes the act of articulating the relation of active tentative theories to active policy proposals and vice versa, to actions in the problem space (problem articulation).

7   Active perceived states (AS) are drawn from a potentially infinite set of competing latent actual states *vis-à-vis* the social construction of reality.
   7.1   These perceived states depend in turn on an infinite cascade of supporting perceived states as to what constitutes the social construction of reality.
   7.2   The political administration of public planning includes the action of including and excluding perceived states from the active set.

8   Active intended states (IS) are drawn from a potentially infinite set of competing latent intended states *vis-à-vis* some notion of a more desirable social construction of reality.
   8.1   These intended states depend in turn on an infinite cascade of supporting intended states as to what constitutes more desirable social constructions of reality.
   8.2   The political administration of public planning includes the action of including and excluding intended states from the active set.

9   The political administration of public planning includes the act of articulating the relation of active actual states to active intended states, and vice versa, to actions in the problem space (problem articulation).

10 These actions lead in turn to a potentially infinite range of problems concerning on the one hand the social construction of reality (exogenous public problems) and on the other the social construction of the political administration of public planning itself (endogenous organisational problems).

11 Active public problems (PP) are drawn from a potentially infinite set of competing latent public problems *vis-à-vis* perceived dysfunction in the social construction of reality.

11.1 These public problems depend in turn on an infinite cascade of supporting public problems as to what constitutes the social construction of reality.

11.2 The political administration of public planning includes the action of including and excluding public problems from the active set.

12 Active organisational problems (OP) are drawn from a potentially infinite set of competing latent organisational problems *vis-à-vis* perceived dysfunction in the organisational capability of public planning.

12.1 These endogenous problems depend in turn on an infinite cascade of supporting endogenous problems as to what constitutes the social construction of the political administration of public planning.

12.2 The political administration of public planning includes the paradoxical action of including and excluding endogenous problems from the active set.

13 The political administration of public planning includes the act of articulating the relation of active exogenous problems to active endogenous problems and vice versa, to actions in the policy space (policy leverage).

14 These actions lead in turn to a potentially infinite range of policies concerning on the one hand attempts to tackle the active public problems (policies), and on the other attempts to tackle the active organisational problems associated with the political administration of public planning itself (organisational policies).

15 Active public policies (PP) are drawn from a potentially infinite set of competing latent public policies.

15.1 These public policies depend in turn on an infinite cascade of supporting public policies.

15.2 The political administration of public planning includes the action of including and excluding public policies from the active set.

16 Active organisational policies (OP) are drawn from a potentially infinite set of competing latent organisational policies.

16.1 These organisational policies depend in turn on an infinite cascade of supporting organisational policies.

16.2 The political administration of public planning includes the action of including and excluding organisational policies from the active set.

17 The political administration of public planning includes the act of articulating the relation of active public policies to active organisational policies and vice versa, to actions in the action space (action programmes).

18 These actions lead in turn to a potentially infinite range of action programmes concerning on the one hand actions to implement active public policies (public programmes) and on the other actions to implement active organisational policies (organisational programmes).

19 Active public programmes (PP) are drawn from a potentially infinite set of competing latent public programmes.

19.1 These public programmes depend in turn on an infinite cascade of supporting public programmes.

19.2 The political administration of public planning includes the action of including and excluding public programmes from the active set.

20 Active organisational programmes (OP) are drawn from a potentially infinite set of competing latent organisational programmes.

20.1 These organisational programmes depend in turn on an infinite cascade of supporting organisational programmes.

20.2 The political administration of public planning includes the action of including and excluding organisational programmes from the active set.

21 The political administration of public planning includes the act of articulating the relation of active public programmes to active organisational programmes and vice versa, to actions in the potential impact space (policy impact).

22 These actions lead in turn to a potentially infinite range of potential consequences – intended and unintended – concerning on the one hand the impact of public policy (potential social change (PC)) and on the other the impact of organisational policy (potential organisational change (OC)).

22.1 Conceptualisation of the potential consequences of these two types of impact is necessarily incomplete.

182

23 Conceptualisable potential intended public policy impacts (ic) are drawn from a potentially infinite set of competing latent intended public policy impacts.

    23.1 These intended public policy impacts depend in turn on an infinite cascade of supporting intended public policy impacts.

    23.2 The political administration of public planning includes the action of including and excluding, *ex ante* fashion, intended public policy impacts.

24 Conceptualisable potential unintended public policy impacts (uc) are drawn from a potentially infinite set of competing latent unintended public policy impacts.

    24.1 These unintended public policy impacts depend in turn on a cascade of supporting unintended public policy impacts.

    24.2 The political administration of public planning includes the action of including and excluding, *ex ante* fashion, unintended public policy impacts.

25 The political administration of public planning includes the act of articulating the relation of conceptualisable potential intended public policy impacts to potential unintended impacts and vice versa, to actions in the impact space of the planning domain (*ex post* policy impact).

26 These actions lead in turn to a potentially infinite range of actual consequences $(C')$ − intended $(ic'')$ and unintended $(uc'')$ − concerning on the one hand the impact of public policy (actual social change), and on the other the impact of organisational policy (actual organisational change).

27 Perceived intended public policy impacts are drawn from a potentially infinite set of competing latent intended public policy impacts.

    27.1 These intended public policy impacts depend in turn on an infinite cascade of supporting intended public policy impacts.

    27.2 The political administration of public planning includes the *ex post* assessment of intended public policy impacts.

28 Perceived unintended public policy impacts are drawn from a potentially infinite set of competing latent unintended public policy impacts.

    28.1 These unintended public policy impacts depend in turn on an infinite cascade of supporting unintended public policy impacts.

    28.2 The political administration of public planning includes the *ex post* assessment of unintended public policy impacts.

29 The political administration of public planning includes the act of articulating the relation of perceived intended public impacts to unintended impacts and vice versa, to actions in the total value system (social change).

30 Conceptualisable potential intended organisational policy impacts are drawn from a potentially infinite set of competing latent intended organisational policy impacts $(ic')$.

30.1 These intended organisational policy impacts depend in turn on an infinite cascade of supporting intended organisational policy impacts.

30.2 The political administration of public planning includes the action of including and excluding, *ex ante* fashion, intended organisational policy impacts.

31 Conceptualisable potential unintended organisational policy impacts are drawn from a potentially infinite set of competing latent unintended organisational policy impacts $(uc')$.

31.1 These unintended organisational policy impacts depend in turn on an infinite cascade of supporting unintended organisational policy impacts.

31.2 The political administration of public planning includes the action of including and excluding, *ex ante* fashion, unintended organisational policy impacts.

32 The political administration of public planning includes the act of articulating the relation of conceptualisable potential intended organisational policy impacts to potential unintended impacts and vice versa, to actions in the impact space of the planning domain (*ex post* policy impact).

33 Perceived intended organisational policy impacts are drawn from a potentially infinite set of competing latent intended organisational policy impacts.

33.1 These intended organisational policy impacts depend in turn on an infinite cascade of supporting intended organisational policy impacts.

33.2 The political administration of public planning includes the *ex post* assessment of intended organisational policy impacts.

34 Perceived unintended organisational policy impacts are drawn from a potentially infinite set of competing latent unintended organisational policy impacts.

34.1 These unintended organisational policy impacts depend in turn on an infinite cascade of supporting unintended organisational policy impacts.

34.2 The political administration of public planning includes the *ex post* assessment of unintended organisational policy impacts.

35 The political administration of public planning includes the act of articulating the relation of perceived intended organisational policy impacts to unintended impacts and vice versa, to actions in the central value system (organisational change).

36 The political administration of public planning includes the act of articulating the relation of tacit political values, active political norms, active tentative theories, active policy proposals, active perceived and intended states, active public and organisational problems, active public and organisational policies, active public and organisational programmes, and potential and actual intended and unintended public and organisational policy impacts of the 'centre' — public planning — to their respective political-, problem-, action-, and impact-, spaces in the central value system and vice versa, to actions in the 'periphery' — the total value system.

These seventy-five organising relationships therefore constitute the essence of the structure for the proposed paradigm of public planning illustrated in Figure 7.3. This paradigm may be distinguished by the emphasis it places on the nature of public planning as problem-oriented, theory-incorporating, dynamic, process-oriented, uncertain, ambiguous, continuously interacting and constantly iterating between problems and solutions, conjecture and refutation, theory and practice, intent and impact — within the context of the forging of public policies in the political area and the implementation of public programmes in the planning domain. Not only does it differentiate between and stress relationships within the 'centre' and the 'periphery' of the political administration of public planning, but it also articulates a distinction between exogenous public problems, policies and programmes, and endogenous organisational problems, etc. The importance of this distinction is fundamental to the problematic paradigm — the idea of consequences of actions, and in particular a differentiation between intended and unintended consequences. But the distinction does not end there because we have differentiated between perceived problems of the total value system and those facing the administration concerned with the tackling of those problems. The implications are worthy of note: not only is public planning explicitly concerned with (a) the understanding and accounting for interconnectedness of problems and solutions (impact and intent) at three levels — 'internal', 'internal-external' and 'external', but equally with (b) the unintended effects associated with policy impacts at those three levels, and also (c) relationships between the interconnectedness of impact and intent and unintended effects at those same three levels.[7] This view of action *qua* public planning as being inherently problematical has been admirably summed-up by Boothroyd:

> It leaves behind the magical belief that somewhere we can find a programme which can provide us with true theories and correct proposals. It pushes sponsoring programmes and intervening programmes *away* from the expectation of certainty toward an expectation of *permanent conjecture, enquiry, review and innovation.*[8] (Italics added.)

**Sketch for a theory of regional planning: a responsive approach**

The idea was touched upon at the beginning of this excursion into the realms of a paradigm for public planning that this paradigm could in turn be extensionalised to provide an outline for a theory of the nature and practice of public planning at the regional level. The building blocks for this sketch consist of an attempt at a synthesis of the concepts developed thus far (in the form of the paradigm just outlined) with those of relevance employed by Popper, Friedmann and Vickers.

That public planning in the context of this paradigm is concerned with change is axiomatic. Likewise that it is concerned with the understanding, influencing, guiding and controlling of that change through institutional arrangements and concrete action programmes. We have already made a case for public planning as a catch-all for different types of government activity and intervention of different kinds and scales in pursuit of different tasks. For example, national defence planning, public expenditure planning, manpower planning, and regional planning. Each was considered a facet of generic public planning. The principal distinguishing characteristic of regional planning was seen to be its concern with space, and in particular with the configuration of spatial relationships within and between different political administrations within subnational and supra-urban contexts of problem regions and regional problems. However, it would be too simple a conclusion to present a sketch of a theory for regional planning which consisted of appending those distinguishing features of regional planning to the paradigm of public planning. For, as Friedmann notes, it is necessary to establish a more formal linkage between the separately treated but clearly interconnected theories of social change (including intervention processes such as public planning) and this spatial organisation. In fact Friedmann has argued a succinct and persuasive case for a kind of regional planning which incorporates this idea of a spatial dimension in public planning:

Society is spatially organized in the sense that human activities and social interactions are space-forming as well as space-contingent. It follows that as a society undergoes development, its spatial structure will be transformed, but the development process will also be influenced by the existing patterns of spatial relation and the dynamic tensions that result from them. *Space is used here in the non physical sense of a field of forces* (e.g. energy levels, decision-making power, communications) . . .[9]

Friedmann makes the point that if regional planning is to be more than a simple descriptive theory of a geographical interpretation of the physical manifestion of public policies ('top down' planning) or a geographical description of the arrangement of the physical location of those policies ('bottom up' planning), then it must incorporate into its processes and structures spatial theories of the development process. In other words, theories accounting for social change which have an explicit spatial dimension – theories which seek to increase our understanding of (a) the spatial ordering of social change, and (b) changing concepts of spatial order. These or any other theories of spatial development must, according to Friedmann, be capable of fulfilling three basic conditions:

1   they must be able to account for spatial development as a set of related social processes;
2   they must be capable of being expressed in terms of a single unifying concept to which all spatial development processes may be explicitly related; and
3   they must be able to encompass all relevant phenomena in a context of systemwide relationships.[10]

It is just this kind of theory which Friedmann has attempted to postulate – what he refers to as 'a general theory of polarised development'. Central to Friedmann's thesis is the dual relationships between social change and spatial development. It is therefore a dynamic emphasis which he argues for – a general theory of spatial development.[11]

So what constitutes the set of related social processes which may account for spatial development? To posit some suggestions which might yield insights into this question we have to refer back to the basic principles underlying the problematic approach to consider the problem of change and development. We have already outlined Popper's conception of societal problem-solving, together with his notion of 'plastic' control. It is the combination of these two ideas which provides a useful starting point to tackle the problem of social change in its more positive rôle – that of social development.[12]

It is the concept of plastic control which is in many respects the catalyst between problem-solving activity and an evolutionary perspective of development and change. Briefly reiterating Watkins' three suppositions regarding organisms and their controlling and controlled mechanisms, we may begin to outline Popper's approach to the idea of evolutionary development: (a) an organism comprises a complex of plastic controls, (b) an organism is a polycentric system in which controls operate simultaneously at various levels, and in which a control may shift from one locus to another; (c) despite this polycentricity, we can roughly distinguish an organisms 'central' control system from its 'executive' parts. Watkins refers to this structure as a quasi-hierarchical system of plastic controls.[13]

It is with respect to the relational nature of the central control system to the executive parts of an organism which paves the way for an account of evolutionary change.[14] The central control system is responsive to changing situations occurring in the executive parts, and vice versa — what Watkins calls 'give and take'. There are two ways in which change can take place within an organism: (a) change in the central control system, leading to some measure of corresponding change in the executive parts, or (b) change in the executive part(s), leading to some measure of corresponding change in the central control system. In the former case, if — as Watkins refers to it — a prima facie favourable mutation occurs within the central control system such that control-skill is enhanced (control-skill outruns executive-power), the result could be advantageous to the organism. Should this also result in some increase in executive-power brought about by mutation then, as Watkins puts it, the organism would be altogether more powerful and effective. In the latter case, however, that is if a favourable mutation occurs within an executive part — a corresponding increase in the organisms executive-power with no change in the central control system (executive-power outruns control-skill) — then the organism is more likely to destabilise and hence, potentially anyway, disintegrate. For evolutionary progress the implications are clear:

1    favourable mutations in the central control system are the distinguishing characteristics of evolutionary development; and
2    mutations in the executive parts are improvements only if they are in parallel with prior control developments.

In terms of social development it is possible to abstract from Popper's account of organismic evolution by simply switching terminology, thus retaining his basic explanatory powers and original meanings. Firstly, the concepts of organism, plastic control, control-skill, and executive-power may all be usefully retained in the sense with which Popper outlined them. Secondly, the idea of the 'central control system' of an organism may be considered synonymous with the notion of what has been referred to as the central value system, and in the context of public planning its political administration. Thirdly, the idea of 'executive parts' may be considered at two levels of synonymous meaning: (a) at the level of the 'internal' components of the political administration of public planning itself, and (b) at the broader level associated with the 'external' components of the planning domain (those key attributes of the total value system over which public planning attempts to exert control and influence). Finally, the concept of 'favourable mutations' may be considered synonymous with Boothroyd's interpretation of the qualities associated with a problematic approach to methodology — permanent conjecture, enquiry, review and innovation.

The key contructs of Popper's account of evolution in organisms can therefore be broadly reconciled with the notion of social development considered to be integral features of both Friedmann's tentative theory and the paradigm outlined earlier. The connections are provided via Dahrendorf for the former, and Shils and Dahrendorf for the latter. [15]

In fact it is the distinction between Shils notion of 'centre' and 'periphery', in terms of the social value system, that can be seen to tie-in with Dahrendorf's idea of 'authority-dependency' relations as cornerstones for a conflict theory approach to a theory of social change. But whereas Shils argues against the notion of a spatial configuration of 'centre-periphery' relations as a basic organising device or determinant, Friedmann injects Dahrendorf's 'model' with an explicit spatial dimension. To Dahrendorf's formalised statement of a summary of coercion theory — consisting of thirty-nine basic propositions in the form of a set of four relational suppositions [16] — Friedmann has added to and extensionalised. His synthetic statement — consisting of 124 basic propositions — is structured in the form of a set of five relational suppositions labelled as (a) development as innovation, (b) the conditions of innovation, (c) innovation, power, and authority in spatial systems, (d) authority-dependency relations in a spatial system, and (e) polarised development in a hierarchy of spatial systems.[17]

Friedmann's 'general theory' has not been the subject of universal acclaim by, or even seen to be of especial interest to, many public planners; indeed it has been the subject of a good deal of criticism of one form or another. But it is this author's contention that much of what has passed for criticism has emanated from one disciplinary source and has been based largely on a misunderstanding associated with Friedmann's original claims for it. These criticisms have emanated largely from economists, and have in the main concerned comments about the economic, or rather lack of, a substantive formal economic thrust to his argument. [18] The validity of these comments, however, must be set into the context of Friedmann's original formulation — which is a claim for a 'general theory'. In fact he has not provided a theory in the accepted sense of that word at all. What he has provided, and which at this stage of the development of social enquiry is arguably of much greater significance, corresponds to what Dahrendorf perceived to be the utility of his own original statement:

> It may appear premature, if not overambitious, to have used the word 'theory' in connection with the approach outlined ... I have suggested a number of premises, concepts, models, and empirical generalizations which appear to have a bearing on problems of social conflict and social change, but these suggestions do not display a degree of formalization and rigidity that would warrant calling them a theory.[19]

Indeed, as most critics have pointed out, Friedmann's theory is not capable of operationalisation in the accepted sense; that is, for example in the context of economics, of formal statements corresponding to a set of mathematically formulated equations which can be opened-up to rigorous analysis, refutation and reformulation. But Friedmann appears to have purposefully presented his claim for a general theory from the perspective of a narrow single disciplinary base — that of economics. As Brookfield points out, this is undoubtedly the result of personal commitment to the integration of theory and practice in the economics of development, of which the Ciudad Guayana experience appears to have had an instrumental impact. His general dissatisfaction with the state of planning theory and regional economic development theory — and a perceived 'ideal-real' gap between what theory predicted and what was the resultant — made for a reassessment of their component and interconnected parts, and hence to demands for the development of a general theory of development. [20] It is in the formal expression of this claim for a general theory that has led to further basic misunderstandings. The contextual setting within which he originally presented his case was that of economics, in the form of a broad critique of classical location theory, spatial organisation theory, and regional growth theory. And yet the alternative he painted was more comprehensive in terms of coverage, and yet shallower with respect to an equivalent explicit single-discipline formulation; stronger with respect to explanatory power, and yet weaker in terms of an equivalent simple single-discipline operational model. In other words the result

190

was a perceived mismatch between what was the latent intention and what was actually achieved in terms of impact on the public planning fraternity. Overgeneralising, Friedmann's claim for a general theory was criticised mainly by economists because it appeared that it was being directed almost exclusively at them. This seems to have had some unfortunate unintended consequences, because it came to be assumed by non-economists to be principally an economic theory. The fact that it was relatively harshly treated by economists therefore led to a general view that it was too abstract and not capable of being made operational or applied in any accepted planning sense. That this was not Friedmann's original intention is manifestly clear.

Having broadly set-the-scene with respect to this 'general theory' – as being more in sympathy with 'a number of premises, concepts, models, and empirical generalizations' than a fully worked-out theory – we are in a position to present Friedmann's thesis from a perspective which is in many respects substantively different from the 'good currency' view associated with it. This perspective is principally from the public planning point of view, which incorporates the economic dimension – not vice versa. Friedmann-as-economist needs to be separated from and subsumed within Friedmann-as-planner.

A central theme of Friedmann's thesis, articulated in most of his more recent writings, concerns the interaction between analysis and action as the two principal components of a single process of what he calls 'societal guidance systems' (including public planning). Complimentary to this theme is the idea of social development ($\equiv$ progress) as a process of social innovation. The synthesis is completed by forging a link between innovation and its guidance – what he refers to as transactive planning: 'A style applicable to both *allocative* and *innovative planning* in which processes of *mutual learning* are closely integrated with an organized capacity and willingness to act'.[21]

It is within this schema that Friedmann sets his heavily annotated 'general theory', or rather five – what has been referred to as – relational suppositions which, when taken together, may be seen as a formalised statement of Friedmann's thesis.

The first supposition set – the platform for his thesis – concerns the fundamental idea of development as innovation.[22] Here he distinguishes between complex development and simple growth, arguing that the latter may be subsumed within the former but does not constitute a prerequisite for development in and of its own volition. Development is therefore historical progress, a temporal succession of social and culture change transformed by the forging and diffusion of epochal innovations (after

Kuznets). These innovations can be technical and institutional — social, economic, political and cultural — and include borrowing and imitation. Development may be seen therefore as a discontinuous, cumulative process — the merging of discrete innovations through time — which attracts and encourages the formation of new values and attitudes and hence further innovation. Societies which fail to achieve such transformations become either 'arrested' or begin to 'degenerate'.

The second supposition set stresses the idea of the process of this innovation in society — the conditions of innovation. [23] Here Friedmann distinguishes between invention and innovation, the former being the conceiving of new ideas whereas the latter concerns the perception, introduction, and diffusion of them. Innovation also requires some element of guidance, an innovative agent (individuals or institutions) which organises the resources and assumes the risks of failure. He argues that there are six basic conditions associated with the likelihood of innovations being generated: (a) the relationship between the number of problems resistant to solution by traditional means and the effective demand for their resolution; (b) the proximity of previously unconnected 'mental frames of reference' in the 'communication field' and the probability associated with their possible confrontation, exchange of information and connection; (c) the capacity of the existing social system to absorb proposed innovations without itself undergoing major structural change: at one extreme are hierarchical, centrally controlled social systems (Type 1) which have a lower capacity for generating and absorbing innovations than the other — non-hierarchical, multi-centric, horizontally integrated social systems (Type II). (Friedmann considers these two types are by no means mutually exclusive; indeed, he argues a case for their complimentarity — 'vertical' type I leadership, central information, and certain conflict-resolving functions can be integrated with 'lateral' type II functions.); (d) the frequency of innovative 'personality traits' in a society at any one point in time; (e) the ability to organise and guide resources (human and material) sufficient for the process of effective innovation from initial ideas to ultimate adoption to diffusion; and (f) the level and kind of social rewards offered by society for innovative activity.

Friedmann supplements these six basic conditions of innovation by setting them within a specific territorially organised kind of social system — a spatial system (in the non-physical sense). He then proceeds to structure this kind of spatial system by arguing that, historically, the seed-beds for innovations have been in the large and rapidly growing urban areas — and cites ten further conditions which emphasise the relationship: (i) the pressures to resolve urban problems; (ii) the inadequacy of traditional

192

approaches and their inability to solve them; (iii) the constant search for new methods and solutions; (iv) the relatively heavy flows of information between urban areas and the rest of the spatial system; (v) the relatively high potential for interaction between different 'mental frames of reference'; (vi) the loose, complex social structure of urban areas and their concomitant diffused centres of power; (vii) the propagation of creative personality types in and their attraction to urban areas; (viii) the provision of opportunities conducive to innovation; (ix) the reinforcement of creative responses to new situations by an extensive rewards system; and (x) the institutionalisation requirements associated with the process of innovation through time.

The third supposition set concerns four relationships between innovation and Dahrendorf's power-authority relations in the territorially organised social system — innovation, power and authority in spatial systems. [24]

First, the concept of power itself: the exercise of a measure of autonomy in decisions over a given environment and to have the ability to implement those decisions. Successful innovation, according to Friedmann, tends to increase the potential power of innovators. This innovation may be realised when the potential power inherent in it is institutionalised and accepted as legitimate. Second, the concept of authority as socially legitimate power. Innovators may seek to translate a potential gain in power into a form of legitimate authority, since society rewards innovation with esteem and a certain measure of authority. In some instances, however, this reward of authority may be in conflict with the existing pattern of authority élites, leading to the formation of potential counter-élites. Third, the idea of authority-dependency relations within a territorially organised social system. Friedmann proposes, following Dahrendorf, that the presence of centres of authority presumes the presence of centres of dependency. Moreover, that spatial systems are integrated through this lattice-like structure of authority-dependency relations, relations which are maintained partly by a perceived legitimacy of the relation itself and partly by means of coercion. Finally, the repercussions associated with attempts at conflict resolution between established authority and, what Friedmann refers to as, 'innovating counter-élites'. This process of conflict resolution is a continuum which can have four types of outcome: suppression, neutralisation, cooptation or replacement. At one extreme suppression implies that existing authority has the powers of inclusion and exclusion with respect to internalising an innovation or conflict situation. Neutralisation is one step removed from suppression. Existing authority does not exert the power of outright suppression, but it can nevertheless include or exclude certain key attributes with respect to internalising an innovation or conflict situation — for example, by simply 'managing' the innovation. Both suppression and neutralisation effectively excludes innovatory counter-élites from assuming access to authority. Cooptation is one step removed from neutralisation.

Existing authority can include or exclude only in a more limited fashion. Internalisation is attempted by coopting into existing authority the offending counter-élites, allowing their innovations to be adopted but in a more restricted form than was perhaps originally intended by them. Counter-élites therefore exercise some measure of authority, but more or less within the framework provided by existing authority. Replacement lies at the other end of the continuum, and implies that counter-élites replace existing authority by substituting their own. Here existing authority has no powers of inclusion or exclusion with respect to internalisation.

The fourth supposition set of Friedmann's thesis consists of an attempt to expand on the authority-dependency relations theme — authority-dependency relations in a spatial system. [25] There are three basic components to this set. First, the idea that development is concentrated in a relatively small number of centres of change. Innovations tend to spread outward from these centres to those areas where the probability of potential interaction is correspondingly lower. Second, these relationships may be distinguished with respect to their capacities for engineering such innovations. Friedmann labels the centres of change 'core regions', and the rest of the spatial system the 'periphery':

> ... core regions are territorially organized subsystems of society which have a high capacity for innovative change; peripheral regions are subsystems whose development path is determined chiefly by core region institutions with respect to which they stand in a relation of substantial dependency. [26]

Friedmann thus translates an aspatial concept of authority-dependency relations into a formal spatial context that is focussed on the idea of dominant core regions. Peripheral regions may be identified by their relations of dependency to core regions, where core and periphery constitute a complete spatial system.

Finally, Friedmann makes four major propositions concerning relationships between core regions and peripheral regions: (a) core regions impose a condition of dependency on the part of peripheral regions, resulting from the penetration of institutions from the 'centre' which are in turn controlled by the authority of the 'centre'; (b) this process of domination tends to be self-reinforcing, which may be ascribed to six major 'feedback effects': (i) a dominance effect, a steady weakening of the strength of the economies of the periphery by a net transfer of factors to the core, (ii) an information effect, the increase in potential interaction within a core region resulting from the change in population, etc., (iii) a psychological effect, the creation of opportunities and conditions favourable to continued innovation in core regions, (iv) a modernisation effect, the transformation of social values and institutions leading to greater acceptance and conformity with change through innovation, (v) linkage effects, the idea that innovation breeds innovation, creating demands for additional services, etc., (vi) production effects, the exploitation by innovators of a temporary monopoly position, and the creation of an attractive reward structure; (c) the introduction of core region innovations into peripheral regions supplements information flows to those regions, further reinforcing core region dominance. Sustained contact with core regions tends to either arouse frustrations and hostility, leading to potential conflict with the 'centre' over the powerlessness of the 'periphery', or stimulate emigration to core regions, hence to be subsumed within the established structures of existing authority-dependency relations; (d) if this kind of spatial alienation results in open hostility to the 'centre', core region élites may move to implement a policy of limited decentralisation — thus creating an environment conducive to the emergence of embryo core regions.

The fifth and final supposition set is an attempt to provide a structure for these core-periphery, authority-dependency relations — polarised development in a hierarchy of spatial systems. [27] Friedmann outlines four basic components to this set. First, core regions are located in a nested hierarchy of spatial systems. Second, whether or not a particular territorially organised subsystem constitutes a spatial system is dependent on the pattern of its internal relations. If such a subsystem can be shown to be dominant with respect to the actions of other external subsystems, then a spatial system of core-periphery relations may be identified. Third, any particular spatial system identified in this way may have more than one core region, the territorial extent tending to vary with the size and scope of that spatial system of which it forms a part. Finally, Friedmann suggests five major propositions concerning the primary rôle of core regions vis-à-vis the development of spatial systems: (a) core regions organise the dependence of their respective peripheries through networks of supply, market and administrative areas; (b) for any spatial system, a loose hierarchy of core regions may be identified corresponding approximately to their respective functional importance within that particular spatial system; (c) core regions transmit impulses of innovations to the peripheries they dominate; (d) the self-reinforcing character of core region growth will tend to be beneficial for the development of the particular spatial system up to a certain point. Unless either the positive effects of core region growth can be accelerated or the peripheral dependency reduced or both, the spatial system will become dysfunctional. Growing political and social tension between core and periphery are likely to drain core region strength and reduce its capacity for further development; (e) the probability of innovation is a function of the probability of information exchange of a given spatial system. This relationship will induce the spread of existing core regions, a weakening of the hierarchical order, conditions favourable to the emergence of embryo core regions in the periphery, and the incorporation of parts of the periphery into one or more core regions of the spatial system.

This completes the outline of Friedmann's attempt to construct a general theory of polarised development. Summarising, it concerns interdependencies within and between development and innovation, the conditions for innovation, power and authority, authority and dependency, within a hierarchical framework of territorially organised social (spatial) systems. Although it is couched in a structural-functionalist style, it is nonetheless a pioneering piece of work in the field of planning theory. As Brookfield notes, it represents one of the closest approaches to a single general theory thus far developed. [28] However, it is this author's contention that, had it not been presented as the filling to a pie called economic development, its profound richness would have resulted in an impact considerably greater than has so far been achieved, and been recognised for the important contribution to social inquiry which it clearly merits.

In this respect three further points can be made which have implications for the operationalising of this model. Firstly, Friedmann's overt commitment to the idea of innovation and its crucial rôle in social development. As Brookfield stresses, [29] the precursor to the derivation of this attempt at a general theory was the notion of a disequilibrium explanation for national and regional economic development. In particular, the cumulative causation thesis propounded by Myrdal and the unbalanced growth thesis suggested by Hirschman, both published in the late 'fifties. Friedmann's original attempt at the development of a core-periphery model may therefore be seen as a logical extension of these two approaches, grounded as they are in economics, but translated into a formal spatial context. This first attempt was thus an explicit economic formulation of a regionally aggregated spatial disequilibrium model. Writing in the early 1960s Friedmann argued that:

196

... centres not only grow so rapidly as to create problems of an entirely new order, but they also act as suction pumps, pulling in the more dynamic elements from the more static regions. The remainder of the country is thus relegated to a second-class, peripheral position. It is placed in a quasi-colonial relationship to the center, experiencing net outflows of people, capital, and resources, most of which redound to the advantage of the center where economic growth will tend to be rapid, sustained, and cumulative.[30]

The subsequent experience of his attempts to relate this tentative theory to practice in the Venezuelan context resulted in a move away from the original formulation of a narrow economic base to a more general approach as to what constituted the underlying 'causes' of spatial development. An understanding of social change was one strand, social interaction the other. The link was provided by the Kuznets thesis of epochal innovation. However, the interpretation of Friedmann's use of the concept of innovation, emanating from Kuznets, is – as Brookfield lucidly illustrates [31] – based on the work of Schumpeter. In particular, the idea that it is not possible to explain economic change solely in terms of previous economic conditions, but rather from the preceding total situation. Also that the essence of development concerns qualitative differences in society brought about by the replacement of old with new combinations of production, engineered by entrepreneurs. The parallels with Friedmann's interpretation are obvious:

> Schumpeter's entrepreneurs are the innovators while and where they are innovating, and this only ... Entrepreneurs respond to opportunity, and this tends to occur in waves after one surge of innovation has been absorbed or as new demands are created by some new situation ... hence development is jerky ...[32]

Secondly, Friedmann's use of the concept of space. It is clear from his idea of a 'territorially organised social system' as a 'spatial system' – coupled with the emphasis on 'interaction' in a 'communications field' – that he is not referring to the geographic concept of space as the primary organising context. Rather he refers to space in the non-physical sense of a 'field of forces'. But he does make explicit use of physical space by way of reference to the rôle of urban areas in the development process. The difference is a difference in emphasis. Physical space is used by Friedmann in the sense of a description of the result of the tensions created by the space-forming and space-contingent nature of social interaction – not its cause.

The final point concerns an observation made by Brookfield in assessing the contextual history of Friedmann's contribution to development studies. It is simply that this kind of centre-periphery model, wedded as it is to a conflict-coercion theory of social change, constitutes as much a theory of revolutions as one of spatial development. This appears to be borne out by Friedmann himself in his concluding sentence: '. . . the transformation of authority-dependency patterns in spatial systems is a fundamental condition of development . . .'[33]

It is therefore perhaps of interest to note that, writing in 1971, he appears to not only broadly concur with this observation but accord it a definite status. His contemporary working definitions of 'planning', 'societal guidance', and 'guidance system' correspond very closely indeed to the Marxian concept of praxis: as Giddens puts it, the union of theory and practice, the conjunction of theoretical understanding and practical political activity — the integration of the emergent transformations potential in history with a programme of practical action which actualises that change. [34] Or as Friedmann describes what he means by, respectively, planning, societal guidance and guidance system:

> The process by which a scientific and technical knowledge is joined to organized action. Planning forms a critical subprocess of societal guidance.[35]

> The processes by which the incidence, rate, and direction of change in society are controlled. The exercise of societal guidance may be intentional or not, and its results may be both favourable and unfavourable.[36]

> The pattern of institutional arrangements . . . that guides the processes of change in society. A 'complete' guidance system involves elements of command, policies, corporate, and participant planning.[37]

This idea of praxis was made an explicit feature of Friedmann's work in a review of Faludi's text on planning theory in late 1974. In that review he takes Faludi to task not only for adopting a rational model for the underpinning of his theory, but also for neglecting the importance of 'action-implementation' relationships — a natural outcome of accepting the premises of a mode of planning which emphasises decisions rather than action, Friedmann argues. He continues:

> Implementation is a form of action, and planning becomes joined to ongoing actions in such a way that any distinction between them must ultimately become artificial. Where this occurs, as it does in all

successful actions — actions which are journeys of exploration into the future — planning becomes the highest form of human praxis. It is praxis which must become the starting point for a reconstruction of social planning and the theory underlying it.[38]

Friedmann's collation of premises, concepts, models and empirical generalisations — his tentative theory of spatial development — may be taken together with the accompanying implications, as one of the four principal cornerstones on which a sketch for a theory of regional planning may be based. It provides an interpretation of the territorial organisation of the social system which is broadly in sympathy with the other three cornerstones: the deductive process of responsiveness, the schema for error-controlled regulation, and the paradigm for public planning. In fact the proposal to outline such a sketch may be seen as an attempt to forge a synthesis from these four cornerstones.

A point of entry can be made by — paradoxically — keeping these four cornerstones initially separate, and to focus attention on the public and problem-oriented nature of regional planning. This can be facilitated by way of Steiss's typology of 'problem encounters' as outlined in the last chapter. In the context of this typology, four distinguishing characteristics were identified: (a) the idea of different types of problem, (b) their frequency of occurrence, (c) the availability of existing expertise to tackle them, and (d) the nature of the response demanded. Steiss argues that it is the manner in which these four characteristics interact and interconnect which makes them an important feature of the nature and practice of public planning. For the purposes of a sketch for a theory of regional planning, the key characteristic concerns the interdependency between types of problem and responses to them. This interdependency implies that low frequency occurrences of problem encounters require a substantively different treatment and response from those whose frequency is more common. The difference is one between an adaptive response and an innovative response on the part of the political administration of public planning, in this case at a regional level. Between the political realisation that a problem exists and the implementation of tentative solutions is to be found this responsive mechanism.

There appear to be at least seven reasonably differentiated facets of responsiveness which — potentially at least — might be capable of providing a coherent framework for a responsive approach to a theory of regional planning. These seven facets consist of a sequence of processes of action which when taken together constitute integral parts of a deductive responsive approach to regional planning. This sequence consists of:

1   the broad type of response envisaged by the political administration;
2   the fundamental objective of the political administration's response;
3   the basic political and administrative form which the response takes;
4   the method of response by the political administration;
5   the political and administrative orientation of the response;
6   the explicit responsive action which the political administration proposes; and
7   the performance of the responsive action.

This sequence may be formally translated into the idea of *problem encounter* ⟶ *responsive mechanism* ⟶ *responsive action* by structuring it along the lines of a conceptual framework for the study of planning proposed by John Friedmann in 1967. [39] That framework draws on the distinction between forms of planning and styles of planning, as well as their respective underlying assumptions, objectives and characteristics. The critical assumption on which he based this framework – and one which is shared in this volume – is that societal guidance *qua* planning encompasses both the maintenance of and change in social systems. Armed with this assumption Friedmann asserts that implicit and sub-sumed within it are two apparently diammetrically-opposed fundamental objectives as to the *raison d'être* of planning itself. The two objectives are, respectively, (a) to maintain a given system in a state of equilibrium or balance and (b) to induce major changes in that systems performance. And moreover, to drive this apparent paradox really home, to do both simultaneously. This paradox, argues Friedmann, makes for two very different forms of planning activity: one which is geared to ensuring system-maintenance – allocative planning – the other to the inducing of system-change – innovative planning. The link between Friedmann and Steiss may be forged through the notions of adaptation and innovation, and hence between Friedmann's framework and Steiss's typology.

Two reasonably distinct kinds of responsiveness may therefore be detected – one which emphasises the more adaptive requirements associated with high frequency problem encounters, hence allocative planning, the other the more innovative requirements associated with low frequency problem encounters, and hence innovative planning. The former we can refer to collectively as the adaptive responsive approach, the latter the innovative responsive approach – with respect to regional planning. That these are mutually interdependent approaches is taken as axiomatic. Indeed it may be more appropriate to consider them not even as reason-ably distinct but perhaps as the respective 'ends' of a continuum of responsiveness. In fact it makes for a considerably simpler form of analysis if they are treated in this manner, as 'ideal types' or 'pure forms'. But as we shall see, if a responsive approach to regional planning is to be articulated and eventually mobilised, then it will clearly be a combination of elements from both approaches interacting simultaneously.


**An adaptive responsive approach**

Consider firstly the adaptive strand of this dual relationship, illustrated in Figure 7.4. In this context the characteristics of an adaptive responsive approach are matched to the notions of problem encounter and the seven facets of responsiveness. Taking each in turn it is clear that the kinds of problem encounter which demand an adaptive response are what Steiss refers to as the recurrent generic and the non-recurrent generic problem type. In these situations the availability of existing expertise is correspondingly high. What specific responses are demanded to cope with these particular encounters? On the assumption that adaptive responsive planning is concerned with and for change, we can assert that the type of response envisaged by the political administration would have to be a substantively adaptive one. In other words, the response would have to be to alter and redistribute commitment at the margin – a process of marginal adjustment – of adapting to a marginally different situation. The fundamental objective associated with this type of response would therefore be to restore some sense of balance both within the 'internal' political administration itself and the 'internal-external' planning domain. The form of response adopted in this instance would therefore approximate to Friedmann's allocative planning mould – the formulation and application of criteria for the allocation and distribution of resources, at the margin, among competing uses.[40]

Having identified the form associated with this kind of responsive mechanism, the method of that response would depend upon the relative autonomy of the 'centre' *vis-à-vis* the 'periphery' – the authority-dependency relations of the fundamental ability to plan argument. In fact Friedmann distinguishes between four levels of autonomy and four kinds of planning method reflecting the distribution of power within society:[41]

Power strongly centralised⟶method in form of plan
Power weakly centralised⟶method in form of policies
Power fragmented⟶method in form of processes
(normative compliance)
Power dispersed⟶method in form of processes
(voluntary compliance)

Fig. 7.4    Adaptive responsive mode

| Mode of response / Responsive mode | Adaptive responsive mode |
|---|---|
| 1  Type of *problem encounter:*<br>— available expertise *high* | — recurrent generic problems<br>— non-recurrent generic problems |
| | **PLANNING FOR CHANGE** |
| 2  *Type* of response | Substantively adaptive-functional |
| 3  *Objective* of response | Maintenance of balance in the planning domain and its political administration |
| 4  *Form* of response | Allocative planning mode |
| 5  *Method* of response:<br>— autonomy *high*<br><br><br>— autonomy *low* | — plan<br>— policies<br>— processes (normative)<br>— processes (voluntary) |
| 6  *Orientation* of response:<br>— autonomy *high*<br><br><br>— autonomy *low* | — command planning<br>— policies planning<br>— corporate planning<br>— participant planning |
| | **RESPONSIVE ACTION** |
| 7  *Responsive action:*<br>— intended change — endogenous<br><br>— exogenous<br><br>— impact of intent — endogenous<br><br>— exogenous | — proposals for adaptive change within adaptive mode<br>— proposals for adaptive change in planning domain<br>— adaptive change engineered within adaptive mode<br>— adaptive change engineered in planning domain |
| | **ACTUAL CHANGE** |
| 8  *Responsive performance:*<br>— proposals for change:<br>endogenous ⟶ not intended (−)<br>exogenous ⤬⟶ intended (+)<br>— impact of proposals:<br>endogenous ⟶ no change (−)<br>exogenous ⤬⟶ change (+) | — material stability (−−)<br>— *material adaptation* (−+) ⎫<br>— *unsuccessful adaptation* (+−) ⎬<br>— successful adaptation (++) ⎭ |

202

If autonomy is high, then it should be possible to adopt a more blueprint response in the form of a highly crystallised plan. If autonomy is low, however — that is, fragmented or dispersed — then such a response is clearly out of the reckoning, a more process-oriented response being more relevant. (That this represents a simplification of a continuum is taken as axiomatic.)

Corresponding to this differentiation between planning methods, based on relative autonomy, is the orientation of that response. Friedmann makes similar distinctions here, asserting that very different orientations are demanded depending again on the level of democratisation and the concomitant distribution of power between centre and periphery:

Power strongly centralised ——▶ orientation in form of
command planning

Power weakly centralised ——▶ orientation in form of
policies planning

Power fragmented ——————▶ orientation in form of
corporate planning

Power dispersed ——————▶ orientation in form of
participant planning

If democratisation is very low then demands for compliance may be correspondingly high. The orientation of the response would thus be in sympathy with the proposed method. If the latter is in the form of the blueprint kind of response, then the orientation would be planning more by command. Vice versa, if democratisation is very high, then participation (in the true meaning of that word) would be by definition correspondingly high. If the method of response is therefore to be based on voluntary compliance, with emphasis on processes rather than plans, then the associated orientation would be what Friedmann refers to as participant planning. (That this represents a simplification of a continuum is also taken as axiomatic.)

These five adaptive responses — by type, objective, form, method and orientation — together constitute what may be referred to as the planning for change component of a responsive problematic methodology. What this component is concerned with is primarily the intent side of the equation. The relationship between intent and impact is, we have argued, as equally if not more important than intent itself. This other side of the equation may be referred to as the responsive action component of a responsive problematic methodology.

In terms of an adaptive responsive approach, the two interrelated ingredients to action which have to be considered are clearly those of intent and impact. But we need to distinguish between two broadly different types of actions — those which are directed at the planning domain (exogenous social change) and those directed at the political administration (endogenous organisational change). That is, between those measures which are intended to engineer changes in society at large and those which are intended to engineer change within, in this case, the practice of regional planning itself. As was outlined earlier, the two are substantively different. In fact there are four broad dimensions to this intent-impact relationship in the context of adaptive responsive action. The first of these concerns proposals for responsive action directed at the planning of marginal change within the adaptive approach itself — the political administration of adaptive planning. As Hart notes, these proposed actions (intent) may be in the form of, for example, marginal changes in the statutory framework within which planning operates, in the type and manipulation of budgetary controls, and/or in the formal organisation of planning itself.[42]

The second concerns the impact of these endogenous proposals. If these kinds of change are implemented — in other words marginal changes have been brought about in, for example, the statutory framework, budgetary controls and formal organisational structure — then it is possible to assert that adaptive change has been engineered within the political administration of the adaptive mode itself. (Whether or not these changes have concerned only the desired consequences will be considered in the context of the treatment of the responsive performance component below.)

The third of these dimensions concerns proposals for responsive action directed at the planning of marginal change within the planning domain via allocative planning. These actions (intent) may take the form of, for example, proposing marginal changes in certain key variables over which planning has legitimate authority or in exerting some degree of control between variables in spatial, functional, temporal, economic and/or social terms.[43]

The fourth dimension concerns the impact of these exogenous proposals. If these kinds of change have been wrought — in other words if marginal changes have been brought about by manipulating certain legitimately regarded variables — then it is possible to assert that adaptive change has been engineered in the planning domain. (Whether or not these changes have concerned only the desired consequences will be considered also in the context of the treatment of the performance component below.)

These four dimensions of action — by intent (end- and exogenous) and impact (end- and exogenous) — together constitute the responsive action component of an adaptive responsive problematic methodology for, in

204

this case, regional planning. The third and final component concerns an assessment of the nature and kind of consequences — intended and unintended — associated with this action. In other words with the performance characteristics of the adaptive intent-impact relationship measured in terms of impact. [44] Like the previous component there are four dimensions which may be associated with the consequences of adaptive responsive action: (a) intended consequences, (b) unintended consequences, resulting in (c) no substantive change, and (d) substantive change. However, differentiation must also be made between changes (a) within the political administration itself (endogenous change), and (b) within the planning domain (exogenous change).

The first of these performance dimensions concerns proposals for intended marginal changes which were *not* implemented, and in which the planning domain continued to be in some form of acceptable balance. This situation may be referred to as 'material stability in the planning domain'. The same relationship holds for the political administration. If no intended change was implemented and no change took place within the administration, then there may be said to exist 'material stability in the political administration'. The second dimension concerns proposals for marginal change which were *not* implemented, but nevertheless unintended change occurred in the planning domain. This situation may be referred to as 'material adaptation in the planning domain'. Likewise for unintended change in the political administration. If no intended change was implemented, and yet change took place within the administration, then this situation may be referred to as 'material adaptation in the political administration'.

The third of these dimensions concerns proposals for intended marginal changes in the planning domain which were implemented but which resulted in no material change taking place, or change which was wholly or substantially unintended. This may be referred to as 'unsuccessful adaptation in the planning domain'. Similarly with the political administration. If proposals for marginal change were implemented, and yet no change or substantially unintended change took place, then a situation emerges which may be referred to as 'unsuccessful adaptation within the political administration'. The fourth and final dimension of responsive performance concerns proposals for marginal changes which were implemented and which resulted in material changes being wrought in the planning domain. If these changes corresponded to what were intended, then the result may be termed 'successful adaptation in the planning domain'.

The same holds for changes taking place in the political administration.

If these were intended changes the situation may be referred to as 'successful adaptation in the political administration'.

This constitutes an adaptive responsive approach to, in this case, regional planning. However, in earlier chapters we presented a case which stressed the idea that public planning could be neither 'successful' in the accepted sense of that word, nor necessarily confine itself to or be associated with the perjorative political overtones associated with 'natural stability'. But the performance component just presented appears to present a case for both successful planning and natural stability. The point is a fundamental one. The proposed solution to it does little to overcome the apparent paradox. This solution simply asserts that both notions are conceptual abstractions which may be hypothesised in theory only. Because of the messy and complex nature of reality, our social constructions of it, and the profound uncertainties and ambiguities which may be associated with it, the idea that intent will neatly correspond to impact on a one-to-one basis is as misleading as it is illusory. Likewise with the relationship between balance and its perfect maintenance.

If this is indeed the case, then it pin-points two areas of particular importance for an adaptive responsive approach to concern itself with in terms of relationships between intent and impact, and intended and unintended consequences. These two are, respectively, the areas of unsuccessful adaptation (why did adaptation not happen, or in the directions which were not intended?) and material adaptation (why did adaptation appear to have taken place independently of our intentions?) — both in terms of the planning domain *and* its political administration.


### An innovative responsive approach

The diametrically opposed strand to this adaptive approach is the innovative responsive approach, illustrated in Figure 7.5. An analysis of the components of this alternative may be considered in similar terms: (a) problem encounter, (b) planning for change, (c) responsive action, and (d) responsive performance. The conceptual basis for this alternative is provided again by Steiss's notion of the problem encounter, matched in turn to the seven facets of responsiveness.

It is clear that the kinds of problem encounter which demand a more innovative than adaptive response are the truly unique and first occurrence of generic problem type. The availability of existing expertise to cope with these new, hence low frequency, problems is correspondingly low. So what specific kind of responses are required to cope with these kinds of

Fig. 7.5   Innovative responsive mode

| Mode of response ╲ Responsive mode | Innovative responsive mode |
|---|---|
| 1  Type of *problem encounter:*<br>  — available expertise *low* | — first occurrence generic problems<br>— truly unique problems |
| 2  *Type* of response | PLANNING FOR CHANGE<br>Substantively innovative-normative |
| 3  *Objective* of response | Inducement of change in the planning domain and its political administration |
| 4  *Form* of response | Innovative planning mode |
| 5  *Method* of response:<br>  — autonomy *high*<br><br>  — autonomy *low* | — legitimation of new norms<br>— realisation of existing norms (strong)<br>— realisation of existing norms (weak)<br>— articulation of existing norms |
| 6  *Orientation* of response:<br>  — autonomy *high*<br><br>  — autonomy *low* | — competitive institution building<br>— action programme development<br>— resource mobilisation<br>— inducing organisational competition |
| 7  *Responsive action*<br>  — intended change — endogenous<br><br>        — exogenous<br><br>  — impact of intent — endogenous<br><br>        — exogenous | RESPONSIVE ACTION<br>— proposals for innovative change within innovative mode<br>— proposals for innovative change in planning domain<br>— structural change engineered within innovative mode<br>— structural change engineered in planning domain |
| 8  *Responsive performance*<br>  — proposals for change:<br>  endogenous ⤬→ not intended (−)<br>  exogenous ⤬→ intended (+)<br>  — impact of proposals:<br>  endogenous ⤬→ no change (−)<br>  exogenous ⤬→ change (+) | ACTUAL CHANGE<br>– material stability (−−)<br>– *material innovation* ( +)<br>– *unsuccessful innovation* (+−) ⎫<br>– successful innovation (++)  ⎭ |

situation? On the assumption that innovative responsive planning is concerned with and for change, we can assert that the type of response proposed by the political administration would have to be a substantively innovative one. The response would have to be to initiate, mobilise, and organise commitment in a substantively new way — a process of structural upheaval and potential transformation. The fundamental objective associated with this type of response would therefore be with the inducing of limited but significant change both within the planning domain and the political administration of planning itself. The form which the response would take would therefore conform to Friedmann's notion of innovative planning — a limited form of action intended to significantly change the nature of reality itself; with the institutionalisation of functions, rôles, frameworks, and action programmes which were not previously part of the repertory of the political administration of planning. Planning and action become coterminous.[45]

If the response is to take the form of innovative planning, then the method corresponding to it depends in turn on the relative level of autonomy of the 'centre' *vis-à-vis* the 'periphery' — the authority-dependency relations of the fundamental ability to plan argument. Friedmann's distinction between levels of autonomy as a function of the distribution of power is also applicable in this context:

Power strongly centralised⟶method in form of legitimation
of new norms
Power weakly centralised⟶method in forms of realisation
of existing norms (strong)
Power fragmented⟶method in form of realisation
of existing norms (weak)
Power dispersed⟶method in form of articulation
of existing norms

If autonomy is high and centralised, then an innovative response would be concerned with the articulating and legitimating of new norms in the planning domain with the avowed aim of inducing structural rather than marginal change. If however autonomy is low and fragmented or dispersed then, as Faludi notes, the ability to forge structural change diminishes considerably — if one is to agree with Friedmann that implementation, and hence impact, are, to some extent determined by the distribution of power and authority throughout society. (That this typology represents a simplification of a continuum is also taken as axiomatic.)

The orientation of the response will likewise reflect differentials in levels of autonomy, reflecting the method of innovative response. Friedmann's schema is therefore of direct relevance here also:

Power strongly centralised——▸ orientation in form of building new institutions

Power weakly centralised——▸ orientation in form of action programme development

Power fragmented————▸ orientation in form of resource mobilisation

Power dispersed————▸ orientation in form of inducing organisational competition.

If democratisation is low then the task of creating new institutions to set about the legitimation of new norms is correspondingly simpler. As the level of autonomy diminishes, this task becomes increasingly more difficult and more bounded. For example, where power is dispersed — democratisation being high — the only really substantive rôle which an innovative approach can undertake is to attempt to be the euphemistic 'grit in the oyster' — that is, either to be physically ejected or to form the platform-cum-base for innovatory change. (That this typology represents a simplification of a continuum is also taken as axiomatic.)

These five innovative responses then, when taken together, constitute what may be referred to as the planning for change component of a responsive problematic methodology — the intent side of the equation. Impact — the responsive action component — or rather the intent-impact relationship, is broadly similar to the treatment given to its adaptive counterpart. That is, intent and impact in terms of (a) changes forged in the planning domain (exogenous change) and (b) change forged in the political administration of planning (endogenous change). The same four dimensions may therefore be discerned.

The first of these concerns proposals for responsive action directed at the planning of structural change within the innovative approach itself — the political administration of innovative planning. Hart's distinctions are again applicable. For example, proposed structural rather marginal changes (intent) in the statutory framework within which planning operates, in the type and manipulation of controls, and in the setting-up of new dynamic organisations and/or closing-down of others which have outlasted their utility.

The second dimension concerns the impact associated with these endogenous proposals. If these kinds of change are implemented, then it is possible to assert that innovative change has been engineered within the political administration of innovative mode itself. (Whether these have brought about desired change will be considered in the treatment of the responsive performance component outlined below.)

The third dimension concerns proposals for responsive action aimed at the planning of innovatory change within the planning domain, via innovative planning. These kind of actions (intent) may take the form of, for example, proposals for innovations in spatial, functional, temporal, economic, social, and/or political terms.

The fourth and final dimension concerns the impacts associated with these proposals for innovatory change in the planning domain. If these kinds of change have been forged — in other words if structural changes have been brought about by innovative means — then it is possible to assert that structural change has been engineered in the planning domain. (Whether or not these have been desired changes will be considered below.)

In similar fashion to the analysis of the adaptive approach, these four dimensions of action together constitute the responsive action component of an innovative responsive problematic methodology for planning, of in this case regional planning. The remaining component which requires some comment concerns the performance characteristics of the innovative intent-impact relationship. There are four dimensions to this interaction: (a) intended consequences, (b) unintended consequences, resulting in (c) no substantive change, and (d) substantive change. Differentiation must also be made between changes (a) within the political administration itself (endogenous change), and (b) within the planning domain (exogenous change).

The first performance dimension relates proposals for intended innovatory changes which were not implemented, the planning domain continuing to be in some kind of balance. This may be referred to as 'material stability in the planning domain'. For the same relationships to hold within the political administration, it may also be referred to as 'material stability' but 'within the political administration'. The second performance dimension concerns proposals for structural change which were not implemented but unintended structural change occurred in the planning domain. This may be referred to as 'material innovation in the planning domain'. Similarly, if structural change took place within the political administration — 'material innovation in the political administration' of planning.

The third dimension, however, concerns proposals for structural change in the planning domain which were implemented, but which resulted in structural change occurring, or change which was wholly or substantially unintended. This relationship may be termed 'unsuccessful innovation in the planning domain'. The corresponding situation for the political administration may also be termed unsuccessful innovation. The fourth and final dimension of performance concerns proposals for structural change which were implemented and which resulted in structural change being forged in the planning domain. If these changes corresponded to what was intended, then the result may be referred to as 'successful innovation in the planning domain'. If structural impact mirrored structural intent for the political administration, then this may also be termed successful innovation.

In similar fashion to the outline of the adaptive approach, this concludes and constitutes an innovative responsive approach to, in this case, regional planning. But can there be such a thing as 'successful' planning or 'natural stability' in bringing about structural change? In the sense that impact mirrors intent 100 per cent, then the answer must clearly be in the negative, for similar reasons to those outlined earlier. Our knowledge of what constitutes reality, with its attendant uncertainties and ambiguities, negates the idea of totally successful planning. The implications for the practice of innovative planning are worthy of note. It pin-points the same two areas on which regional planning *qua* public planning needs to focus attention − areas which have been the subject of woeful neglect in the recent past. Respectively, of unsuccessful innovation (why did structural change not occur, or in directions which were not originally intended?) and material innovation (why did structural change appear to occur independently of our actions?) − both in terms of the planning domain and its political administration.

### Responsive planning: adaptive plus innovative modes

It should be clear from this rather formal analytical treatment that the adaptive and innovative approaches to public planning are by no means mutually exclusive. Indeed they are inextricably interwoven approaches to responsive planning. In more formal terms they constitute it. So instead of artificially separating them, we are now in the position to bring them together. Or as Friedmann describes the relationship:

> These two facets of societal guidance − maintaining a complex social system in balance and, *simultaneously,* inducing new performance characteristics through changes in some of its structural relations − interpenetrate in many ways.
>
> Innovations may be needed, for example, to restore a system to a healthy balance . . . On the other hand, a measure of balanced order may be prerequisite to the introduction of planned innovations.[46]

However, this apparent complimentarity shields some rather interesting paradoxes and conflicts between the two approaches, as Friedmann notes.

In fact he takes his argument to its apparently logical conclusion by asserting that where allocative planning is most feasible it is generally superfluous and subsumed within innovative planning, and where it is most needed it is not feasible. [47] A simple key to this apparent paradox is to be found in the two analyses of the four dimensions of responsive action. There Hart's action strategies were noted for both the political administration of planning and the planning domain. In the former these strategies consisted of marginal changes in the statutory framework, in the type and manipulation of budgetary controls, and in the formal organisation of planning itself. In the latter these strategies were couched in spatial, functional, temporal, economic and social terms. In the innovative analysis these same strategies for action were employed — with two notable exceptions. Two additional features were added — the idea of creating new institutions and making others redundant, and the idea of change in the political component of society. The former was associated with what Friedmann refers to as 'competitive institution building', the latter to the very authority-dependency relations themselves. But innovative planning clearly incorporates many if not most of the characteristics associated with the adaptive approach. Therein lies the key as to why there may be a rôle for adaptive planning, albeit within the compass of its innovative stable-mate. Adaptive planning has certain qualities if and only if it is not possible to implement in full the innovative planning mode. In other words if the contextual setting within which planning operates is incapable or not capable of implementing a substantively innovative approach. The two modes may therefore be brought together within this contextual setting — the political administration of public planning (Figure 7.6).

However, a potentially more fruitful way of considering the way in which these two facets interact concerns the facet of responsive performance. If we are to agree with Friedmann's assertion that planning is about action and impact, then it is in this area that some tie-up may be expected if not identified. In fact there are three components to this facet which need to be considered and compared: (a) *ex ante* intent — the interaction between proposals for change within the planning modes (endogenous) and proposals for change in the planning domain (exogenous); (b) *ex post* impact — the interaction between intended and unintended consequences of these endogenous and exogenous proposals; and (c) *ex post-ante* responses to relations between *ex ante* intent and *ex post* impact.

With the proposed emphasis on material and unsuccessful adaptation on the one hand, and material and unsuccessful innovation on the other, a responsive approach to planning is clearly not considered to be a serial or sequential one-off ends-oriented mode of planning. Responsive planning

212

## Fig. 7.6  Responsive planning – adaptive *plus* innovative modes

| Adaptive responsive mode | Mode of response | Innovative responsive mode |
|---|---|---|
| – recurrent generic problems<br><br>– non-recurrent generic problems | Problem encounter | – first occurrence generic problems<br>– truly unique problems |
| substantively adaptive-functional | Type | substantively innovative-normative |
| maintenance of balance in the planning domain and its political administration | Objective | inducement of change in the planning domain and its political administration |
| allocative planning mode | Form | innovative planning mode |
| – plan<br>– policies<br><br>– processes (normative)<br><br>– processes (voluntary) | Method | – legitimation of new norms<br>– realisation of existing norms (strong)<br>– realisation of existing norms (weak)<br>– articulation of existing norms |
| – command planning<br><br>– policies planning<br>– corporate planning<br>– participant planning | Orientation | – competitive institution building<br>– action programme development<br>– resource mobilisation<br>– inducing organisational competition |
| – proposals for adaptive change within adaptive mode<br>– proposals for adaptive change in planning domain<br>– adaptive change engineered within adaptive mode<br>– adaptive change engineered in planning domain | Responsive action | – proposals for innovative change within innovative mode<br>– proposals for innovative change in planning domain<br>– structural change engineered within innovative mode<br>– structural change engineered in planning domain |
| – material stability (– –)<br>– *material adaptation* (–+)<br>– *unsuccessful adaptation* (+–)<br>– successful adaptation (++) | Responsive performance | – material stability (– –)<br>– *material innovation* (–+)<br>– *unsuccessful innovation* (+–)<br>– successful innovation (++) |

has no obvious starting point or finishing place. The process of fusion which translates the intent-impact relations of responsive performance back into the setting of problem encounters is to be found in the way the three aforementioned components of the responsive performance facet interact and iterate. The key to this particular process is to be found in the perception, assessment and articulation of the consequences associated with the implementation of action programmes. We have already differentiated between intended and unintended consequences, and between those consequences which impact on either the political administration of planning or its planning domain counterpart. But this is a wholly unsatisfactory and artificial distinction. It is not an either-or situation. The consequences of action in the planning domain will have some impact on its political administration, and vice-versa – irrespective of whether these were intentional or not. The other unsatisfactory and arbitrary distinction concerns the way in which what was deemed to be a consequence of, for example, adaptive planning remained within the boundaries of the adaptive mode. Similarly for the consequences associated with innovative planning. This situation is therefore a ridiculous and intolerable one. For what it implies is that once a problem has been cast as one requiring either a substantively adaptive or innovative response, then it keeps within those administrative boundaries throughout its recurrent life. Also that all the consequences associated with the implementation of responsive strategies – both intended and unintended – are and will continue to be within the constraints of either the adaptive or the innovative mode. There appears to be little or no room for, for example, unintended consequences of an adaptive responsive strategy being redefined or recast as a further problem requiring a more innovative response. This is clearly an absurd proposition. There has to be some degree of interaction between modes – the problem is to locate it.

There appear to be at least two points of potential connection, one which has already been implied in the outline above, the other concerning the political administration of planning itself. This latter connection will be explored in the next chapter. It is the former which is of interest here. In fact it may be outlined with the aid of a simple diagram, illustrated opposite (Figure 7.7).

The three components labelled A, B, and C correspond to, respectively, intent, impact and response – the three components of responsive performance. The way in which these interact may be more appropriately referred to as a typology of problem recasting – the process of fusion which translates intent-impact relations back into problem encounters.

The simple modal relationships described earlier under the labels of the facets of responsive action and responsive performance are therefore combined and illustrated in this diagram. The difference here reflects the idea that there is continuous interaction and constant iteration between intent (intended and unintended – endogenous, exogenous, adaptive, innovative) on the one hand, impact (intended and unintended – endogenous,

214

Fig. 7.7   Typology of problem recasting

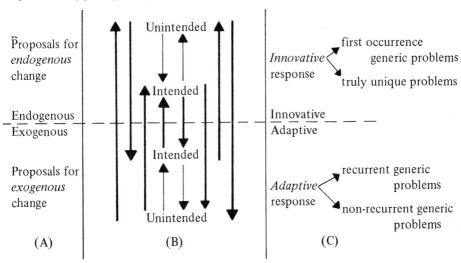

exogenous, adaptive, innovative) on the other, and the responses (adaptive, innovative) to them. The picture is therefore considerably more complex and open than the simple modal analysis might appear to indicate. The dual relationship between intended and unintended effects for each mode, categorised by impact in terms of either mode or domain, is indicated by the smaller arrows. The more important links are now deemed to be those between the two types of proposals for change with respect to the links between their respective impacts (indicated by the thicker arrows), and the responses to the intended and unintended consequences associated with those original actions. Instead of the four original basic relationships there are now twelve. These illustrate the differential impacts of, for example, proposals for change in the planning domain which are then implemented, and which result in a variety of unintended consequences which impact on proposals for change in the political administration of planning itself. As a result it may prove necessary to radically alter policy proposals put forward for change within the political administration, for example, from a primarily adaptive to a more innovative response. In other words, as a result of the consequences of actions associated with the prosecution of change in the planning domain, proposals will reflect, be reflected in, and in part, be determined by an assessment of those exogenous consequences, and vice versa.

As a result of the consequences of actions associated with the prosecution of change within the political administration of planning, proposals for change in the planning domain will reflect, be reflected in, and in part be determined by an assessment of those endogenous consequences. These assessments will therefore be concerned within the kinds of response needed to tackle these consequences – to 'internalise' the desirable and intended, and to suggest the forms, methods, orientations and actions of response appropriate to the undesirable and unintended consequences. In both cases the result is the generation and perception of 'new' problem situations – of both 'good' and 'bad' varieties. The consequences of actions – particularly the unintended variety – have therefore a persistent, almost inevitable, habit of not respecting political, administrative and technical boundaries; of spilling over, into and permeating both the planning domain and its concomitant political administration – even though the original intentions were mistakenly or otherwise directed solely at one or the other. The key word in this last phrase has to be 'mistakenly'. And so we arrive at the rather unattractive conclusions that the problems associated with the planning for change outside its political administration cannot usefully be divorced from problems associated with the planning of change within it, and vice versa. In other words we can usefully differentiate neither between the consequences of change without and within nor between innovative and adaptive approaches. The two are inextricably intertwined. They may only be differentiated by degrees of artificiality associated with our general lack of knowledge and the ways in which we construct, alter and reconstruct our interpretations of what constitutes reality. [48] Hence the dashed line which runs laterally through the typology of problem recasting. Endogenous proposals for change fuse with exogenous proposals (A), intended and unintended endogenous impacts fuse with intended and unintended exogenous impacts (B), and innovative responses fuse with adaptive responses (C). As a result problems originally cast as requiring a substantively innovative or adaptive response are recast in the form of new problem encounters requiring potentially different responses. Problems, then, not only change through time but our perceptions of them change; our basic understanding of them and their attributes changes.

So we arrive at the two strands which constitute the core of a responsive approach to regional planning: (a) the continuous interaction and constant iteration between material adaptation and innovation at national/regional and regional/local levels (change which has occurred irrespective of planned intent) and unsuccessful adaptation and innovation at national/regional and regional/local levels (unintended consequences of the implementation of planned intent) in both the planning domain and its political administration, and (b) the processes by which this interaction and iteration takes place – between intent, impact and response in terms of the national/regional and regional/local time-space continuum. In terms

216

of the institutionalising of this problem recasting device, it is perhaps more appropriate to consider it as a strategic monitoring device of a responsive approach to public planning. Not only does it perform the tasks of 'pulse taker' and 'midwife', but it also acts as a pressure point and, its corollary, that of a point of leverage. The proposal for the establishment of a Regional Performance Evaluation and Policy Review Unit for the North West would appear to 'fit' the requirements of this recasting device to the last detail. For example, the rôle of this proposed Unit is: '. . . to both *evaluate* previous *performance* and at the same time to *review* existing and proposed *policy* to determine its continued applicability'.[49]

Thus we have a responsive approach to planning and regional planning which compliments, and in some respects mirrors, what Hart has referred to as — in the context of urban policy development — a policy chain or spiral. Paraphrasing, we can assert that this emphasis on process allows for a more meaningful assessment to be made of, in this instance, the utility of regional planning than would otherwise be the case by either (a) simply examining each mode in turn, or (b) treating the modes together as if they were part of some simple historical progression.[50]

To summarise the position thus far, this chapter — together with those earlier chapters which have provided the underpinnings to it — constitutes an attempt to sketch an outline for a theory of what a responsive approach to regional planning would need to incorporate. At this stage of formulation it is clearly in a very loose, embryonic and conceptual state. But nevertheless it does serve to illustrate a number of the more crucial ideas inherent in a responsive approach, together with an assessment of some of the implications which that implies. For example, the focus of attention on the fundamental schema of problem encounter⟶ response mechanism⟶responsive action, particularly its action-orientation. But perhaps most importantly of all the shadow it casts on our ability to plan 'successfully', and the concomitant opening-up of the need to reorientate and recast planning problems in a form which focuses attention on the less attractive notion of the reasons why intervention has been 'unsuccessful'. This chapter has stressed the process component of just such a form of responsiveness within the context of its political administration. But the political dimension has largely been 'held constant', if not treated as an independent variable — an unrealistic and untenable assumption. It is this missing dimension which provides the point of entry into the next and last chapter.

# Notes

[1] Boothroyd, 1974, op. cit.; compare with the concept of 'reflective experience' suggested by J. Dewey, 1916, p. 150; for a critique see I. Scheffler, 1974, Part 4, especially Chapter VI.

[2] Boothroyd, 1974, op. cit., p. 7; compare with Dewey, 1916, op. cit., pp. 139 and 150—1.

[3] Boothroyd, 1974, op. cit., p. 20.

[4] Boothroyd, 1974, op. cit., pp. 69—70.

[5] Boothroyd, 1974, op. cit., p. 71.

[6] Boothroyd, 1974, op. cit., p. 71.

[7] On the relationship between interconnectedness and unintended effects see Vickers, 1974b, op. cit., p. 8; see also Hirschman, 1967, op. cit., Chapter 1, particularly his concept of the 'hiding hand'.

[8] Boothroyd, 1974, op. cit., p. 27.

[9] J. Friedmann, 1973c, p. 42.

[10] Friedmann, 1973c, op. cit., p. 17.

[11] This 'theory' was first couched in an economic context in an attempt to explain the process of regional *economic* development (J. Friedmann, 1966). The 'general theory' was first published as a background paper to the Ford Foundation Programme in Chile (J. Friedmann, 1967c). The first published version is to be found in N. Hansen, 1972, pp. 82—107; also Friedmann, 1973c, op. cit., pp. 42—56; see also Friedmann, 1973b, op. cit., pp. 143—70.

[12] Popper, 1972, op. cit., prefers to refer to it by its biological equivalent — evolution. See especially Chapter 7, 'Evolution and the tree of Knowledge'; also Popper, 1963, op. cit., p. 342, in connection with the social sciences.

[13] Watkins, 1974, op. cit., p. 389.

[14] See Watkins, 1974, op. cit., pp. 389—93.

[15] It is perhaps of interest to point out that much of the groundwork for both approaches is provided by Dahrendorf, 1959, op. cit.

[16] Dahrendorf, 1959, op. cit., pp. 237—40.

[17] J. Friedmann, 1972a, pp. 86—99.

[18] This could be partly accounted for by Friedmann's original attempt at an economic formulation along disequilibrium/cumulative causation lines (Friedmann, 1966, op. cit.). See Brookfield, 1975, op. cit., pp. 101—4; also H. Richardson, 1972, pp. 37—38; H. Richardson, 1973, pp. 138—43, especially p. 52; H. Siebert, 1969, p. 199.

[19] Dahrendorf, 1959, op. cit., p. 236.

[20] Brookfield, 1975, op. cit., pp. 101–4; for a personal reflection see Friedmann, 1973b, op. cit., pp. 13–17.

[21] Friedmann, 1973b, op. cit., p. 247.

[22] See Friedmann, 1972a, op. cit., pp. 86–7; compare with Schon, 1971, op. cit., pp. 80–115.

[23] See Friedmann, 1972a, op. cit., pp. 87–90; compare with Schon, 1971, op. cit., pp. 31–60.

[24] See Friedmann, 1972a, op. cit., pp. 90–3; compare with Schon, 1971, op. cit., pp. 116–79. See also J. Friedmann, 1972b, on the spatial organisation of power in urban systems.

[25] See Friedmann, 1972a, op. cit., pp. 93–6; compare with Schon, 1971, op. cit., pp. 81–4.

[26] Friedmann, 1972a, op. cit., p. 93.

[27] Friedmann, 1972a, op. cit., pp. 96–9.

[28] Brookfield, 1975, op. cit., p. 122.

[29] Brookfield, 1975, op. cit., pp. 101–4.

[30] J. Friedmann and W. Alonso, 1964, Introduction, especially p. 3.

[31] Brookfield, 1975, op. cit., p. 119.

[32] Brookfield, 1975, op. cit., pp. 89–90.

[33] Friedmann, 1972a, op. cit., p. 101.

[34] Giddens, 1971, op. cit., p. 20.

[35] Friedmann, 1973b, op. cit., p. 246.

[36] Friedmann, 1973b, op. cit., p. 245.

[37] Friedmann, 1973b, op. cit., p. 245.

[38] J. Friedmann, 1974, p. 311, a review of Faludi's book on planning theory – Faludi, 1973b, op. cit.

[39] Friedmann, 1967b, op. cit., pp. 311–18; see also Friedmann, 1973b, op. cit., Chapter 3.

[40] Friedmann, 1973b, op. cit., p. 52; J. Friedmann, 1969a, p. 313. On allocative planning see Friedmann, 1973b, op. cit., pp. 52–9; also Friedmann, 1967b, op. cit.

[41] Friedmann, 1973b, op. cit., pp. 70–9, especially Table I; for an alternative approach see Hart, 1974, op. cit.

[42] See Hart, 1975, op. cit.

[43] See Hart, 1975, op. cit.

[44] On the idea of performance in planning see Wedgewood-Oppenheim et al., 1975, op. cit.

[45] See Friedmann, 1969a, op. cit., p. 313; Friedmann, 1973b, op. cit., pp. 59–65; also Friedmann, 1967b, op. cit.

[46] Friedmann, 1973b, op. cit., p. 52.

[47] See Friedmann, 1973b, op. cit., pp. 60–70.

[48] On this relationship see H. Simon, 1969; also Berger and Luckmann, 1971, op. cit.

[49] Wedgewood-Oppenheim et al., 1975, op. cit., p. 1.

[50] Hart, 1974, op. cit., p. 40.

# 8  Regional Planning:
# The Art of the Possible

The theme for this last chapter is derived from the introduction to Sir Peter Medawar's provocative series of essays entitled *The Art of the Soluble: Creativity and Originality in Science.* In particular his assertion that scientific research is the art of the soluble, politics the art of the possible, but that both are immensely practical-minded affairs.[1] Since we have well and truly nailed our planning colours to the political rather than the scientific mast, it therefore follows that planning, and in this case regional planning, is a practical-minded affair corresponding to the determining of what is possible in an environment characterised by the problems of uncertainty and ambiguity. This activity is therefore what Medawar refers to as an art — for two reasons. First, because it is above all else a creative activity involving not simply the application of processes of adaptation and innovation to change and changing circumstances but to the very social construction of reality itself. Second, it is therefore an activity which demands originality on the part of the political administration of planning — originality not solely on the part of bringing about change 'out there', but originality in responding to changing conditions within and between the organisations and agencies which together constitute that political administration. To do justice to this notion — that planning is also the art of the possible — we need to map-out the features of this 'missing dimension' which contributes to and guides this creating and originality: the processes of the political administration of planning.

### The missing dimension — the political process

In consideration of the two 'ideal-type' responsive planning modes outlined in the last chapter, and in particular with the attempt to draw them together in the form of a multifaceted, multiresponse-type framework, the political administration component was treated as a determinant of responsive planning. This is clearly an unsatisfactory treatment because, as we argued in earlier chapters, the processes of planning to some extent shape if not determine its political administration — which in turn moulds and is moulded by relations with the legitimately regarded domain of planning, and so on. The relationships are therefore messy, confused and confusing. They are far from causal.[2]

Having attempted to fuse the dual modes of responsive planning in terms of their respective processes, we need to extend that analysis to include this missing dimension. In other words, to consider the processes of the political administration of planning which constitute and to some extent are constituted by planning. Since the earlier analysis was concerned with the development of the idea of responsiveness it seems logical that the analysis which is to follow should be couched in similar terms. That is, to outline some of the principal characteristics of a responsive administration which would incorporate and be incorporated within the dual mode of responsive planning.[3]

The basic relationships between the two may be approached by way of reference to a fundamental flaw in the interaction associated with the facets of the responsive mechanism outlined previously. This flaw concerns the facets of the method of response and the orientation of that response. There the distinction was made between differentials in levels of autonomy associated with differences in characteristics of political administrations. The levels were deemed to vary from high to low, reflecting the fundamental ability to plan. What this categorisation implies is that responsive planning as a mode of planning cuts across different types of political administration (Figure 8.1). One measure of these differences, and the one used earlier, is autonomy — the ability to propose and dispose processes and authority on those facets which make up the planning domain and its administration. But autonomy is only one measure, albeit perhaps a useful and general one. As such it can not be considered as the measure which equates differences in planning style with political administrations. Indeed it is possible to argue that a set of measures or criteria is more appropriate — and which includes autonomy as one explanatory variable.

It is tempting to simply adopt Friedmann's account of differences between types of social system and their political administrations outlined as part of his attempt at a 'general theory'. In particular, the distinction noted earlier between his Type I and Type II systems of capacities for the generation and absorption of innovations. The former corresponding to hierarchical, centrally controlled social systems — with a relatively low capacity; the latter to nonhierarchical, multi-centric, horizontally integrated social systems — with a relatively high capacity.[4] But this would be unsatisfactory for our purposes on at least three counts. First, because as Friedmann notes the categorisation is in some respects a spurious one —

Fig. 8.1   Responsive planning and political administration

*Types of political administration*

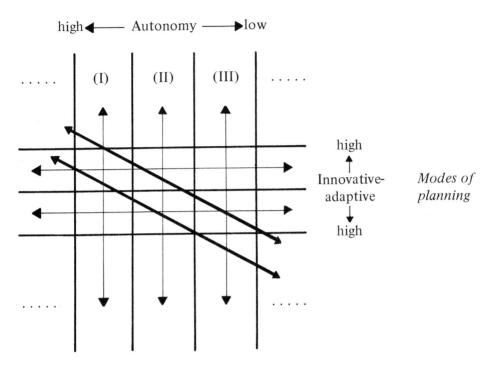

not all hierarchical systems have low capacities, and not all poly-centric systems have high capacities. Indeed it is perhaps more appropriate to consider each as an 'ideal-type', representing the diametrically-opposed poles of a single continuum. In other words, we would then have to consider in what ways Type I systems coexist and mesh with Type II systems *vis-à-vis* the political administration of responsive planning.

The second criticism, which stems out of the last, concerns Friedmann's underlying methodological approach to the problem of these relationships. Here we come to a methodological impasse which to some extent precludes its adoption. Friedmann's position with respect to these Type I and Type II systems is based primarily on stressing the importance of relationships between their respective structures and functions. This functionalist position, wedded as it is – and noted in Chapter Two – to a particular view of society emphasising cohesion and integration, is in many respects not capable of being reconciled with Friedmann's action-framework approach which has been proposed for the foundations of a responsive planning mode. It is therefore unsatisfactory for our purposes because it tends to preclude other important methodological accounts which are potentially capable of reconciliation with an action-framework.

The third reason for not adopting this distinction between Type I and Type II systems represents a combination of the above two points. This concerns their general neglect of the rôle of the processes associated with relationships between social systems and political systems, and their administration *vis-à-vis* public planning. A structural-functional approach is capable of including the idea of processes, but only in terms subservient to it. A comparative analysis of 'ideal-types' in this particular context also neglects the fundamentally important status which we have attributed to the role of process in public planning.[5] For these three reasons we need to search elsewhere for a more suitable and internally consistent account.

An alternative and particularly useful and important contribution to the understanding of the processes associated with the political administration of planning has been provided by Hart.[6] In that contribution he identifies and distinguishes between three different strands to relationships between the casting of public policy and the premises on which that policy is based. Although the gist of Hart's argument is directed primarily at accounting for the development of public policy at the urban level, it is nonetheless capable of extension into the general field of the development of public policy *per se*. These three strands, cast in the form of 'policy modes', correspond to the cohesive, factored and diffused. Each, Hart argues, is characterised by a number of reasonably distinct qualities which are capable of being subjected to critical analysis on at least ten, what he refers to as, 'explanatory levels'. These correspond to (i) the orientation of the planning process, (ii) the method of operationalising that process, (iii) the concept of order (e.g. urban, regional, economic, etc.) which underpins it, (iv) the type of prescription associated with the process, (v) relationships between the operating components of the planning process, (vi) the primary initial constraints acting on the process, (vii) the political climate associated with the planning process, (viii) the nature of its administrative coordination, (ix) relationships between the objectives of the process, and (x) the level of proposed finality associated with outputs from the planning process. The principal attribute associated with utilisation of this rather than, for example, Friedmann's approach is that it attempts not only to consider the ways in which these facets interact within each policy mode but, and perhaps more importantly for our purposes, also: '. . . to consider the way in which they *interrelate* to form the spatial, functional and temporal basis of the planning strand of the policy-making process'[7] (Italics added).

224

As such they may be taken as more suitable proxies for the 'vertical' types of political administration outlined in Figure 8.1 than, for example, Friedmann's Type I and Type II systems.

Briefly summarising, and running the risk of oversimplifying the analysis, the first of these 'vertical' policy modes, the cohesive, means pretty much what it implies: a mode whose internal construction is characterised by, permeated with, and soaked in the ideology of cohesion. Or, as Hart puts it:

> Policy is *formulated* on the basis of intelligible and explicable objectives on the part of the planners which are formally cohesive, administratively integrated and above all, rationally determined. This type of centralised rationality . . . is both one of the characteristic features of the planning process and one of its principal legitimations.[8]

In terms of the ten explanatory levels, the principal orientation of the process of planning is with the formulation of policy. The method by which this is operationalised is therefore the model of rational analysis. The concept of order which underpins this approach is organic, and analogous to viewing regions, Hart notes, as living organisms or 'organic complexes':

> According to this model, after a careful comprehensive survey and a detailed analysis of the material collected it is possible to plan for the resolution or reduction of those difficulties which have prevented (a region) from developing in an orderly manner and achieving a full and balanced maturity.[9]

The type of prescription associated with this approach is one based on an understanding of the region as a whole, leading to a careful construction of the design of a set of measures to overcome the stumbling blocks to a stable state. The relationships between the components which make up this set of measures are therefore complementary in the sense that they are seen to neatly interlock and to be mutually reinforcing. The initial constraint which to some extent determines if not influences the mapping-out of the boundaries to this design is the spatial one − the original delimitation of the physical boundaries of the region.

These technical attributes of this cohesive policy mode are primarily concerned with the fitting and modification of parts to the whole. The emphasis is therefore a holistical one: the whole is somehow seen to be greater than the sum of the parts of which it is made. The technical attributes are perceived by planners to reflect and be reflected in the broader contextual setting of the political climate on the one hand, and its administrative coordination on the other. The technical strand becomes reinforced by this additional perception in two ways:

> In the first place it is assumed that the planning process rests on a broad-based *political consensus* regarding ultimate objectives . . . Political consensus of this type means that the nature of what constitutes the public interest is widely accepted and the planner is freed to play a strictly technical role . . . Secondly, the planner as a technician is aided in his task by a high level of administrative coordination which gives coherence to the process of implementing the plan. The major problem after the formulation of the plan . . . (is) of ensuring that it (is) properly executed and . . . that deviations and alterations to the approved plan (are) either limited in scope or (are) only raised at uniform intervals when the plan (is) officially reviewed.[10]

Relationships between the objectives of the process are therefore highly integrated and the levels of finality associated with the outputs from this mode are therefore typically cast in the form of masterplans – or what we referred to in Chapter Four as the blueprint mode of planning. This proposed finality is therefore complete in and of itself. As a proposal for change it is complete from the moment it is officially accepted (Figure 8.2). Hart cites as examples of this kind of finality the Abercrombie plans for the London region produced in the 1940s. Other examples include the first round of regional strategies prepared for the Regional Economic Planning Councils for each of the English planning regions in the middle 'sixties.[11]

The second 'vertical' policy mode, the factored, concerns the tensions between the making of policy and the administrative requirements associated with its implementation. This policy mode therefore gives recognition to the idea that its internal construction is characterised by, permeated with, and soaked in the ideology of fragmentation. Or, as Hart puts it:

> Policy, it can be argued from this perspective, must be considered within a broader and more realistic context and that context has a substantial bureaucratic component. The Factored Mode . . . holds that the central point of the planning process is the *articulation* of policy . . .[12]

The factored mode is therefore substantively different from the cohesive policy mode. In terms of the ten explanatory levels the principal orientation of the process of planning is with the articulation of policy. This takes place at two levels. At one level policy is simply published beyond the boundaries within which it was forged. At the other, and more important, level policy is articulated in administrative terms. Hart identifies four broad components to this form of articulation: (a) the political administration is not a monolith but rather a constellation of departments and agencies; (b) the kind of problems associated with planning are broken down into component parts and allocated to these departments on the basis of expertise and interest; (c) these component parts are perceived and redefined by departments on the basis of their respective expertise and interest as to what constitutes, for example, acceptable performance, operating procedures, etc; and (d) these administratively-separate components, having been recast as the problem of the problem, are therefore articulated and often equated with solving the problem in its entirety, and hence with serving the public interest. [13] According to Hart, this implies that: '. . . disaggregation of the problem means that the planning process may have rational elements but it is not wholly or even mainly rational . . .'[14]

The method of operationalising this approach to the process of planning and policy-making is therefore, as Hart admirably puts it, less the result of rational analysis and more the product of organisational output. The concept of order underlying this factored approach is likewise substantially different. The principal interest is rather less than with the region as a whole and rather more with the specific problems associated with planned public intervention. It is therefore more with a mechanistic sense of order; the region is perceived to be more an artificial man-made construct than a 'natural' process of evolution. As such it is geared more to the provision of public goods directed at the satisfaction of human wants and needs. The type of prescription associated with this fragmented mode is to assess and make estimates − predictions − of these wants and needs. The initial constraint is therefore more of a functional than a spatial one, although clearly this assessment is made more often than not within the physical boundaries and aerial subdivisions associated with that particular heterogeneous-organised political administration. The relationships between the operating components reflect this functional categorisation. Far from being wholly complementary, interlocking and reinforcing, they are of a more contiguous nature − spatially and functionally − relying heavily on means of coordination as an instrumental variable in forging them into a coherent whole.

These then constitute the technical attributes of the factored policy mode. The tensions result partly in this attempt at coordination. Power and authority is not usually to be found uniformly distributed either between departments or within the political administration itself. Instead it is more fragmented, correlating more often than not positively and highly with size of department. As Hart notes:

Some measure of coordination at the administrative level is usually secured but the large, well-funded departments often act in an almost *semi-autonomous* fashion as implementation proceeds . . . In this type of situation . . . there are important and evident differences of opinion regarding the timing and order of priority of projects. As these differences become more pronounced, although there may be nominal political agreement regarding the long-term objectives of planning, shorter term measures can become political issues. [15] (Italics added.)

In such cases the political climate will reflect and ultimately be reflected in these kind of issues. The implication is such that if these issues persist or become of increasing political significance, the political environment may move away from a climate of relative consensus to a more fragmented and alternating pattern. In these situations power and authority may alternate between competing political interests. The relationships between the objectives of the process may therefore become far removed from the idea of total integration associated with the cohesive mode. Rather they may be characterised by a similar fragmentation and become segmented. The levels of finality associated with outcomes may also correspond to and reflect this segmentation. Solutions which are articulated in response to differentiated problems and present and projected administrative difficulties emerge in the form of a continuous extrusion:

Suggestions become increasingly specific and resource expenditure considerations become steadily more important as they progress from the planning authority to the various operating departments involved. Ultimately the proposals are put into effect — backed by a high degree of organizational commitment. It is the administrative proposals rather than the (region) in its entirety which develops according to this point of view.[16]

Hart cites as an example of this particular mode the ring-and-radial road proposals contained in successive post-war plans for London, and culminating in the *Greater London Development Plan* of 1970. One further example includes the setting-up, history, and fate, of the now defunct Department of Economic Affairs (1964 to 1968), the department deemed responsible for the coordination of national/regional development and middle- and long-term economic planning (previously and now the prerogative of the Treasury)[17] (Figure 8.2).

The third and final 'vertical' policy mode is the diffused mode. This particular view of the way policy is made rejects both cohesive and factored explanations as, Hart notes, unattainable in theory and unworkable in practice. This policy mode gives substance to the idea that its internal construction is characterised by, permeated with, and soaked in the ideology of diffuseness. Or, as Hart puts it:

> Diffused policy asserts that decision making is far more decentralised and informal than either of the previous modes would seem to suggest. Policy, from this stance, is much more shaped by *political outcome,* rather than being the result of rational analysis or the consequence of organizational output.[18]

In terms of the ten explanatory levels associated with the diffused approach, the principal orientation of this process of making policy is by modification. Hart suggests two reasons why this should be the case. First, because it is argued that planning is as much a matter of opinion as a matter of facts. Opinions are continuously subject to change, and this has to be reflected and incorporated within the process of making policy. Second, planning itself has to be sympathetic to changing circumstances 'out there'. Assessments of these changes become an integral component of and as significant as the formulation of the original proposals. In this respect, policy and the policy machine itself must be capable of modification with respect to the method associated with its operationalising — that of political outcomes. The concept of order which underpins this mode is therefore that of, what Hart calls, a particularly sophisticated, higher-order machine concerned with the exchange and processing of information — a cybernetic concept of order. The type of prescription which is associated with this view of order, with respect to the interaction between modification of policy and political outcomes, is almost exclusively that of evaluation:

> *Evaluation* of policy therefore becomes at least as important as the design of solutions or the prediction of future activity patterns even given the most imaginative designs or the most far-sighted of surveys.[19]

This diffused policy mode is therefore based on the kind of processes which are characterised as sequential and incremental, a view which is attributable to the belief that planning has a restricted and limited amount of control that it is capable of exercising. Since control is limited, and policy is seen to be based on political outcomes, the approach to the making of policy implies, as Hart describes it, some degree of conflict among organisations of which the administration of planning is but one competitor. The relationships between the operating components constituting and contributing to the making of policy are therefore competitive in nature:

This conflict which is based essentially on a *problem-oriented* approach turns on differing views regarding benefit and loss at . . . various levels. 'Political facts' are marshalled to support the resulting opposing points of view.[20]

As such attention is drawn to those policy proposals which are particularly contentious, leaving the traditional less-contentious bed of policies largely undisturbed. The continuation of existing non-controversial policy becomes an implicit facet of planning, and departed from only in increments at the margin if at all. The initial constraint which operates on this schema of things is the temporal one. Time, especially that discounted at the 'political rate', becomes of increasing significance, although this assessment must inevitably be associated with what is regarded as the legitimate boundaries of public planning – physical, functional, but more importantly, political.

These technical attributes of the diffused policy mode are obviously located within and form a part of the broader political environment. The emphasis on conflict resolution, competition between agencies, and incremental change geared to political outcomes indicates that the political climate is largely an adversarial one. The impact on the administrative coordination of the policy-making process of this highly politicised mode of planning implies that it too is incremental and sequential with respect to its orientation:

> The struggle may thus assume an *adversarial* character in political terms and administrative coordination becomes as a result more *piecemeal* and fragmented. The cumulative effect of this type of activity is that it becomes increasingly difficult in either political or organizational terms to execute any large-scale (proposals).[21]

Since this conflict is based on a problem-oriented approach it implies that the relationships between the objectives associated with the process are problem-oriented also. The levels of finality associated with this problem-oriented political outcomes-based approach are correspondingly loosely woven and largely unstructured, or at least not corresponding to some neat and orderly package of coherent policies which is supposed to be part and parcel of the cohesive mode. Rather the degree of finality is described by Hart as iterative (see Figure 8.2):

> . . . because planning is becoming increasingly politicised and pluralistic, lengthy inquiries are required to hear objectives and to incorporate modifications. The planning process thus has a pronounced and time-consuming *iterative* character.[22]

Fig. 8.2   Hart's policy modes compared

| Explanatory Levels | Policy mode characteristics | | |
|---|---|---|---|
| | cohesive | factored | diffused |
| Planning process stage | formulation | articulation | modification |
| Method of operation | rational analysis | organizational output | political outcome |
| Underlying concept of order | organic | mechanistic | cybernetic |
| Prescriptive requirement | design | prediction | evaluation |
| Component relationships | complementary | contiguous | competitive |
| Primary initial constraint stress | spatial | functional | temporal |
| Political climate | consensus | alternating | adversarial |
| Administrative coordination | coherent | semi-autonomous | sequential |
| Goal relationships | integrated | segmented | problem oriented |
| Proposed finality | complete | continuous extrusion | iterative |

Source: Hart, 1974

The example which Hart cites to illustrate this complexity and iterative character is the public inquiry into the *Greater London Development Plan*. Further examples are provided by pretty well any major development proposal, from the size and location of new motorway links to the location of aluminium smelters.[23]

Three broad explanations, each put forward as an attempt to describe and account for the development of public policy. On the one hand, the cohesive mode, stressing the virtues of rational analysis, integration and consensus in terms of the political environment, and above all a concept of order which accords the whole a greater significance than that of its component parts. On the other hand the factored mode. Rational analysis is relegated to the status of being *a* component, organisational output being considered a better explanatory variable. Recognition that integration and consensus are special cases to be found in politics and its administration rather than the norm. In 'reality' the situation is much more complex and confusing; political hetero- rather than homogeneity is

231

the more relevant distinguishing characteristic. Similarly with the concept of order — each individual component is so complex that it has to be accorded a greater significance than that of the whole itself.

And in contrast to both cohesive and factored modes, the diffused mode. Rational analysis and organisational output are confusing abstractions and impossible to operationalise, if not illusory anyway. The only appropriate method and measure is that based on political outcomes and their evaluation. Consensus and coherence are mythical creatures divorced from the real 'reality' — that of conflict and competition. Better to try and improve on what we already know and basically understand than attempt to institutionalise myths! After all, the order which prevails 'out there' is neither holistic nor mechanical, but a complex set of social interactions — a veritable engine of communication, of information exchange and processing.

Three modes of policy development, each based on a set of competing if not diametrically-opposed premises. But are they that radically different? Are they not different ways of viewing the same thing — that of public policy-making — but with different emphases? Is not each after all simply an oversimplified extreme, an ideology, a distorted view, of what is and what is not the process by which policy is forged and implemented in the public arena in the name of government for the governed? In other words, is it not more appropriate and relevant to view these three modes not as differentiated, free-standing competing alternatives but rather as three strands which are differentiated and competitive to some degree but which are nonetheless capable of being detected in various degrees in any analysis of public policy or indeed any development of public policy? On this basis the emotive issue of which of these three modes is the 'correct' one is therefore misplaced if not irrelevant. It is not a choice between rational planning, functional planning or disjointed incrementalism. Rather it is combinations of all three — the more interesting questions therefore concern the various emphases given to each in any public policy situation. Or as Hart admirably puts it:

> ... policy cannot be satisfactorily explained as if it were only the result of rational analysis, or the consequence of organizational output, or the product of political outcome. *It is an interweaving of all three of these elements* because no single agency — however logical and well informed — has the power to put its proposals into effect without having them altered — and in some cases completely transformed — by the complex interaction of ideas, of organizations and of political interests which continuously occurs within the (regions). [24] (Italics added.)

These three 'vertical' components of the political administration of planning, taken together, are illustrated in Figure 8.2. Between each mode, and at each of the ten explanatory levels, there is some measure of interaction which is of a continuous nature. Within each mode there is some measure of iteration which is constantly occurring between each of the explanatory levels. These facets of continuous interaction and constant iteration may therefore be taken to represent the distinguishing characteristics of the processes associated with the development of public policy. By themselves, or treated individually, they do not constitute those processes. In fact Hart argues that this kind of interaction forms a policy chain or spiral, and it is this very internal dynamic which shapes and gives shape to the process of planning itself.[25]

To briefly summarise, this analysis was embarked upon as an attempt to map-out the components of the processes of types of political administration associated with regional *qua* public planning. The concept of autonomy was found to be wanting in this respect. The object of this analysis was thus to understand this 'missing dimension', which was considered to be fundamental to the processes of a responsive approach to planning. Hart's three policy modes were therefore utilised as proxies for these types of political administration, creating the 'vertical' thrust needed to complete the conceptual framework outlined in Figure 8.1. The dimension of autonomy may now be formally dispensed with and replaced by Hart's policy modes of cohesive, factored and diffused — on the understanding that they are compartmentalised largely for purposes of simplifying the analysis. In terms of the development of a responsive administration within which responsive planning may be located and in turn be located within, for the moment we shall simply make the assertion that the ability to facilitate switching between modes constitutes responsiveness with respect to the political administration of planning.

Having replaced the single dimension of autonomy with the triple dimensions of cohesive, factored and diffused policy modes, it is possible — at the risk of further overgeneralisation — to consider some of the ways in which they might form a responsive policy chain or spiral. In other words, to outline the kind of processes which in turn influence, if not determine in certain respects, the way in which these modes are interwoven and interlocked. There are at least two possible avenues of entry: first, to consider on what basis one or other of the three modes — in the sense of the characteristics of their respective components — emerges as the predominate one at any particular stage in the development of public policy; and second, to focus on the relationships between the internal dynamics of each interacting mode and the dynamics associated with the iterative nature of responsive planning.

One approach to the first avenue is to treat each policy mode not solely in terms of a triad — cohesive to factored to diffused to cohesive — but as a differentiated triad, where each mode is considered as a continuum of, respectively, cohesion, factorisation and diffuseness according to some acceptable measure:

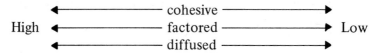

The interesting questions therefore concern in what ways these continuums interact and what measures may be appropriate for their assessment. That the two are in turn interrelated is axiomatic. But one approach which has some relevance to tackling both at the same time is that of authority-dependency relations — of which autonomy may be one such measure! It is suggested, however, that the kind of composite measure suggested by Dahrendorf, based on the degree of internal cohesion and coercion relations, may be more appropriate. For example, if cohesion-coercion relations were noticeably high, then a substantive cohesive mode could be expected to rise to the fore. If, however, cohesion-coercion relations were noticeably low, then a substantive diffused mode could be the resultant. If cohesion-coercion relations may be considered in this manner, as representing a composite measure of interconnectedness, the following kind of picture emerges (Figure 8.3).

Fig. 8.3    Policy mode interaction (I)

*Degree of internal cohesion-coercion relations*

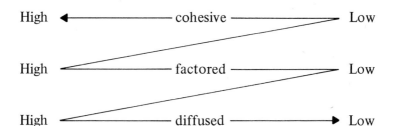

For example, if the initial policy situation exhibits a high degree of cohesiveness, then cohesion-coercion relations may be expected to be correspondingly high. If the situation and/or the relations begin to deteriorate, the degree of cohesiveness may be expected to deteriorate likewise.

One outcome of this deterioration might be a tendency to fragmentation which may begin to assume the characteristics associated with the factored mode. Should the situation and/or relations continue to deteriorate through time, the emphasis may shift further, possibly corresponding to the characteristics of the diffused mode. But should the circumstances surrounding the policy situation change their ground, the result could be further deterioration (negative change) or improvement (positive change). If the latter were the case then it could be expected that the relations between the policy mode, the policy problem and the degree of coercion-cohesion would exhibit less fragmentation and greater cohesion or coercion. This process corresponds to one view of the internal dynamic associated with Hart's policy mode triad, albeit based on cohesion-coercion relations of the kind which underpins Friedmann's 'general theory'. As a measure of these cohesion-coercion relations it would seem that the original ten explanatory levels would be particularly relevant.

The second point of entry concerns this internal dynamic with regard to the dynamics associated with responsive planning itself. In particular with the two modes of responsive planning — innovative and adaptive. The relationships may be illustrated quite simply as the balance between innovative and adaptive modes with respect to the demands associated with the three policy modes. Reference back to Figure 7.6 and in particular to the facets of method and orientation of response, gives some indication of this relationship. A truly innovative capacity demands a type of political administration where internal cohesion is particularly strong — as reflected in cohesion-coercion relations. If this cohesion is weak, fragmented or even diffused, the fundamental ability to plan in an innovative capacity becomes increasingly remote and unrealistic. A truly adaptive capacity requires none of these trappings, it is capable of being made operational in any one or combination of the three policy modes (Figure 8.4).

Fig. 8.4   Policy mode interaction (2)

| Ability to plan | Policy mode | | |
|---|---|---|---|
| | Cohesive | Factored | Diffused |
| Innovative capacity | + + | + − | − − |
| Adaptive capacity | + + | + + | + + |

From this diagram it follows that innovative-adaptive capacity reflects and is reflected in the kind of cohesion-coercion relations suggested by Friedmann. Where these increase innovative capacity increases correspondingly, and vice versa. But adaptive capacity remains roughly constant irrespective of the strength of these relations. There is thus some hazy area of grey where adaptive capacity merges with innovative. If cohesion-coercion relations become stronger it would appear that an environment more conducive to innovative planning becomes an increasingly realistic proposition, and vice versa. If cohesion-coercion relations fragment or weaken, innovative capacity weakens and eventually becomes no longer tenable. The interesting questions in this respect therefore concern the set of circumstances and conditions at the point where innovative-adaptive relations broadly correspond, together with the requirements associated with the dynamics of each.

Abstracting from this analysis it becomes clear not only that the three policy modes are heavily interconnected, but also the two modes of planning. But there is one further fundamental connection — the links between the two. In fact we can argue that what binds the three policy modes into a policy spiral can be seen in terms of the characteristics of the interaction between the two modes of planning, and what binds the two planning modes into a policy spiral can be seen in terms of the characteristics of the interaction between the three policy modes. The links between the lateral and vertical components illustrated in Figure 8.1 are therefore identified. The political administration of planning 'controls' public planning, and public planning in turn 'controls' the political administration of it. These 'controls' are also differentiated according to some measure of the contextual authority-dependency relations *vis-à-vis* cohesion-coercion relations and innovative-adaptive capacity (the broad diagonal band in Figure 8.1).

### Recasting regional planning

On the basis of what has been outlined in this and earlier chapters, it may seem presumptuous in the extreme to suggest that the practice of regional planning needs to be recast along some of the lines proposed in this book. However, it would be equally presumptuous to argue that regional planning practice should not be tampered with until a fully-worked up theory of regional planning exists. As was noted earlier, this either-or categorisation is wholly arbitrary, spurious and artificial. Regional planning practice is neither sufficiently remote to make it unreachable nor sufficiently private to make it politically untouchable. Regional planning is grounded in politics and the political process — a component of public planning which, as Hart neatly points out, floats on the surface of a pool of values, beliefs and assumptions.[26]

The sketch for a theory of regional planning was developed out of the earlier sketch for a theory for the process of public planning, together with the proposed paradigm for public planning. The conceptual framework thus far developed is therefore potentially applicable to most kinds of public planning. It consists of a loosely-knit set of concepts grounded in the basic assumption that planning, like politics, is concerned with 'the art of the possible'. It is contended that this is as equally true for the internal configuration of planning itself as it is for politics or the relationships between them. It is also a framework which stresses the importance of interaction between theory and practice via the twin strands of problem-orientation and theory-incorporation. As Friedmann notes:

> Anyone can prepare plans without theory. The making of plans poses less of a problem than planning analysis capable of withstanding sophisticated criticism ... The planner ... can defend alternative proposals on technical grounds, he can reduce the area of choice by showing what is feasible and what is not, he can sharpen the issues for political decision. And *this special ability is nourished by theory.*[27]

The theory which Friedmann refers to in this context is not solely confined to those from, for example, the disciplines of economics, sociology, geography, etc., which are of direct use and applicability in planning. It includes theory which is of relevance to the very nature and practice of planning itself. As Faludi notes, planners need to be concerned with both types — theories in planning, and theories of planning. [28] It is this kind of relationship that has been a central concern of this and previous chapters. The concern of this book has therefore been not so much with a manifesto for a complete overhaul of the practice of regional planning. Only to suggest that perhaps there are other meaningful avenues which need to be explored before we crystallise and institutionalise basic forms and processes associated with 'current best practice' and those 'ideas in good currency'. Planning, and in particular regional planning, has suffered considerably in the past from fads and fashions — for example, the pursuit of the 'systems approach' (what Wildavsky has cynically referred to as the search for the eleventh commandment [29]), also the almost magical properties which have been accorded to the use of techniques with 'social physics' properties (in particular the gravity model, which has found its way into almost all areas of planning practice — even into attempts to measure proxies of authority-dependency relations [30]). But perhaps the biggest fad to date — and which has come in for the severest criticism of all — has concerned the apparent internalisation of rationality, exemplified in the rational model of policy-making. Indeed, as we illustrated earlier, this methodology represents a cornerstone of both 'current best practice' and the 'good currency' view. Because of its almost universal application in practice, it is debatable whether we have yet felt its full impact in terms of the policies and programmes which have been pursued in its name and as a result. The emerging picture is admirably described by Hart with respect to the cohesive policy mode:

> . . . the Mode is internally consistent and in many ways is intellectually appealing but the picture which it conveys regarding the nature of the policy-making process is a false one. As an explanation of how the planning process works it is at best incomplete and at worst positively misleading — often for the planners themselves — regarding the manner in which considered intent is translated into actual effect.[31]

It is this latter point which is perhaps most pertinent. At the risk of another oversimplification, the rationality school of planning asserts that it is the formulation of policy (considered intent) which is the most important facet of the process of planning, if not its *raison d'être*. If it is possible to tune this process fine enough, by including all the right variables at the right time, and presenting it in the correct way, then any implementation of that policy is bound to be 'come up with the goods'. If the goods do not materialise, then that is a problem of implementation — for example, 'if only we had $x$ per cent more resources', etc. But planning is more than simply the making of policy or the production of a neat publishable document of intent. Making policy has to be seen as *a* critical component and a condition of public and regional planning, but it is not the component or a sufficient condition. Just as history is more than a chronological listing of key dates, so planning is more than the formulation of policy or the production of a plan. It is also, and perhaps more importantly, concerned with the impact side of the equation. It is this component which has been the subject of serious neglect, both in theory and in practice.

If regional planning is to be recast in some way, no matter how trivial or insignificant it might appear, the analysis presented thus far suggests twelve critical areas of contention concerning 'current best practice'. First, that planning is more than the making of policy. It is also about actions — implementation and impact, 'within' as well as 'without'. Second, that there is an alternative methodology to deterministic rational analysis —

238

deductive-indeterminism, the process of responsive planning. This suggests that the focus of attention should shift from end-reduction of goals/objectives to a more action-centred problem-oriented approach. Third, that 'successful' planning is illusory – we can only plan by degrees of relative failure. Nonetheless, as Arctander notes, we still need to plan – albeit in an alternative fashion. Fourth, that planning is as much concerned with learning about and coordinating action and intent, particularly with attempts at understanding the interconnected nature of problems and solutions to impact and intent to intended and unintended consequences of actions. Fifth, that if planning is instrumentally concerned with bringing about and guiding change, then it must be willing to apply to itself (the process of planning) what it is apparently willing to apply to others (the planning domain). In other words, it must be as equally concerned with the bringing about and guiding of change within the institutions and mechanisms, directions and instruments, of which it is constituted and indeed constitutes. Sixth, that planning must therefore be responsive to change – changing circumstances and conditions, changing political values, etc. – rather than merely responding to or indeed pre-empting or proscribing such change. Seventh, planning must continuously and consistently make assessments of its general utility (in terms of levels and methods of expertise) in relation to the perception of problems and abilities to incorporate and contribute to theories which have some bearing on strategies for action. Eighth, planning must therefore dispense with its banner-waving about being 'comprehensive'. It can be nothing of the kind, at least in spatial, functional and temporal terms. Our knowledge and understanding, as well as our basic inability to comprehend 'facts' (the problem of uncertainty and ambiguity), means that planning must strive for, what Hart refers to as, process comprehensiveness – the consideration of, for example intent and impact rather than one or the other. [32] Ninth, that planning – again as Hart puts it – is at least as concerned with continuously incorporating changing concepts of order as it is with simply ordering change. [33] Tenth, that notions of space and region must be extended beyond the idea of geographical space as the determinant of and framework for social and political actions. Friedmann's perceptive interpretations need to be incorporated – the idea of a region as a time-space continuum in the non-physical, supra-Euclidean sense of a 'field of forces' (e.g. communications, economic linkages, authority-dependency relations, etc.) operating within social, economic, temporal, physical and political space. These broader more complex concepts of space and region are therefore open and, what Norton Long has referred to as, 'unwalled'. Eleventh, that planning is an inherently ideological and utopian form of

239

human activity. It is therefore an important task of planning to unmask and constantly question the values and premises concerning the patterns of behaviour and their relationships on which it is based. For example, it is as equally important to assess why strategies, proposals, policies, actions, etc. were not considered or implemented as much as with justifying the courses of action which were operationalised (the inclusion-exclusion concept). Finally, to give explicit recognition to the view that planning is based and legitimated upon assessments as to what constitutes 'reality' and how it is changing. This reality is conceived and internalised within the minds of mortals — it is necessarily an incomplete image. It is therefore the task of planning to construct interpretations of this reality, to articulate them and open them up for criticism and comment. To leave them as implicit assertions, or as assumptions dressed up as facts is neither tenable nor necessary. These constructions may be seen as integral parts of the creativity and originality associated with a view of planning as 'the art of the possible'.

**Entry points for change**

Like Braybrooke, [34] we have to point out that these twelve broad areas represent one way — not the only way, not the best way, not even by themselves an adequate way — for the recasting of planning. Nonetheless they are based on a framework, albeit a loosely-knit, highly conceptual one, which has attempted to outline the principal attributes of regional planning as public planning. If these areas are to be the basis for a recasting, however tentative that might be, it nevertheless makes sense to try to identify those critical points of entry by which change may be brought about. The approach to be utilised in this context is one developed by Silverman in outlining an action-framework analysis of the origins of organisations and organisational change. [35] It should perhaps be noted that Silverman's interest was more with the analysis of change rather than with a more normative prescription for change. This author is therefore in danger of being euphemistically hoisted by his own petard with respect to mixing description with prescription. However, it is suggested that an action-framework — whilst not legitimising such an action — is at the least less susceptible to the methodological and philosophical switch from positive to normative. In some respects it is a normative treatment anyway. As Silverman describes it:

> An explanation in terms of the Action approach . . ., would begin from the fact that organizations are created by a specific person or

240

group. It therefore becomes necessary to ask: who are these people and what is the nature of the ends and definitions of the situation which cause them to form an organization with a particular goal? How does the pattern of expectations and type of legitimate authority within the organization relate to the stock of knowledge characteristic of the society and to the finite provinces of meaning of its founders?[36]

In terms of entry points for recasting change within regional planning, Silverman's observations and model are particularly relevant. According to him organisational change may be considered as a change in either the rules of the game or in the attachment of actors to those rules. [37] Both are therefore related, for if attachment weakens sufficiently changes will take place in the rules of operation. Change is thus a facet arising out of the interaction of actors within the organisation. On this premise Silverman constructs an action-framework for the analysis of organisations and organisational change. He outlines six interrelated areas which are suggestive of points of entry. These concern:

1   the nature of the rôle system and the pattern of interaction that has been built up in the organisation; also the extent to which it represents the shared values of all or some or none of the actors;
2   the nature of the involvement of principal actors (e.g. moral, alienative, instrumental) and the characteristics of the reward system (e.g. work satisfaction, material rewards, security);
3   the actor's present definitions of their situation within the organisation together with their expectations of the likely behaviour of others with respect to the strategic resources which they perceive to be at their and others disposal (degree of coercive power);
4   the typical actions of different actors and the meaning which they attach to their action;
5   the nature and source of the intended and unintended consequences of action, with particular respect to impacts on other actors and on the expectations associated with the rôle system; and
6   changes in the involvement and objectives of respectively actors and the rôle system with regard to outcomes (e.g. political or legal changes).[38]

If any recasting is to be attempted, by adaptation or innovation or both, it is suggested that these six interrelated areas are the most critical from the points of view of articulating proposals and their mobilisation. It is also clear that if recasting is to take place at all realistically then it is also intimated that it must be directed at each of the six areas. A focus of attention on one area alone, if not exactly doomed to failure, is liable to experience minimal organisational impact. It is perhaps interesting to note in passing why it is that legislative changes may have an impact on the involvement of actors in certain areas (area six), but unless that impact is matched or followed-up by attempts to introduce or induce change in most if not all of the remaining five areas, the net result may more often than not be met with disappointment if not disillusion − not only on the part of those experiencing change but perhaps more importantly on the original proposers. A good example of this syndrome is provided by attempts to introduce change into the operation of 'The City' in London solely by legislation and codes of conduct. It is therefore perhaps not surprising that the City has remained largely dynamically conservative in response, and innovative changes have not been wrought. Other more relevant examples include the history and fate of the Development Plan-making procedures under the immediate post-war legislation and, more recently, the attempts to reorganise and 'reform' local government via the administrative machine.[39]

The problem of recasting is therefore a gargantuan and complex problem in and of itself (the inducement-of-change-within-the-political-adminis-tration argument). If we are also to agree with Stewart that the contextual situation within which proposals for change are cast are more often than not organisations which are not only differentiated with respect to rôle systems but multi-levelled and multi-functioned, then the problems which recasting gives rise to are what Vickers calls the problem of multi-valued choices.[40] Proposals of internal change therefore represent but one facet of this choice spectrum along with a multiplicity of others. On this basis it would appear that the capacity for inducing internal change from the outside in formal terms would seem to be somewhat limited in scope. If this is the case, then is it perhaps of greater utility to attempt to cast change in more informal terms from the inside? That is, away from the macro, 'big bang' attempt at change, and more to the micro, process-oriented progression based on trial-and-error, loose-knit, pragmatic strategies. Modifying the context within which he originally proposed it, Friedmann makes a case for a pragmatic approach to the inducing of change, at the same time sustaining political commitment. Experience suggests, he writes, that policies for change should conform to three pragmatic criteria: (a) it must be simple in concept and dramatic in its implications; (b) it must be embodied in new organisational arrangements which are capable at least of outlasting periodic changes in government, and (c) it must be capable of producing visible results quickly.[41] Above all they should be responsive.

If change within the political administration of planning is to be wrought in this fashion then, assuming that the high degree of interaction between the process of planning and the planning domain is maintained, should proposals for change within the planning domain reflect this pragmatic responsive approach also? If the answer is to be in the affirmative then it raises a number of implications of significance for the nature and practice of planning itself. In fact, according to Sir Geoffrey Vickers, it raises six inferences which can be couched in terms of pragmatic guidelines or strategies for an action-framework approach. These are:

1   identify the minimum number of variables so interconnected that they must all be considered in order to understand the problem and to estimate the probable result of any action or inaction;
2   identify the minimum number of values which cannot be ignored in deciding what results are significant in terms of 'costs' and 'benefits';
3   identify the constraints which limit the planner's powers of intervention in terms of resources, maintenance of the existing order of things, consistency with other policies, etc.;
4   identify points of increasing or diminishing returns with respect to the pursuit of alternative possible policies;
5   identify elements of risk and uncertainty, their possible range, scale and magnitude in terms of their relative importance and relation to different time horizons — for example, political, private, social, etc.; and
6   identify the relevant time relations, notably lead times and fruition times (lead-lag relations) and their relation to the time horizons beyond which significant uncertainties and risks defy estimation.[42]

In terms of the minimum requirements necessary to attempt to inject some element of responsiveness into and within an existing organisation, these six inferences may be taken as first-order conditions. If any one or more of these 'conditions' are not carried through or insufficient it is more than likely that the result will conform to what Schilling refers to as another example of the policy syndrome. That is, where policy is associated with a particular brand of sterile inaction with certain pejorative associations; for example, where comments — or whose symptoms — are in the form of 'no policy at all', 'a compromised policy', 'a paper policy', 'a blind policy', or 'a gyroscopic policy'. Each is based on perceptions of apparently irreconcilable differences; for example, such as the realisation that problems have no 'right' answers; where policy differences stem from both intellectual and institutional differences on the part of participants; when the processes which distribute authority and advantages do so differentially among participants; where critical stresses and tensions emerge leading to compromise and consensus; and where outcomes result more from open conflict, coalition and bargaining.[43]

The other problem of potential significance concerns the so-called 'ideal-real' gap — the difference between what, in this case, planners say they are doing, as compared to what they appear to be doing, with respect to what they should be doing. These kinds of situation emerge routinely, and are associated with the problems of endogenous uncertainties and ambiguities with respect to both endogenously and exogenously determined actions. In order to respond and be responsive to these kinds of problem it is necessary that some internal strategic monitoring device be instituted on similar lines to the device proposed for the problem recasting component of responsive planning outlined in the last chapter. That is, to evaluate past performance whilst at the same time reviewing existing and proposed policy to determine whether it is still of relevance. To operationalise a responsive approach to planning in its minimum form would therefore also require a monitoring device such as the one proposed here in order to assist the closure of the intent-impact, 'ideal-real' gap within the context of the political administration itself.

### The problem of planning

*'A solved problem is as useful to a man's mind as a broken sword on a battlefield.'* (Idris Shah.)

One of the principal threads to the argument around which this book has been based is a concern for the dangers and irrelevancies associated with the splitting of planning into the separate compartments of theory and practice. This split is a wholly arbitrary and artificial one, based as it is — and as we have seen — on one particular interpretation as to what constitutes society and social change in combination with one particular model of the process of planning. Neither can be accorded, as O'Neill points out, the status of a god-given gift or of being the 'natural' approach. [44] Another of the threads to permeate these pages has been concern for the development of an approach to the problem of planning based on an alternative set of premises and assertions to those propping-up the rationality thesis. The impression which may have been created is that rationality is a 'bad thing'. This would be a misrepresentation of the argument: there clearly is room *for* rationality as one component of the processes which constitute planning, but to treat it as the component is to accord it a status of reified proportions which it — or any other methodology — simply does not merit. As Rapoport has illustrated in a different context,

244

once a particular view of planning is defined and formalised, for example, as 'the science of rational decision-making', a general feeling may be in danger of being created that a mastery of the theory will lead down the path to 'successful' planning, and hence to becoming a 'successful' planner.[45] That this is a mistaken interpretation is clear, but it still manages to manifest itself in 'current best practice' if not in the 'good currency' idea that if somehow policy can be forged 'correctly' and according to the 'right' processes, then the implementation side of the equation will occur automatically and naturally like manna from heaven.

It is largely as a result of this kind of distortion about the nature of public planning that much of this book has been purposively given over to the idea of public planning as the generic, inherently-political, umbrella-like core of other but constituent kinds of planning. Regional planning has therefore been considered in these terms − as one vital strand of public planning and of its political administration. The avenue which has been explored in this respect has been based on the assertion that there can be no such thing as regional planning in and of its own apolitical right − as some writers and practitioners would have us believe. It is one form, and one form only, of this broader umbrella and core-activity − albeit at some regional scale along the subnational/supra-urban continuum. Regional planning therefore can no longer be considered solely in terms of a technical exercise, that is, with the application of technical solutions to technically-defined problems. The technical component clearly has a rôle to play, but it would be stretching credulity beyond the bounds of legitimate actions to accord it a status of the rôle. Nonetheless, there are indications that in both British and North American practice this has indeed been the case.[46] The problems with this obsession for technics are two-fold: first, however much some practitioners would like to pursue the technical avenue to its logical conclusion, they can never exploit it to the full. Technical problems cannot be divorced from their contextual settings, and the primary contextual setting for regional planning is the political one. Technical problems contain some measure of, and shade imperceptibly into, political problems. The two are interwoven, one with and within the other. Political problems never remain static for long enough to enable purely technical solutions to be applied and assessed. Second, and following on from the latter point, practitioners are neither problem-neutral nor policy-neutral. In other words, as we have seen, they are part and parcel of the central value system, and as such form a substantive part − the expertise − of the core itself. The evidence which is beginning to emerge from studies of the politics of British and North American regional planning suggests that the balance between these technical and political strands have been more than inextricably intertwined — they have also been heavily dependent on each other. Indeed, in some cases it has been argued that the technical component has been manipulated to reorientate and depoliticise issues from a substantive social and political base to a more apolitical and abstract base. For example:

> . . . the main purpose of the regional organizations has remained constant — to persuade the people of the (region) to accept a certain range of policies and assumptions about policy, and to mobilize to achieve these aims in a socially comprehensive way on 'regional' rather than on area, industry, party or interest basis . . . The significance of this (approach to) regional problems lies . . . in alternative approaches which have been repressed . . . In emphasizing the regional, attention is directed away from the social. The causes of legitimate grievances are displaced from the area of general or societal politics into an area of purely regional politics.[47]

The substance of regional, if not all styles of public, planning is therefore characterised by, permeated with, and soaked in controversy of various forms at various levels. For example, at one level controversy about planning and planned action within the planning domain, as well as within the political administration of public planning, but perhaps most importantly within the very processes of planning itself; and at the other level controversy about planning and planned action between different facets of the planning domain, as well as between the planning domain and its political administration with respect to the processes of planning. In other words, controversy between planning and its critics. These kinds of controversy have arisen, and in all probability will continue to arise from disagreements not only about the means and directions of public planning, but also about the very substance of planning itself. As Beneviste notes, public planning can only be as process comprehensive as the basic ability of its protagonists to create and maintain support, commitment and hence legitimation. [48] In terms of these relationships — between political processes and planning processes — these interrelated areas of controversy, as Marsden illustrates, usually concern five fundamental issues: (a) controversy surrounding the adequacy and scope of the mechanisms of public planning — the quality of planning — in terms of the basic ability to meet the demands of the planning domain and its political administration with respect to; (b) controversy surrounding the balance between, as Marsden puts it, 'economy and generosity, zeal and tact' at the interfaces between the processes of planning and the planning domain, and those processes and the ability of the political administration — to use Crick's argument

246

once more — to not only balance but reconcile between conflicting interests. These kind of controversies may raise additional issues concerning (c) the provision and (d) the urgency with which the processes of the political administration and the processes of planning respond to issues concerning the adequacy and scope, and the need to balance and reconciliate — what Marsden refers to as the sensitivity of the mechanisms of those processes to not only detect new needs but to reach out and meet them. In other words, (e) controversy concerning the speed of this responsiveness, and in particular, as Marsden notes, the speed with which discretionary provision becomes consolidated into legalised rights, and the security of those rights once established in law.[49]

To therefore say that regional planning *qua* public planning is, for example, a process, concerned with continuity, comprehensive, about politics, even about people, or any other similar 'ideas in good currency', is indicative of the kind of 'ideal-real' gaps which permeate the contemporary practice of regional planning. In fact it is possible to argue that these assertions are nothing more than a set of truisms which add little of substance to resolving those issues which are characteristic of the five areas of controversy outlined above. They are therefore remarkably weak in explanatory power and as such are largely irrelevant to an understanding of what constitutes the nature and practice of planning. If these truisms are to have some substance or utility then they need to be recast, and not in the same mould. The critical issues associated with them concern, for example, not whether planning is a process, or indeed whether it is a continuous or comprehensive process, but in what way planning is a continuous and comprehensive set of processes. In other words, what are the ingredients of this kind of planning which distinguish it from other, potentially competing forms? What are the characteristics — and hence implications — associated with a perspective which stresses the virtues of comprehensiveness, of process? It is these kinds of issues — an amalgam of the five areas of controversy — which constitute the heart of a study of the nature and practice of planning. Neither planning practice nor the study of planning can be exclusively concerned with, or the exclusive concern of, the creativity and originality which permeates the view of planning as the forging of intended action. It is also and equally about a concern for the controversy and emotion which surrounds the inherently political nature of planning as implementation.[50] The problem of planning is therefore about the art of the possible. And regional planning can be no exception.

# Notes

[1] Medawar, 1969, op. cit., p. 11.

[2] See Silverman, 1970, op. cit., especially Chapter 10.

[3] See Stewart, 1974, op. cit., for the idea and attributes of a responsive administration.

[4] Friedmann, 1972a, op. cit., pp. 88—9.

[5] See for example Silverman, 1970, op. cit., pp. 126—46.

[6] Hart, 1974, op. cit.; Hart, 1975, op. cit.

[7] Hart, 1974, op. cit., p. 29.

[8] Hart, 1974, op. cit., p. 29.

[9] Hart, 1974, op. cit., p. 30.

[10] Hart, 1974, op. cit., pp. 30—1.

[11] See for example the regional strategy entitled 'Challenge of the Changing North' (Northern Regional Economic Planning Council, 1966).

[12] Hart, 1974, op. cit., p. 32.

[13] Hart, 1974, op. cit., pp. 32—3.

[14] Hart, 1974, op. cit., p. 33.

[15] Hart, 1974, op. cit., p. 34.

[16] Hart, 1974, op. cit., p. 34.

[17] See for example the comments made on this conflict, and the fate of the DEA, by the late R.H.S. Crossman in the serialisation of diary extracts (*The Sunday Times,* especially February 9, 1975).

[18] Hart, 1974, op. cit., p. 35.

[19] Hart, 1974, op. cit., p. 36.

[20] Hart, 1974, op. cit., p. 37.

[21] Hart, 1974, op. cit., p. 37.

[22] Hart, 1974, op. cit., p. 37.

[23] See for example Dell, 1973, op. cit.

[24] Hart, 1974, op. cit., pp. 39—40.

[25] Hart, 1974, op. cit., p. 40.

[26] Hart, 1974, op. cit., p. 39.

[27] Friedmann, 1973c, op. cit., pp. 308—9.

[28] Faludi, 1973a, op. cit., Introduction.

[29] Wildavsky suggested these comparisons during the proceedings of a conference on 'Approaches to Policy-making in Local Government', London, 24—5 June 1974.

[30] See for example the comments by Power, 1971, op. cit.; also see K. Cox et al. (eds.), 1974.

[31] Hart, 1974, op. cit., p. 31.

[32] Hart, 1974, op. cit., p. 41.

[33] Hart, 1974, op. cit., p. 27.

[34] D. Braybrooke, 1974, p. 1.

[35] Silverman, 1970, op. cit., Chapter 7.

[36] Silverman, 1970, op. cit., pp. 147–8.

[37] Silverman, 1970, op. cit., p. 152; for the derivation of the model see p. 151.

[38] Silverman, 1970, op. cit., p. 154.

[39] In this context Silverman's account of the dynamics of Gouldner's 'Wildcat Strike' is of particular interest, Silverman, 1970, op. cit., pp. 155–63; compare with Schon, 1971, op. cit., for other examples.

[40] See Vickers, 1971, op. cit., Chapter 6; also Vickers, 1967, op. cit.; Vickers, 1972, op. cit., p. 134.

[41] Friedmann, 1973c, op. cit., pp. 239–42.

[42] Vickers, 1974b, op. cit., pp. 8–9.

[43] W. Schilling, 1962, pp. 21–6. Quoted in Allison, 1971, op. cit., pp. 154–6.

[44] J. O'Neill, 1974, p. V.

[45] A. Rapoport, 1964, p. 4.

[46] See for example Rowntree Research Unit, 1974, on UK experience; on US experience see Derthick, 1974, op. cit., especially Chapters 1 and 8.

[47] Rowntree Research Unit, 1974, op. cit., p. 143.

[48] Beneviste, 1973, op. cit., p. 114.

[49] D. Marsden, 1973, p. 227.

[50] Compare with Dewey, 1916, op. cit., and Dewey, 1927, op. cit.; also the observations made by Edmund Leach on the open and fluid nature of planning, E. Leach, 1969, p. 4:

> What I am suggesting . . . is not that there should be no planning, but that when there is planning it must be justified by quite arbitrary principles such as aesthetic fashion or religious dogma or even military convenience. The 'needs of society', which it is now fashionable to invoke, won't work at all. No plan can ever be defended on the grounds that it represents 'the only sociological solution', because sociological solutions are infinitely adaptable.

# Bibliography

Ackoff, R., *A Concept of Corporate Planning,* Wiley, New York 1970.

Alden, J. and Morgan, R., *Regional Planning: A Comprehensive Approach,* Leonard Hill, Heath and Reach, Beds. 1974.

Allen, J., 'Review of Metropolitan Plan Making', *Urban Studies,* vol. 9, no. 2, June 1972, pp. 237–9.

Allison, G., *Essence of Decision: Explaining the Cuban Missile Crisis,* Little, Brown and Co., Boston 1971.

Arctander, P., 'The Process is the Purpose', *Journal of Royal Town Planning Institute,* 1972, pp. 313–5.

Armstrong, Sir W., *Professions and Professionalism in the Civil Service,* Oration Paper, London School of Economics 1970.

Ashby, W., *An Introduction to Cybernetics,* Chapman and Hall, London 1956.

Barras, R. and Broadbent, T., 'A Framework for Structure Plan Analysis', *PRAG Technical Papers,* TP8, Centre for Environmental Studies, London 1975.

Bauer, R. and Gergen, K. (eds.), *The Study of Policy Formulation,* Free Press, New York 1968.

Beckman, N., 'The Planner as a Bureaucrat', *Journal of American Institute of Planners,* vol. 30, 1964, pp. 323–7.

Bell, D., 'Twelve Modes of Prediction – a Preliminary Sorting of Approaches in the Social Sciences', *Daedalus,* vol. 93, no. 3, Summer 1964, pp. 845–80.

Bendix, R., 'Bureaucracy and the problem of power', in Merton, R. et al. (eds.), *Reader in Bureaucracy,* Free Press, New York 1952.

Beneviste, G., *The Politics of Expertise,* Croom Helm, London 1973.

Benington, J. and Skelton, P., 'Public Participation in Decision-Making by Governments', Programme Budgetting in 1984, Institute of Municipal Treasurers and Accountants Seminar, London, mimeo 1972.

Berger, P. and Luckmann, T., *The Social Construction of Reality: A Treatise in The Sociology of Knowledge,* Penguin Books, Harmondsworth 1971.

Bićanić, R., *Problems of Planning – East and West,* Mouton, The Hague 1967.

Boothroyd, H., *On the Theory of Operational Research,* WP 51 Centre for Industrial Economic and Business Research, University of Warwick 1974.

Boyce, D., Day, N. and McDonald, C., *Metropolitan Plan Making,* Regional Science Research Institute, University of Pennsylvania, Philadelphia, Pa. 1970.

Boyce, D., McDonald, C. and Farhi, A., *An Interim Report on Procedures for Continuing Metropolitan Planning,* mimeo, University of Pennsylvania, Philadelphia, Pa. 1972.

Bray, J., *Decision in Government,* Gollancz, London 1970.

Braybrooke, D. and Lindblom, C., *A Strategy for Decision: Policy Evaluation as a Social Process,* Free Press, New York 1963.

Braybrooke, D., *Traffic Congestion Goes Through the Issue Machine: A Case-Study in Issue-Processing, Illustrating a New Approach,* Routledge and Kegan Paul, London 1974.

Brittan, S., *Participation Without Politics: An Analysis of the Nature and Role of Markets,* Institute of Economic Affairs, Hobart Paper Special 62, London 1975.

Broady, M. (ed.), *Marginal Regions: Essays on Social Planning,* Bedford Square Press, London 1973.

Brookfield, H., *Interdependent Development,* Methuen, London 1975.

Brown, A., *The Framework of Regional Economics in the United Kingdom,* Cambridge University Press, for NIESR XXVII, Cambridge 1972.

Cameron, G., 'The Regional Problem in the United States: Some Reflections on a Viable Federal Strategy', *Journal of Regional Studies,* vol. 2, no. 2, 1968, pp. 207–20.

Cartwright, C., 'Problems, Solutions and Strategies: a Contribution to the Theory and Practice of Planning', *Journal of American Institute of Planners,* vol. 39, no. 3, May 1973, pp. 179–87.

Catanese, A., 'Frustrations of National Planning: Reality and Theory in Colombia', *Journal of American Institute of Planners,* vol. 39, no. 2, March 1973, pp. 93–105.

Cattell, R., 'Patterns of Change: Measurement in Relation to State Dimension, Trait Change, Lability and Process Concepts', in Cattell, R. (ed.), *Handbook of Multivariate Experimental Psychology,* Rand McNally, Chicago 1966.

Cattell, R. (ed.), *Handbook of Multivariate Experimental Psychology,* Rand McNally, Chicago 1966.

Central Office of Information, *Regional Development in Britain,* HMSO, London 1974.

Chadwick, G., *A Systems View of Planning: Towards a Theory of the Urban and Regional Planning Process,* Pergamon Press, Oxford 1971.

Chapin, F., Jr., *Urban Land Use Planning,* University of Illinois Press, Urbana, Ill. 1965, 2nd ed.

Civil Service Commission, *Government Departments and Their Work,* HMSO, London 1972.

Civil Service Department, *Her Majesty's Ministers and Senior Staff in Public Departments,* HMSO, London May 1974, no. 1.

Coddington, A., 'Positive Economics', *Canadian Journal of Economics,* vol. V, no. 1, February 1972, pp. 1–15.

Cohen, P., *Modern Social Theory,* Heinemann, London 1968.

Coleman, J., 'Collective Decisions and Collective Action', in Laslett, P., Runciman, W. and Skinner, Q. (eds.), *Philosophy, Politics and Society,* Blackwell, London 1972, 4th ed.

Committee on the Civil Service 'Report' (Fulton Committee), June, Cmnd 3638, HMSO, London 1968.

Cowling, T. and Steeley, G., *Sub-Regional Planning Studies: An Evaluation,* Pergamon Press, Oxford 1973.

Cox, K. et al. (eds.), *Locational Approaches to Power and Conflict,* Sage, Beverley Hills, California 1974.

Crick, B., *In Defence of Politics,* Penguin Books, Harmondsworth 1964.

Crick, B., 'Politics and Planning', Royal Town Planning Institute Summer School Proceedings, University of St. Andrews 1972.

Crossman, R., 'The Crossman Diaries', *The Sunday Times,* January 26 – February 23 1975.

Dahrendorf, R., *Class and Class Conflict in Industrial Society,* Routledge and Kegan Paul, London 1959.

Dalton, M., *Men Who Manage,* Wiley, New York 1959.

Davidoff, P. and Reiner, T., 'A Choice Theory of Planning', *Journal of American Institute of Planners,* vol. 28, May 1962, pp. 103–15.

Dell, E., *Political Responsibility and Industry,* Allen and Unwin, London 1973.

Department of the Environment, *Management Networks: A Study for Structure Plans,* HMSO, London 1971.

Department of the Environment, *The Water Services,* HMSO, London 1974.

Department of the Environment, *Structure Plans,* Circular 66/74, HMSO, London 1974.

Derthick, M., *Between State and Nation: Regional Organizations of the United States,* Brookings Institution, Washington 1974.

Deutsch, K., 'On Political Theory and Political Action', *American Political Science Review,* vol. LXV, no. 1, March 1971, pp. 11–27.

Dewey, J., *Democracy and Education,* MacMillan, New York 1916, 1961 ed.

Dewey, J., *The Public and its Problems,* Swallow Press, Chicago 1927, 1973 ed.

Dror, Y., 'The Planning Process: a Facet Design', *International Review of Administrative Sciences,* vol. 29, no. 1, 1963, pp. 46–58.

Dror, Y., *Public Policy-Making Reexamined,* Chandler Pub. Co., Scranton, Penn. 1968.

Dror, Y., 'Policy Analysis for Local Government', Conference, Approaches to Policy-making in Local Government, London, 24–25 June 1974.

East Midlands Regional Economic Planning Council, *Opportunity in the East Midlands,* HMSO, London 1969.

Eckstein, H., *The Theory of Stable Democracy,* Princeton University Press, Princeton 1961.

Eddison, T., *Local Government: Management and Corporate Planning,* Leonard Hill, Heath and Reach, Beds. 1973.

Etzione, A., *A Comparative Analysis of Complex Organisations,* Free Press, New York 1961.

Etzione, A., 'Mixed Scanning: A Third Approach to Decision-Making', *Public Administration Review,* vol. 27, December 1967, pp. 385–92.

Etzione, A., *The Active Society: A Theory of Societal and Political Processes,* Free Press, New York 1968.

Faludi, A., Mimeo notes, unpublished 1969.

Faludi, A., 'The Planning Environment and the Meaning of Planning', *Journal of Regional Studies,* vol. 4, no. 1, May 1970, pp. 1–9.

Faludi, A., *A Reader in Planning Theory,* Pergamon Press, Oxford 1973a.

Faludi, A., *Planning Theory*, Pergamon Press, Oxford 1973b.

Feldstein, M., 'The Social Time Preference Discount Rate in Cost Benefit Analysis', *Economic Journal,* vol. 74, 1964, pp. 360–79.

Firestone, O. (ed.), *Regional Economic Development,* Ottawa University Press, Ottawa 1973.

Foster, C., 'Public Finance Aspects of National Settlement Patterns', *Urban Studies,* vol. 9, no. 1, February 1972, pp. 79–97.

Fried, R., *Planning the Eternal City,* Yale University Press, New Haven, Conn. 1973.

Friedman, M., *Capitalism and Freedom,* University of Chicago Press, Chicago 1962.

Friedmann, J. and Alonso, W., 'Introduction', in Friedmann, J. and Alonso, W. (eds.), *Regional Development and Planning: A Reader,* MIT Press, Cambridge, Mass. 1964.

Friedmann, J. and Alonso, W. (eds.), *Regional Development and Planning: A Reader,* MIT Press, Cambridge, Mass. 1964.

Friedmann, J., 'Planning as Innovation: the Chilean Case', *Journal of American Institute of Planners,* vol. 32, 1964, pp. 194–204.

Friedmann, J., 'A Response to Altshuler: Comprehensive Planning as a

Process', *Journal of American Institute of Planners,* vol. 31, August 1965, pp. 195–7.

Friedmann, J., *Regional Development Policy: A Case Study of Venezuela,* MIT Press, Cambridge, Mass. 1966.

Friedmann, J., 'Planning as a Vocation', *Plan (Canada),* vol. 6, 1966/7, pp. 99–124; vol. 7, 1966/7, pp. 8–26. (Quoted in Faludi, A., *Planning Theory,* 1973, p. 172.)

Friedmann, J., 'The Institutional Context', in Gross, B. (ed.), *Action Under Planning,* McGraw-Hill, New York 1967a.

Friedmann, J., 'A Conceptual Model for the Analysis of Planning Behavior', *Administrative Science Quarterly,* vol. 12, no. 2, September 1967b, pp. 225–52.

Friedmann, J., *A General Theory of Polarized Development,* Ford Foundation Urban and Regional Advisory Program in Chile, mimeo, Santiago 1967c.

Friedmann, J., 'The Guayana Program in a Regional Perspective', in Rodwin, L. (ed.), *Planning Urban Growth and Regional Development,* MIT Press, Cambridge, Mass. 1969, chapter 7.

Friedmann, J., 'Notes on Societal Action', *Journal of American Institute of Planners,* vol. 35, no. 5, September 1969a, pp. 311–8.

Friedmann, J., 'A General Theory of Polarized Development', in Hansen, N. (ed.), *Growth Centers in Regional Economic Development,* Free Press, New York 1972a, pp. 82–107.

Friedmann, J., 'The Spatial Organization of Power in the Development of Urban Systems', *Comparative Urban Research,* vol. 1, 1972b, pp. 5–42.

Friedmann, J., 'The Public Interest and Community Participation: Toward a Reconstruction of Public Philosophy', *Journal of American Institute of Planners,* vol. 39, no. 1, January 1973a, pp. 2–12.

Friedmann, J., *Retracking America: A Theory of Transactive Planning,* Anchor Press/Doubleday, New York 1973b.

Friedmann, J., *Urbanization, Planning and National Development,* Sage, Beverley Hills, Calif. 1973c.

Friedmann, J., 'Review of Planning Theory', *Journal of Regional Studies,* vol. 8, nos. 3/4, November 1974, p. 311.

Friend, J. and Jessop, N., *Local Government and Strategic Choice,* Institute of Operational Research, Tavistock Publications, London 1969.

Friend, J., Power, J. and Yewlett, C., *Public Planning: The Inter-Corporate Dimension,* Institute of Operational Research, Tavistock Publications, London 1974.

Garrett, J., *The Management of Government,* Penguin Books, Harmondsworth 1972.

Giddens, A., 'Power in the Recent Writings of Talcott Parsons', *Sociology*, vol. 2, 1968, pp. 268–70.

Giddens, A., *Capitalism and Modern Social Theory,* Cambridge University Press, London 1971.

Giddens, A., 'Elites in the British Class Structure', in Stanworth, P. and Giddens, A. (eds.), *Elites and Power in British Society,* Cambridge University Press, London 1974.

Gouldner, A., *The Coming Crisis of Western Sociology,* Heinemann, London 1970.

Grabow, A. and Heskin, A., 'Foundations for a Radical Concept of Planning', *Journal of American Institute of Planners,* vol. 39, no. 2, March 1973, pp. 106–14.

Greater London Council, (undated), *Greater London Development Plan Statement,* GLC Press, London.

Gross, B. (ed.), *Action Under Planning,* McGraw-Hill, New York 1967.

Gutch, R., 'Planning, Philosophy and Logic', *Journal of Town Planning Institute,* vol. 56, no. 9, November 1970, pp. 389–91.

Hall, R., *The Theory and Practice of Regional Planning,* Pemberton Books, London 1970.

Hall, P., *Urban and Regional Planning,* Penguin Books, Harmondsworth 1974.

Hampshire County Council, *South Hampshire Structure Plan Draft Written Statement,* South Hampshire Plan Advisory Committee, Winchester 1972.

Hansen, N. (ed.), *Growth Centers in Regional Economic Development,* Free Press, New York 1972.

Hart, D., 'Ordering Change and Changing Orders: A Study of Urban Policy Development', *Journal of Policy and Politics,* vol. 2, no. 1, 1974, pp. 27–41.

Hart, D., *Strategic Planning in London: A Study of the Rise and Fall of the Primary Road Network,* Unpublished PhD, London School of Economics, University of London, (forthcoming, Pergamon Press, Oxford 1975.)

Harvey, D., *Social Justice and the City,* Edward Arnold, London 1973.

Hayek, von, F., *The Road to Serfdom,* Routledge and Kegan Paul, London 1944, 2nd ed. 1962.

Heclo, H. and Wildavsky, A., *The Private Government of Public Money: Community and Policy Inside British Politics,* MacMillan, London 1974.

Hilhorst, J., *Regional Planning: A Systems Approach,* Rotterdam University Press, Rotterdam 1971.

256

Hill, M., *The Sociology of Public Administration*, Weidenfeld and Nicolson, London 1972.

Hirschman, A., *The Strategy of Economic Development*, Yale University Press, New Haven, Conn. 1958.

Hirschman, A., *Development Projects Observed*, Brookings Institution, Washington 1967.

House of Commons, *Second Report from the Trade and Industry Sub-Committee of the Expenditure Committee, Session 1973–1974: Regional Development Incentives*, HC Paper 85, HMSO, London 1973.

Kuklinski, A., 'Regional Development, Regional Policies and Regional Planning: Problems and Issues', *Journal of Regional Studies*, vol. 4, no. 3, October 1970, pp. 269–78.

Laslett, P., Runciman, W. and Skinner, Q. (eds.), *Philosophy, Politics and Society*, Blackwell, Oxford 1972, 4th ed.

Lasswell, H., 'The Study of Political Elites', in Lasswell, H. and Lerner, D. (eds.), *World Revolutionary Elites: Studies in Coercive Ideological Movements*, MIT Press, Cambridge, Mass. 1965.

Lasswell, H. and Lerner, D., *World Revolutionary Elites: Studies in Coercive Ideological Movements*, MIT Press, Cambridge, Mass. 1965.

Leach, E., 'Planning and Evolution', *Journal of Town Planning Institute*, vol. 55, no. 1, January 1969, pp. 2–8.

Levin, P., 'On Decisions and Decision-Making', *Public Administration*, vol. 50, Spring 1972, pp. 19–44.

Lindblom, C., 'The Science of "Muddling Through" ', *Public Administration Review*, vol. 19, Spring 1959, pp. 79–99.

Lindblom, C., *The Intelligence of Democracy: Decision-Making Through Mutual Adjustment*, Free Press, New York 1965.

MacKaye, B., *The New Exploration: A Philosophy of Regional Planning*, Harcourt, Brace and Co., Illinois 1928, 1962 ed. University of Illinois Press.

MacRae, D., *Weber*, Modern Masters Series, Fontana, London 1974.

Magee, B., *Popper*, Modern Masters Series, Fontana, London 1973.

Mannheim, K., *Ideology and Utopia*, Routledge and Kegan Paul, London 1936.

March, J. and Simon, H., *Organisations*, Wiley, New York 1958.

Marcuse, H., *One Dimensional Man*, Sphere Books, London 1964.

Marris, P. and Rein, M., *The Dilemmas of Social Reform*, Routledge and Kegan Paul, London 1967.

Marsden, D., *Mothers Alone: Poverty and the Fatherless Family*, Penguin Books, Harmondsworth 1973.

Mayer, R., 'Social System Models for Planners', *Journal of American Institute of Planners*, May 1972, pp. 130–9.

257

McLoughlin, J., *Urban and Regional Planning: A Systems Approach,* Faber and Faber, London 1969.

McLoughlin, J., *Control and Urban Planning,* Faber and Faber, London 1973.

Medawar, Sir P., 'Hypothesis and Imagination', *The Art of the Soluble: Creativity and Originality in Science,* Penguin Books, Harmondsworth 1969.

Merton, R. et al. (eds.), *Reader in Bureaucracy,* Free Press, New York 1952.

Michael, D., *On Learning to Plan and Planning to Learn,* Jossey-Bass Pub., San Francisco 1973.

Miliband, R., *The State in Capitalist Society,* Weidenfeld and Nicolson, London 1969.

Mills, C., 'Corporate Planning in the British Gas Industry', *Public Administration,* vol. 52, Spring 1974, pp. 27–40.

Ministry of Housing and Local Government, *Development Plans: A Manual on Form and Content,* HMSO, London 1970.

Mishan, E., *Cost Benefit Analysis,* Allen and Unwin, London 1971.

Musgrave, R., *The Theory of Public Finance,* McGraw-Hill, New York 1959.

Northern Regional Economic Planning Council, *Challenge of the Changing North,* HMSO, London 1966.

North West Joint Planning Team, *Strategic Plan for the North West,* HMSO, London 1974.

O'Neill, J. (ed.), *Phenomenology, Language and Sociology,* Heinemann, London 1974.

Peters, G., *Cost Benefit Analysis and Public Expenditure,* Institute of Economic Affairs, Eaton Papers 8, London 1966.

Pile, Sir W., 'Corporate Planning for Education in the DES', *Public Administration,* vol. 52, Spring 1974, pp. 13–26.

Polyani, G. and Polyani, P., *Failing the Nation – the Record of the Nationalised Industries,* Fraser Ansbacher Ltd., London 1974.

Polyani, M., *The Logic of Personal Knowledge: Essays Presented to Michael Polyani,* Routledge and Kegan Paul, London 1961.

Popper, K., *The Logic of Scientific Discovery,* Hutchinson, London 1959, 6th ed. revised.

Popper, K., *Conjectures and Refutations,* Routledge and Kegan Paul, London 1963, 4th ed. revised.

Popper, Sir, K., *Objective Knowledge: An Evolutionary Approach,* Oxford University Press, London 1972.

Popper, Sir, K., 'Autobiography of Karl Popper' in Schilpp, P. (ed.), *The*

*Philosophy of Karl Popper,* The Library of Living Philosophers, Open Court, La Salle, Ill. 1974, vol. 1, Part One.

Power, J., *Planning: Magic and Technique,* Conference on 'Beyond Local Government Reform', Institute for Operational Research, Tavistock Institute, London 1971.

Pressman, J. and Wildavsky, A., *Implementation: How Great Expectations in Washington Are Dashed in Oakland,* University of California Press, Berkeley, Cal. 1973.

Pugh, D. et al., *Writers on Organizations,* Penguin Books, Harmondsworth 1971, 2nd ed.

Rapoport, A., *Strategy and Conscience,* Schocken, New York 1964.

Rawls, J., *A Theory of Social Justice,* Oxford University Press, London 1972.

Reissman, L., 'A Study of Role Conceptions in Bureaucracy', *Social Forces,* vol. 27, 1949, pp. 305–10.

Rhodes, J., 'Review of Regional Economic Analysis for Practitioners', *Economic Journal,* vol. 82, December 1972, pp. 1449–50.

Richardson, H., 'A Critique of Regional Growth Theory', in Firestone, O. (ed.), *Regional Economic Development,* Ottawa University Press, Ottawa 1973.

Richardson, H., *Regional Growth Theory,* MacMillan, London 1973.

Rittel, H. and Webber, M., 'Dilemma's in a General Theory of Planning', *Journal of Policy Sciences,* vol. 4, no. 3, September 1973, pp. 155–69.

Robinson, J., *Economic Philosophy,* Penguin Books, Harmondsworth 1964.

Rodwin, L., 'Reflections on Collaborative Planning', in Rodwin, L. (ed.), *Planning Urban Growth and Regional Development,* MIT Press, Cambridge, Mass. 1969, chapter 25.

Rodwin, L. (ed.), *Planning Urban Growth and Regional Development,* MIT Press, Cambridge, Mass. 1969.

Rowntree Research Unit, University of Durham, 'Aspects of Contradiction in Regional Policy', *Journal of Regional Studies,* vol. 8, no. 2, August 1974, pp. 133–44.

Royal Commission on Local Government in England, *Local Government in England 1966–69* (Redcliffe-Maud Report), Cmnd 4040, HMSO, London 1969.

Royal Commission on the Third London Airport, *Report* (Roskill Commission), HMSO, London 1970.

Russell, B., *The History of Western Philosophy,* Simon and Shuster, New York 1946.

Scheffler, I., *Four Pragmatists: A Critical Introduction to Peirce, James, Mead and Dewey,* Routledge and Kegan Paul, London 1974.

259

Schilling, W., 'The Politics of National Defense: Fiscal 1950', in Schilling et al. (eds.), *Strategy, Politics and Defense Budgets,* New York 1962.

Schilling, W., Hammond, P. and Snyder, G. (eds.), *Strategy, Politics and Defense Budgets,* New York 1962.

Schilpp, P. (ed.), *The Philosophy of Karl Popper,* The Library of Living Philosophers, Open Court, La Salle, Ill. 1974, vol. 14, books I and II.

Schoettle, E., 'The State of the Art in Policy Studies', in Bauer, R. and Gergen, K. (eds.), *The Study of Policy Formulation* Free Press, New York 1968.

Schon, D., *Beyond the Stable State: Public and Private Learning in a Changing Society,* Temple Smith, London 1971.

Scottish Development Department, *Central Scotland: A Programme for Development and Growth,* Cmnd 2188, HMSO, Edinburgh 1963.

Secretary of State for Industry, *Industry Bill,* Bill 73, HC47/1, HMSO, London 1975.

Secretary of State for Industry, Trade and Regional Development, *The North East: A Programme for Regional Development and Growth,* Cmnd 2206, HMSO, London 1963.

Self, P., 'Regional Planning in Britain: Analysis and Evaluation', *Journal of Regional Studies,* vol. 1, no. 1, May 1964, pp. 3–10.

Self, P., *The State Versus Man,* Public Lecture, London School of Economics, January 12 1972a.

Self, P., *Administrative Theories and Politics,* Allen and Unwin, London 1972b.

Self, P., 'Is Comprehensive Planning Possible and Rational?' *Journal of Policy and Politics,* vol. 2, no. 3, 1974, pp. 193–203.

Selznick, P., 'Foundations of the Theory of Organisations', *American Sociological Review,* vol. 12, 1948, pp. 25–35.

Sennett, R., *The Uses of Disorder,* Penguin Books, Harmondsworth 1973.

Shils, E., 'Centre and Periphery', in Polyani, M., *The Logic of Personal Knowledge: Essays Presented to Michael Polyani,* Routledge and Kegan Paul, London 1961.

Siebert, H., *Regional Economic Growth: Theory and Policy,* International Textbook Company, Scranton, Penn. 1969.

Silverman, D., *The Theory of Organisations: A Sociological Framework,* Heinemann, London 1970.

Simmie, J., *Citizens in Conflict: The Sociology of Town Planning,* Hutchinson, London 1974.

Simon, H., *Administrative Behavior: A Study of Decision-Making Processes in Administrative Organization,* Free Press, New York 1957, 2nd ed.

Simon, H., *The Sciences of the Artificial,* MIT Press, Cambridge, Mass. 1969.

Sleeman, J., *The Welfare State: Its Aims, Benefits and Costs,* Allen and Unwin, London 1973.

Smith, A., *An Inquiry into the Nature and Causes of the Wealth of Nations,* 1776, Book IV, Penguin Books, Harmondsworth, 1970 ed.

Solesbury, W., *Policy in Urban Planning,* Pergamon Press, Oxford 1974.

South East Joint Planning Team, *Strategic Plan for the South East,* HMSO, London 1970.

Stanworth, P. and Giddens, A. (eds.), *Elites and Power in British Society,* Cambridge University Press, London 1974.

Steiss, A., *Public Budgeting and Management,* Lexington Books, Lexington, Mass. 1972.

Stewart, J., *Management in Local Government: A Viewpoint,* Charles Knight, London 1971.

Stewart, J., *The Responsive Local Authority,* Charles Knight, London 1974.

Taylor, P., *A Dictionary of Economic Terms,* Routledge and Kegan Paul, London 1968, 4th ed.

Thayer, L. (ed.), *Communication Concepts and Perspectives,* Spartan Books, New York 1967.

Urwick, L., *Elements of Administration,* Pitman, London 1947.

Vickers, Sir G., *The Art of Judgement: A Study of Policy Making,* Methuen, London 1965.

Vickers, Sir G., 'The Multi-Valued Choice', in Thayer, L. (ed.), *Communication Concepts and Perspectives,* Spartan Books, New York 1967.

Vickers, Sir G., *Value Systems and Social Processes,* Penguin Books, Harmondsworth 1970.

Vickers, Sir G., *Freedom in a Rocking Boat: Changing Values in an Unstable Society,* Penguin Books, Harmondsworth 1972.

Vickers, Sir G., 'Values, Norms and Policies', *Journal of Policy Sciences,* vol. 4, no. 1, March 1973, pp. 103–11.

Vickers, Sir G., 'Projections, Predictions, Models and Policies', *The Planner,* vol. 60, no. 4, April 1974a, pp. 636–40.

Vickers, Sir G., 'Policy Making in Local Government', *Journal of Local Government Studies,* February 1974b, pp. 5–11.

Watkins, J., 'The Unity of Popper's Thought', in Schilpp, P. (ed.), *The Philosophy of Karl Popper,* The Library of Living Philosophers, Open Court, La Salle, Ill. 1974.

Wedgewood-Oppenheim, F., Hart, D. and Cobley, B., *An Exploratory Study in Strategic Monitoring,* Institute of Local Government Studies, University of Birmingham, (forthcoming, Progress in Planning, Pergamon Press, Oxford 1975).

Wildavsky, A., 'Rescuing Policy Analysis from PPBS', *Public Administration,* April 1969, pp. 189–200.

Wildavsky, A., 'If Planning is Everything, Maybe its Nothing', *Journal of Policy Sciences,* vol. 4, no. 3, September 1973, pp. 127–53.

Winch, D., *Analytical Welfare Economics,* Penguin Books, Harmondsworth 1971.

Ylvisaker, P., 'Diversity and the Public Interest', *Journal of American Institute of Planners,* vol. 27, no. 2, May 1961, pp. 107–17.

Yorkshire and Humberside Regional Economic Planning Council, *Yorkshire and Humberside Regional Strategy,* HMSO, London 1970.

Zeckhauser, R. and Schaeffer, E., 'Public Policy and Normative Economic Theory', in Bauer, R. and Gergen, K. (eds ), *The Study of Policy Formulation,* Free Press, New York 1968.

# Author index

264

# Subject index

# The Author

Having studied planning at both undergraduate and postgraduate levels, David Gillingwater has had considerable practical experience as Planning Assistant with Norwich City Planning Department and as Planning Officer with Bedfordshire County Council. Since 1973 he has lectured in Regional Planning at the University of Technology, Loughborough.